Inclusion in Higher Education

Inclusion in Higher Education

Research Initiatives on Campus

Edited by
Amanda Macht Jantzer and Kyhl Lyndgaard

LEXINGTON BOOKS
Lanham • Boulder • New York • London

Published by Lexington Books
An imprint of The Rowman & Littlefield Publishing Group, Inc.
4501 Forbes Boulevard, Suite 200, Lanham, Maryland 20706
www.rowman.com

6 Tinworth Street, London SE11 5AL, United Kingdom

British Library Cataloguing in Publication Information Available

Library of Congress Cataloging-in-Publication Data

Library of Congress Control Number: 2020944435
ISBN 978-1-7936-2564-9 (cloth)
ISBN 978-1-7936-2566-3 (pbk)
ISBN 978-1-7936-2565-6 (electronic)

Contents

**SECTION B: UNDERSTANDING THE EXPERIENCES OF
MINORITIZED POPULATIONS ON CAMPUS** 87

**SECTION C: ADDRESSING ISSUES FACING
UNDERREPRESENTED STUDENTS IN VARIED
FIELDS OF STUDY** 129

Acknowledgments

The completion of this edited collection was only possible due to the time, energy, resources, and passionate engagement of a broad coalition of individuals across our community. We are humbled by their excellence and are deeply appreciative. In particular, we wish to express our sincere thanks to the following:

- To the Andrew W. Mellon Foundation for funding support for the "Faculty Formation to Support Liberal Learning for All," the "Faculty Development to Engage Increasingly Diverse Students," and the "Becoming Community" grant initiatives at the College of Saint Benedict and Saint John's University.
- To Mary Dana Hinton, President Emerita of the College of Saint Benedict, who served as PI for the "Faculty Formation to Support Liberal Learning for All" and "Becoming Community" grants and provided inspiring vision and leadership about what it means to truly build community on our campuses through the urgent pursuit of transformative inclusion and justice.
- To Michael Hemesath, President Emeritus of Saint John's University, who served as PI for the "Faculty Development to Engage Increasingly Diverse Students" initiative and provided leadership and support.
- To all of the contributors to this edited collection who, despite incredible challenges in the midst of the COVID-19 pandemic and social uprisings for racial justice, completed this work in a timely and high-quality fashion. We are awed by all of you and are honored to be your colleagues.
- To our collaborators who also completed the work in this volume while juggling life demands, especially the many authors with small children who did not have access to childcare due to COVID-19-related closings, and still somehow managed to complete this excellent scholarly work.

- To Jean Keller, Anna Mercedes, and Brandyn Woodard who served with us as co-administrators of these grant initiatives and fill us with deep admiration and inspiration. We are better professionals and better people for having had the opportunity to work with and learn from you. In profound ways, you have shown us how to do the work, every day. Thank you for guiding us toward a better, more diverse, inclusive, equitable, and just future.
- To Laura Schmitz, Linda Bruner, Linda Larson, Cindy Gonzalez, Diane Van Beck, Ben Stommes, Robert Kachelski, and Kathryn A. E. Enke for their impressive administrative, budget, and research expertise. Implementing the vision of the Mellon grants was only possible through your time and support.
- To student assistants Daniel Welshons, Theresa Slivnick, Quinn Brabok, and Xia Vang for assistance with copyediting and excellent attention to detail.
- To our families. Thank you Jake, Max, and Leo Jantzer for your love and support. Thank you Marian, Lars, Pippin, and Victor Lyndgaard for your love and understanding.
- To all the students who voiced their truth.

Foreword

A Call to Action

Mary Dana Hinton and Kathryn A. E. Enke

The world has shifted. In the time that was spent working on this edited volume, a pandemic engulfed our globe, physically, mentally, and emotionally. We sheltered in place and wondered when and how we would emerge. What would the new normal be like? No longer could we take for granted physical proximity. Thanks to COVID-19, living in close physical relationship and community shifted from a foundation of support and joy to a source of potential danger and fear. Our long-standing habits and ways of being in the world were completely disrupted. In the brave new world of COVID-19, old assumptions and behaviors were no longer acceptable.

But it was not the virus or the months of sheltering in place that prompted the most significant shift in our society during the spring of 2020. Within this context, another significant shift happened. Perhaps it was only in the face of massive death from a virus that we could examine massive death for senseless reasons. Massive death due to systemic injustice. It was 8 minutes and 46 seconds when a white police officer pressed his knee into the throat of George Floyd, killing him, that made our world change.

Of course, George Floyd was not the first black man to die at the hands of police. George Floyd was not the first black person to die due to systemic racism and injustice. In fact, COVID-19 was its own example, as black and brown people were far more likely to die from this insidious virus. It would be impossible to count the people of color who have died due to racism and injustice in the 402 years since the first Africans arrived in the United States. But the killing of George Floyd captured international attention in a way that reflected the disruption of our usual systems and habits.

What does this have to do with inclusion on your college campus? Everything. In the new world, inclusion is no longer a nice to have, good will, altruistic thing to do. When the world shifted in the spring of 2020, inclusion finally assumed its rightful place as a cultural priority and expectation. Further, it became abundantly clear that inclusion is not about providing a proliferation of programming for students. The work of inclusion, while it may be led by students, is work for our faculty, staff, and administrators to do. It is time for us to reconcile the fact that we have dwelt in a system of injustice and racism that has infiltrated every aspect of what we do. We can no longer serve as faculty or institutional leaders if we are not first willing to address our own misconceptions.

BECOMING COMMUNITY

When we first implemented the Becoming Community initiative at the College of Saint Benedict and Saint John's University in 2016, the goals were clear, aggressive, and broadly defined. At the outset, we stated that the work of inclusion must be comprehensive and demands that we look at multiple dimensions and perspectives when we think about our campus and the students we serve. Certainly, economic diversity is and will remain a key consideration, as will race and ethnicity. And we were careful not to limit our gaze to visible and/or easily quantifiable metrics. We intentionally stated that when we think and speak of inclusion, we need to think about geographic, spiritual, and ability diversity. Sexual orientation and gender identity, along with diversity of thought and perspective equally merits our attention. If we commit to all having a voice in our community, then it is essential that we think through the variety of people we serve and what they add to, and expect from, our community.

To do the work of inclusion requires multiple partners and points of influence. Clearly, our work both in the classroom and outside of the classroom is critically important. We challenged ourselves to do the work of nurturing a community that is culturally competent and striving toward inclusive excellence.

Key questions guided us as we began this work: How do we, as a professional community, share the responsibilities and the joys of being an inclusive community? What programming and training are helpful and necessary for us? Where and how do members of our professional community feel included and excluded? How do we, as a professional community, model inclusive excellence? We can grapple with and respond to each of these questions as a community.

Even as we did this work, we began to question a fundamental concept at the heart of our work: the call of community. As we did our broad work, we quickly realized a flaw in our thinking. Most language of diversity and inclusion implies that those on the outside will join those already on the inside, with the implicit expectation that they will adopt or adapt to already established norms. Transformation, by contrast, deconstructs the center in interaction with newcomers, so that the voices, experiences, and cultures of all community members are reflected in institutional norms and self-understanding.

Becoming Community undertakes a practice of ongoing community formation based on transformative inclusion. Our goal for Becoming Community is to prepare and enable our students, faculty, and staff to become agents of change by preparing them to dismantle oppression rather than simply teaching them about oppression. The subject matter itself is transformation. We initially sought to make a substantive shift from the narrative of critique to the narrative of dynamic action, moving from a deficit perspective on diversity and inclusion to a strength, or asset-based, perspective. Yet as the grant has unfolded, and the world was refashioned around us so, too, has our work.

Our efforts to undertake and model an intentional practice of community formation based in transformative, rather than primarily additive, inclusion is a vast departure from the norm. This approach to inclusion seems even more instructive given the reshaping of community due to COVID-19 and the clearer attention to the complete systemic transformation needed in the wake of George Floyd's death.

THE LEADERSHIP IMPERATIVE

Midway through our work, it became clear that grappling with the issue of transformative inclusion needed to go far beyond a community immersed in the work of inclusive excellence. Everyone in the community was going to have to assume the mantle of leadership for us to truly engage in transformational leadership.

We eventually realized that the key to inclusion is not about a secret to a class or text in the curriculum. It's not about a single stated outcome or even a single gap. It's not about resolving higher education's economic model in a particular way or ways. What kept coming up, repeatedly, is that inclusion is really about being willing to lead—from whatever your position or role or location—in a way that places you in relationship with the students you have the privilege of educating. It's about leading in such a way that you are willing to see students whom others may want to render invisible. It's about looking at your syllabus and, with clear eyes, asking, can each student I serve see themselves in this course? Can each student I serve see themselves on this leadership cabinet? In this conference room? Our work of inclusion became about a campus community committing to mentoring every person on the campus to serve as an institutional commitment to doing better and supporting the marginalized.

This work of inclusion, as we focused more on systemic change, is about leadership fearlessly facing discrepant outcomes. System change recognizes that the data that reflects discrepant outcomes can hurt to examine, but that that's an intentional and necessary experience of pain in order to transition your community to a better place. Leaders must help a community see the humanity behind the data, rather than allowing a community to be paralyzed or afraid of the data.

It's about making choices that reflect who we are and to whom we are committed. It's about investing in the difficult soul work of inclusion.

Systemic change reflects the need to invest, and hold accountable, the professional communities of which we are a part. It is our desire in higher education to spend every dollar on students, but to truly pursue inclusion we must ensure the entire community is equipped to lead in this work. We must invest in the development of our professional communities, and we must lead conversations that shift the responsibility to all of us. In a college community, this is work for all of us to do. All of us must lead. How do we move the focus from fret and concern about the need to change to being more self-critical in order to grow?

For faculty and staff, this means that our teaching, research, and service must privilege inclusion. The work of inclusion must not be exempt from the content demands and pedagogical freedom at the heart of our academic enterprise. In fact, because the classroom is the center of the student experience, it is imperative that we do our most difficult work in that context.

As we think about our classrooms and the academic enterprise, we are also challenged to think through how we will authentically hear from others whose experiences may be dramatically different from our own. How do we hear new truths about our culture and create policy reflective of those truths? Just because it's not the truth we want, just because it's not our experience, does not mean it is not true or didn't happen or shouldn't be addressed. How can we hear those truths in a way that binds us, as opposed to alienates us?

Once we acknowledge the need for culture change that begins in the classroom and the existence of multiple experiences, how do we learn from and listen to something new? As faculty and staff, how do we learn and listen to something that interrogates our shared past and calls us to new ways of knowing, being, and acting? And what do we need to learn about why we must be transformed as an institution? How do we embrace that learning? How do I, and each of you as leaders, create an environment wherein that learning can take place? Once that learning has commenced, how do we shape institutional goals that align with where we would like to move? How do we change culture?

THE IMPORTANCE OF EXPLICIT ANTI-RACISM

A broad call to inclusion, the reframing of the notion of community, and the articulation of the leadership imperative within and outside of the classroom were good and right and just as we went through this process. And the tremendous results and models for other institutions are shared within the pages of this volume. But in the shadow of spring 2020, it no longer feels like enough. Not only must we be inclusive, we must also be explicitly and unapologetically anti-racist.

Our institutions have promoted the demand for culture change as one constant from the beginning of this work through today. And, at this moment, we must recognize that at the core of that change must reside an explicit call for anti-racism. To call for anti-racism means that we must explicitly deal with the topic of race. We can no longer lump it in with the other worthy components of inclusion but, instead, we must recognize anti-racism as central to the success of inclusion on campus.

While there are many calls for action in our world, and within this volume, the action must lead to significant cultural change on our campuses. Few people are better equipped to do that within higher education than our faculty and staff. However, for faculty and staff to do that work they must apply the same rigor and standards applied to their research, teaching, and service to the work of anti-racism. We can no longer assume expertise but must do the work ourselves.

We believe the models shared within this volume provide some steps to begin that transformative work. And we continue in our quest to lead the inclusive and anti-racist institutions our students—and our communities—deserve.

Introduction to *Inclusion in Higher Education: Research Initiatives on Campus*

Amanda Macht Jantzer and Kyhl Lyndgaard

OVERVIEW

How can we create more inclusive colleges and universities? How can we pursue data-informed change? How can we make inclusion part of everyone's work rather than just the responsibility of one professional or one university office? These pressing questions face many professionals in higher education. The work in this edited collection examines the value of using inquiry-based approaches to address these sorts of inclusion questions and to seek meaningful, evidence-based change in institutions of higher education. By enlisting the resources that colleges and universities all have—the research and critical thinking skills of faculty, staff, and students—and applying them to pursue important research questions about inclusion on campus, transformative change may be realized.

This approach to inclusion begins by embracing scholarly inquiry. We share information about an Inclusion Research Initiative, supported by the Andrew W. Mellon Foundation, that launched nearly a dozen interdisciplinary research teams at two joint institutions of higher education. These teams were composed of faculty, staff, and students at liberal arts institutions who pursued important lines of scholarly inquiry addressing a central question, "How do the institutions promote or inhibit creating an inclusive community?" The foci of these investigations are diverse, addressing a wide range of diversity, equity, and inclusion issues. While individually important, taken together the results of these investigations provide broadly valuable data and insights to inform transformative organizational change efforts. To facilitate the implementation of data-informed change, the results were compiled and presented to key institutional stakeholders in order to develop an inclusion action plan for institutional leaders with a mechanism in place to support

1

implementation. Thus, we are using these research findings to pursue meaningful, evidence-based change toward a more inclusive community.

In this collection, we encourage readers to consider ways that they may similarly engage in lines of scholarly inquiry to address the pressing diversity and inclusion questions at their own institutions. Moreover, we consider how to create mechanisms so that the results of such inquiries are compiled, presented to key institutional stakeholders, translated into concrete action plans, and sustainably implemented. We call others in higher education to join us in asking urgent inclusion questions, gathering necessary data, and facing the changes we need to create more truly inclusive campus communities.

THEORETICAL FRAMEWORK: PURSUING A VISION OF TRANSFORMATIVE INCLUSION

This work has become part of our larger pursuit of transformative inclusion, which is the focus of our Becoming Community initiative funded by the Andrew W. Mellon Foundation (Drazenovich, Rodriguez, and Mercedes 2017, 30; Hinton, 2017, 1). The vision of transformative inclusion is that inclusion must go beyond merely adding new people to preexisting groups, norms, and power structures. This is particularly important when some preexisting elements of a community structure are exclusive or oppressive in nature. Instead, true inclusion requires engaging in continuing group formation, norm-building, and power distribution. Thus, inclusion requires deep, and ongoing, transformation at multiple levels, beginning with self-reflection and expanding all the way to long-standing institutional practices. We seek to pursue transformative inclusion at our own institutions while using this framework, and we challenge others to do so as well.

Our approach to pursuing this vision was further informed by multicultural organizational change theory. More specifically, Pope, Reynolds, and Mueller (2014, 29) apply the Multicultural Change Intervention Matrix which frames change as occurring on individual, group, and institutional levels. This model is particularly useful within the context of transformative inclusion because it further posits that these multilevel changes occur on both first-order (changes within the existing structure) and second-order (sustained changes to the structures or paradigms themselves) dimensions. While first-order change is necessary and important, colleges and universities typically focus on programming and education aimed primarily at increasing individual-level awareness (32). Therefore, an emphasis on second-order changes, including sustained individual-level consciousness-raising, revision of group-level norms, and pervasive institutional-level shifts, better captures how to conceptualize and assess transformative change.

Similarly, we recommend that professionals at complex organizations like colleges and universities take time to evaluate and adopt a theoretical framework to guide their diversity, equity, and inclusion work. As Pope and colleagues (2014, 19) observed, due to the diffuse, complex organizational structure of institutions of higher education, approaches to inclusion are often well intentioned but piecemeal in nature. Frequently, efforts lack a central, cohesive vision, coordination across units, and mechanisms for assessment and sustainability. Moreover, the responsibility for such inclusion efforts frequently overburdens particular professionals or units, such as chief diversity officers or Student Affairs professionals. Therefore, adopting a theoretical framework can spur important institutional discussions, clarify a vision for inclusion, shape goals, inform interventions, and create a process for ongoing evaluation and change.

We positioned this work within the context of larger institutional inclusion efforts, which made this theoretical framework more effective and more efficient as we saw that much of the first-order change had been addressed in recent years. In particular, a series of initiatives, funded earlier and also with support from the Andrew W. Mellon Foundation, spurred a variety of interventions aimed at creating higher levels of cultural competence and inclusive pedagogy among faculty. These professional development projects were funded through twin grants called "Faculty Formation to Support Liberal Learning for All" and "Faculty Development to Engage Increasingly Diverse Students" which were aimed at faculty in the Humanities and/or those who taught in the interdisciplinary First-Year Seminar program.[1] While much of the professional development in these initial grants was structured to emphasize pedagogical techniques for more inclusive teaching and advising, we learned that there was a great need for faculty and staff to have time for self-reflection in order to create inclusion in and out of the classroom. Personal growth toward cultural competency is what allows faculty to see the need for and to become truly open to transformative inclusion and organizational change.

Much of the work described in this collection has been done with the assistance of external funding. Indeed, in the process of clearly identifying needs and goals for a college or university around inclusion, the question of how to fund these initiatives is important to build in from the beginning. Research projects are possible on a range of budgets. One advantage of external funding, or perhaps by applying internal evaluation and assessment lines in a new way, is that a culture of inclusiveness can be more readily created. We learned from those initial projects that it was possible to create a "buzz" around the projects, garnering broad buy-in. Meanwhile, faculty who were not eligible to apply for them began to ask for similar opportunities. Whatever the case, not only being realistic but also being aspirational about potential resources to support institutional change research is important to build into the initial process.

Studying the local context is critically important when developing the framework and goals for a project of transformative inclusion. Understanding who the community is—particularly in an era when student demographics are changing rapidly—and being self-aware about individual and institutional blind spots is necessary in order to set up meaningful research projects. Mertens (2012, 805) defines cultural competence in research:

> . . . as a systematic, responsive mode of inquiry that is actively cognizant, understanding, and appreciative of the cultural context in which the research takes place; it frames and articulates the epistemology of the research endeavor, employs culturally and contextually appropriate methodology, and uses community-generated, interpretive means to arrive at the results and further use of the findings.

By applying an inquiry-based approach to inclusion after working on what the cultural context and state of inclusion is at an institution, research teams are better equipped to ask the right questions, and in appropriate ways, to include community members who have been historically underrepresented at their institutions. Ultimately, what this framework can do is help guide an institution to apply their energy to a line of action that is sustainable and ongoing, rather than an ephemeral development project that fades in memory and influence after just a few years. By tying research and development to the community and to institutional processes, the inquiry-based approach to inclusion is intended to make lasting and transformative progress.

RATIONALE AND CALL

Building on our theory of change and the momentum of this series of institutional initiatives, the work chronicled in this volume illustrates the value of engaging in scholarly inquiry and evidence-informed interventions. Specifically, we provided resources to research teams at our institutions so that they could pursue a wide variety of pressing inclusion questions on our campuses. This helped us gather data to inform and tailor subsequent interventions around inclusion. Importantly, from the framework of Pope and colleagues' Multicultural Intervention Matrix (2014, 29), this approach helped us address needs at levels that may not have been meaningfully or effectively addressed merely from a traditional top-down approach, driven strictly by positional leaders or those from other privileged social statuses. Instead, leveraging administrative authority as a resource fostered the implementation of multiple programs of research on inclusion from teams of researchers with varied positional perspectives, thereby pursuing important questions among groups of people with unique social positions or needs on campus. For instance, scholars could explore unique barriers to access and success in specific fields, like biology, exercise science, or education. Others could work to amplify the voices of marginalized student groups on campus to identify needs from a community informed perspective, while also engaging them in the process and implementation of change. In addition to the benefits of pursuing evidence-informed change, providing support to individuals and units to explore and examine the pressing questions within their own realms of influence also helps to recruit a more broad-based network of changemakers, increasing buy-in for inclusion efforts across the institution. Altogether, an inquiry-based approach to inclusion increases the possibility of meaningful transformative change.

Through our Inclusion Research Initiative, we pursued an inquiry-based approach to inclusion that embraced scholarly inquiry, collaborative efforts, and evidence-based interventions to inform institutional change. Faculty, staff, and student groups were invited to propose research projects that addressed how the institutions promote or inhibit an inclusive community. Proposals were expected to address a cross section of life at our institutions in an attempt to focus and inform the work to be completed through future large-scale institutional change initiatives. To extend upon prior learning, all initial teams were required to include a member of the original Humanities or First-Year Seminar cohorts from the original Mellon grants. Thus, these funds served as an important bridge between our past, current, and future work, allowing us to build upon the critical momentum we had established.

THEMATIC SUMMARY OF PROJECTS

The Mellon Inclusion Research Initiative received a large and enthusiastic response. We were able to launch research teams composed of several dozen faculty, staff, and students who pursued important lines of inquiry while illustrating dedication to making our community more just and inclusive. Collectively, these researchers illustrated the value of using inquiry-based approaches to address inclusion issues and to seek meaningful, evidence-based change. As featured in this edited collection and described below, the foci of these investigations were diverse, addressing a wide range of diversity, equity, and inclusion issues.

Four projects pursued questions related to systemic organizational issues and make up the first section of the collection. These include the development of an ecological theoretical model for creating social justice in academic settings (Jantzer, Wielkiewicz, and Stelzner), which is the opening chapter that helps further theorize and frame this collection. The authors of this model emphasize the complex ecological context of organizations like colleges and universities, stress the need for diversity of perspectives and meaningful feedback loops, and highlight the importance of emergent leadership. The Inclusion Research Initiative illustrates these aspects of ecological leadership. Next, two projects look at larger realities and basic needs that are inseparable from how students access and sustain themselves during college. One is on the shared responsibility community members have on issues of food security (Heying and Nash), while the second is on access to transportation, particularly in small town and rural settings with limited public transportation options (Kachelski, Jantzer, and Booth). The final project in this systemic, organizational section incorporates a course-based inquiry which empowers students to research exclusionary institutional policies (Bacon, Jantzer, and Kramer).

The second section, "Understanding the Experiences of Minoritized Students on Campus," consists of two chapters that address the experiences of specific minoritized populations. An innovative chapter outlines three distinct and ongoing approaches to redress injustices to Native students (Gordon, Benway, and Winters). The second chapter in this section offers suggestions on how to improve the experiences of students from underrepresented religions and denominations, particularly on a campus with a particular religious affiliation (Sheehan, Conway, Schrupp, Scott, and Lewi). Notably, the projects in this section both include student coauthors.

In the final chapters, which make up a section on underrepresented students in specific fields of study, four chapters offer approaches undertaken by faculty from academic departments in divergent disciplines. The first project outlines a comprehensive equity audit done in a teacher training program, which could be applied more broadly to other departments and programs (Israelson, Fenton, Bohn-Gettler, Cofell, Rodriguez, Spenader, & Woodard). The next project in this section explores inclusive practices in Biology 101, which is a course that enrolls high percentages of first-year students (Furniss, J. Jantzer, Kirkman, and McClure). Another project examines how to build inclusivity into Spanish classrooms which blend Latinx and heritage speakers with second-language learners (Kuffner, Gomez, and Schaff). The final project explores access issues, along with embedding social issues in natural science, in the context of an exercise science department (Stenson, Fischer, Hinchley, and LaFountaine).

The cumulative results of these investigations provided rich, valuable data to guide our own institutional inclusion efforts. We are confident that these projects will also serve as useful models for other colleges and universities who are similarly facing inclusion challenges on individual, unit, and institutional levels. Each of the Inclusion Research Initiative projects in this collection feature a clear articulation of the rationale for the project, a review of relevant literature, a process overview to serve as a model, a summary of outcomes, and recommendations for adoption in other units and institutions.

PROCESS AND RESISTANCE

To aid and support these scholars, we developed a series of professional development opportunities and facilitated communication and implementation of findings. The professional development series included a research proposal workshop in coordination with personnel from our academic budget office and institutional review board, a mixer to address common issues and to build community among the researchers, and a focus group research training session. While all the participants were skilled in their respective fields, not all had experience in the sort of qualitative research that many of the projects needed to include and so that was one area we emphasized in the professional development series. We also provided funding for ten researchers, with representatives from each of the research teams, to attend a national Association of American Colleges & Universities (AAC&U) Diversity, Equity, and Inclusion conference that was relevant to their research and related work around diversity and inclusion.

Moreover, we established a mechanism for creating a feedback loop and for promoting actionable change. The Inclusion Research Initiative researchers received support from the Mellon grant as they finalized, disseminated, and applied their results. Each research team submitted a dissemination plan in order to share their findings with the campus community and through professional conferences and publications. In addition, the results, particularly highlighting marginalized student voices, were compiled and presented to key institutional stakeholders at a retreat in order to prioritize concerns and develop an inclusion action plan presented to the institutional leaders. Thus, our goal was to use these research findings to pursue meaningful, evidence-based change toward more inclusive campus communities, and to do so we needed to find or create venues that would be most effective at reaching decision-makers.

We learned that these projects have deep value as applied research studies with contributions to the existing knowledge base not just on our campuses but also to broader bodies of research literature. Beyond these merits; however, these initiatives are also much more than mere research studies. Applications of the findings and the processes undertaken to conduct these works have already produced remarkable actions and outcomes. For instance, as you will discover in the chapters in this collection, researchers have taken initiative to establish campus task forces to address basic needs like food security. Others, like our colleagues from an education department, have applied the impressive, comprehensive process that they developed to conduct a departmental equity audit to guide new approaches to department program evaluation across our institutions. Our researchers have also fostered changes that extend far beyond our institutions. For instance, our colleagues who are examining issues facing Native students have impressively established new relationships with sovereign tribal governments and have begun to foster discussions about restorative justice. They have already created multiple opportunities for mutual peer learning via a series of student exchanges and created a Native Studies professional development series. Thus, the value of using an inquiry-based approach to inclusion in institutions of higher education is that they create new dialogues, new interdisciplinary collaborations, new processes, new innovations, and ultimately, new solutions to pressing problems. Taken together, an inquiry-based approach to inclusion on our campuses has become truly transformational.

We must also acknowledge potential barriers to this sort of broad, inquiry-based approach to examining inclusion. While valuable, this research enterprise can be complex and charged. For instance, learning the answers to these inclusion questions can be difficult and some may not wish to face or publicize the results, perhaps fearing negative impacts on institutional reputations or enrollment. However, recalling Baldwin's (1962, 38) famed observation: "Not everything that is faced can be changed, but nothing can be changed until it is faced," we argue that it is crucial that we face the changes needed in our colleges and universities, lest we continue to exclude and marginalize those whom we seek to include and help thrive.

By engaging a broad cross section of faculty, staff, and students across varied disciplines, this inquiry-based approach has helped elicit buy-in for change work. This level of interest has allowed for tailoring interventions to the needs of specific courses, departments, and subsets of students. Thus, this broad-based engagement has helped undermine resistance to change at our institutions and we believe that adoption of this approach may help engender similar engagement at other institutions.

THE WAY AHEAD

How may others use the models in this volume to apply these approaches widely? We encourage your consideration of how to institutionalize similar inquiry-based research projects on inclusion at other colleges and universities. In response to urgent calls for changes across the nation, US colleges and universities must find ways to effectively answer calls for increased diversity, inclusion, equity, and justice. These inquiry-based approaches may be one way that institutional leaders can pose important questions about inclusion across the diffuse domains of their complex organizations. Then, as higher education professionals gather responses to these questions and center the voices of those too frequently marginalized in our campus communities, transformational change becomes possible. Together, we hope that the way ahead will be a richer, more varied, and more inclusive path.

NOTE

1. See Jean Keller and Kyhl Lyndgaard, "A Brief Taxonomy of Inclusive Pedagogies: What Faculty Can Do Differently to Teach More Inclusively," *Headwaters* 30. For a more comprehensive overview consisting of articles by many faculty contributors called "Roundtable Discussion—From Intention to Action: Building an Inclusive Community" is at the following: https://digitalcommons.csbsju. edu/headwaters/

REFERENCES

Baldwin, James. 1962. "As Much Truth as One Can Bear; To Speak Out About the World as It Is, Says James Baldwin, Is the Writer's Job." *The New York Times*. January 14, 1962, Section T, Page 11, 38. https://www.nytimes.com/1962/01/14/archives/as-much-truth-as-one-can-bear-to-speak-out-about-the-world-as-it-is.html.

Drazenovich, Dana, Terri Rodriguez, and Anna Mercedes. 2017. "How Far Can Inclusion Take Us? Framing the Narrative for Transforming our Community." *Headwaters,* 30 (1): 211–222.

Hinton, Mary. 2017. *Becoming Community*. Unpublished grant proposal manuscript funded by the Andrew W. Mellon Foundation.

Keller, Jean, and Kyhl Lyndgaard. 2017. "A Brief Taxonomy of Inclusive Pedagogies: What Faculty Can Do Differently to Teach More Inclusively." *Headwaters,* 30 (1): 64–82.

Mertens, Donna M. 2012. "Transformative Mixed Methods: Addressing Inequities." *American Behavioral Scientist*, 56 (6): 802–813.

Pope, Raechele, Amy Reynolds, and John Mueller. 2014. *Creating Multicultural Change on Campus*. San Francisco: Jossey-Bass.

Section A

ATTENDING TO SYSTEMIC ORGANIZATIONAL CONTEXT

Chapter 1

An Ecological Model for Building Multiculturalism and Social Justice in Institutions of Higher Education

Amanda Macht Jantzer, Richard M. Wielkiewicz, and Stephen P. Stelzner

Higher education professionals are being challenged to comprehensively respond to rapidly changing demographics and urgent sociopolitical challenges in a way that will allow all members of campus communities to thrive. This need spurs organizational efforts to create more diverse and inclusive colleges and universities. In response to these common challenges and opportunities, the purpose of this chapter is to describe processes for moving an academic institution toward multiculturalism within a social justice context. We expand upon Wielkiewicz and Stelzner's (2005) theoretical framework for leadership and apply it to address multiculturalism and social justice in higher education. This leadership theory is based upon ecological principles that define leadership as a multidirectional *process* instead of solely the actions and decisions of a positional leader. The central element of the theory is this: "Organizations are more adaptive when there is a diversity of genuine input into the decision-making processes" (Wielkiewicz and Stelzner 2005, 326). This approach emphasizes the role of ecological principles of interdependence among organizational leaders and multiple stakeholders, open systems with an emphasis on feedback loops, and cycling of resources which involves broadly engaging talent across the organization. From our perspective, current models of how to infuse a multicultural perspective on college campuses do not adequately account for the systemic context in which such change must take place. As an alternative, we argue that an extension of this ecological model to the domain of higher education will help move colleges and universities toward diversity, inclusion, and justice.

Wielkiewicz and Stelzner's (2005) theory of leadership developed out of work that was being done on our campuses, two joint liberal arts institutions in the Midwest, nearly thirty years ago. The institutions had received a grant from the W. K. Kellogg Foundation to develop leadership research and programming on campus. A conversation between the head of student development (who initiated the grant process) and one of the theory's developers (Stelzner) culminated in the expression of a mutual frustration with the state of leadership theorizing. Further discussion led to the notion of applying an "ecological lens" to leadership that was based in the literature from community psychology. Leaders at our own institutions recently proposed a similar applied concept called the "inclusion ecosystem" that offers a systemic view of how to create a more inclusive and diverse campus (Hinton 2016, n.p.). Hinton highlighted the need for such approaches to inclusion to represent diverse dimensions of identity, experience, and perspective. Moreover, consistent with a contextual, ecological framework, Hinton and Hemesath (2017) noted that "the work of inclusion requires a number of partners and points of influence" (62). In this ecosystem, they specifically emphasized spheres of influence in institutions of higher education that include the curriculum and cocurriculum, the institutional policies/programs/practices, the professional development designed for employees, and the broader local and regional community. While building upon this conceptualization, our goal here is to provide a more extended, comprehensive, and empirically grounded theoretical framework to guide institutional change processes in higher education.

The process of creating a multicultural campus requires leadership; however, it requires leadership different from the typical top-down or industrial approach that centers on the efforts of positional leaders. Instead, we argue in favor of a modern, ecological approach to leadership (Allen, Stelzner, and Wielkiewicz 1999; Bronfenbrenner 1977; Colarelli 1998; Neville and Mobley 2001; Stelzner and Wielkiewicz 2015; Wielkiewicz and Stelzner 2005). Key ingredients of these modern leadership theories emphasize that "leadership as a process, involves influence, occurs within a group context and involves goal attainment" (Chin and Trimble 2015, 15). As Chin and Trimble (2015, 15) noted, such theories highlight mutuality and interrelationships among organizational leaders and followers where influence does not flow simply from the top-down but is multidirectional in nature. Additional key ingredients include the need to be responsive to contextual factors with an emphasis on flexibility and adaptation. Consistent with these modern perspectives, Wielkiewicz and Stelzner (2005, 330) described the core of the ecological approach to understanding leadership. Yet, the theory argues that there must be a balance between the ecological approach and the more traditional "industrial" approach to leadership. The theory consists of six premises that describe the dynamic process of how leadership works in an organization. In the work that follows, we describe each of these premises and illustrate the applications of these aspects of the model for creating multicultural change and enacting social justice work in the context of higher education.

PREMISE 1: LEADERSHIP IS AN EMERGENT PROCESS

This premise challenges the very notion of traditional leadership, which assumes that leadership consists primarily of the actions and decisions of positional leaders. Wielkiewicz and Stelzner (2005, 330–331) begin with a definition of leadership that moves from centering the positional leader to defining leadership as an *emergent process*; that is, it emerges from the interactions and actions of individuals across the organizational ecological system. From this perspective, the role of positional leaders is still important for institutional change to succeed. For instance, to establish a sense of urgency, institutional leaders must be visibly engaged in the change process and must communicate messages that are consistent with the aims of multicultural and social justice initiatives (Kotter 1996, 97–98; Pope, Reynolds, and Mueller 2014, 4). A lack of such involvement or competing messages from uppermost leadership may undermine or sabotage the ultimate success of change initiatives (Kotter 1996, 51–66, 97–98). However, a multicultural initiative has little chance of success if it is solely the result of decisions imposed upon the institution by positional leaders. For instance, campus leaders can order that a new initiative be undertaken or that faculty and staff attend a workshop, but the outcome of the initiative will be null unless the entire organization engages in processes that influence the nature of the initiative. Beyond the role of a singular institutional leader, a broad network of change-makers is needed to extend buy-in and active engagement in change processes across the institution (Kotter 1996, 51–66; Pope, Reynolds, and Mueller 2014, 6). If positional leaders wish to implement a multicultural initiative or intervention, it requires thorough vetting by the community, and customization to ensure it meets the actual needs of the community.

Importantly, broad-based, decentralized leadership is spurred through engaged social interaction where individuals in a community emerge to take action. This emergent leadership may be sustained action or a single instance of change that is tailored for the needs of a unique organizational domain or broadly focused on institutional change. However, this emergent leadership shifts the focus from a central positional leader toward the engaged actions of a broad coalition across the ecological system. Consistent with biological ecology, change emerges out of interaction among varied life systems.

Organizational change processes around inclusion may evolve through many layers of emergence. For instance, the Mellon Inclusion Research

Initiative was launched through the initial leadership of our college president who communicated an inspiring vision of inclusion and secured resources through external grant funding. The grant administrators then emerged as leaders to implement this vision. Upon creation of the Mellon Inclusion Research Initiative, the grant administrators awarded resources to teams who proposed research questions in specific spheres of influence. Many of these teams then took these initial resources and turned what began as a research project into a means of establishing new relationships, opening up cross-cultural and institutional dialogue, and prompting community engagement. Some of our researchers then took the initiative in leading change on campus and off, and in the process inspired others, including students and faculty colleagues, to also lead subsequent change efforts. This demonstrates multiple layers of emergent leadership. The benefit of this is that by fostering a culture of emergent leadership, an organization elicits broad-based buy-in, deep engagement, and extensive community networks. This enhances the ability of the organization to stay nimble and adapt to the diverse needs of campus stakeholders, including those who have been traditionalized marginalized. Moreover, individuals are more likely to engage in change processes that they had a role in developing; thus, enhancing the likelihood of sustainable success.

The role of the positional leader is to foster this sort of emergent process through cultivation of an organizational culture that encourages people to emerge as inclusion leaders within and across their unique spheres of influence. They may do so by leveraging available resources to incentivize change and by rewarding success. A process view of leadership also encourages a focus on decision-making processes and suggests that a key issue is to determine to what extent the ability to influence decisions is distributed among organization members. Then, this emergent process is translated into adaptive decisions and executive processes. The role of the positional leader is not to *make* decisions, but to ensure that the *process* of decision-making includes a diversity of perspectives. Thus, the leader must communicate clearly that input is welcome and must inspire members of the organization to contribute to decision-making processes.

However, the process of change implementation necessarily includes many feedback loops that allow for adjustments and modifications as the context changes and is better understood. It is important that these feedback loops include the voices of marginalized and minoritized community members to more fully represent a diversity of views. However, one risk of feedback processes is that they become so detailed and time-consuming that the proposed initiative becomes outdated. In other words, the discussion can continue infinitely so that the program never begins. For instance, in the context of institutions of higher education, unreasonable delays may result when campus leaders repeatedly postpone action due to the perceived need to wait to intervene until they first obtain extensive baseline data. Frequently, imperfect conditions or incomplete data produce avoidance instead of engagement in change processes (Pope, Reynolds, and Mueller 2014, 115). In this case, the positional leader may stop deliberations, create consensus, and act, trusting that the ecosystem creates feedback that helps correct flaws in the initiative.

Another role for the positional leader is to use their knowledge of the organizational structure, individual expertise, and interests of members to bring individuals and groups together to discuss issues and formulate action plans. For example, a university president could order formation of a diversity and inclusion committee with faculty, staff, and student representatives, including minoritized voices, to make recommendations about new policies, procedures, and education to advance social justice goals. The role of the positional leader remains important in ecological theory, but it shifts from decision-making to brokering information pathways and inviting participation in the process. Leadership and investment should come from all elements of the organization, or the process becomes top heavy or responsibility is abdicated. It is critical to understand that the various groups/departments are interdependent, and so no initiative will go anywhere without an investment from all elements of the campus ecosystem.

PREMISE 2: EFFECTIVE LEADERSHIP CONSISTS OF FINDING A BALANCE BETWEEN THE INDUSTRIAL AND ECOLOGICAL APPROACHES TO LEADERSHIP

Buenger, Daft, Conlon, and Austin (1996, 557), Quinn (1988), and Quinn and Rohrbaugh (1983, 370) have argued that organizational failure often results from the inability to balance competing values. Dedicated pursuit of only one side of the competing values eventually becomes a failing strategy as the context changes. Kelly, Ryan, Altman, and Stelzner (2000, 153–155) stated that over-focusing on process while excluding structure or hierarchy could cause an organization to disintegrate because it does not implement decisions efficiently. The history of leadership studies has generally been written from the perspective of the industrial paradigm (Rost 1997, 3), emphasizing the preeminence of positional leaders and the machine-like qualities of organizations. By contrast, the ecological theory of leadership was first described by Allen, Stelzner, and Wielkiewicz (1998) and elaborated by Wielkiewicz (2000, 2002), and Wielkiewicz and Stelzner (2005). The theory defines leadership as a process that emerges from the human interactions that make up an organization and asserts in Premise 2 that organizational members must find an optimal balance between the industrial and the ecological perspectives if the organization is to adapt effectively.

This is one of the more challenging premises of the ecological approach to leadership. The industrial approach, centered on the behavior and decisions of positional leaders, is so dominant it may appear that the ecological approach replaces the industrial approach entirely. However, a theory of leadership based entirely on ecological principles is flawed because the amount of information to be considered to address any problem is nearly infinite. For example, college and university libraries must examine numerous potential reference source materials or search tools, and choose which ones meet the needs of various constituents on campus, including faculty, students, staff, administrators, and community members. Merely using the search term "multiculturalism" in the Google search engine results in more than eighty-seven million hits. The task of reviewing all the available information relevant to almost any decision is an impossible task. For this reason, the ecological approach to leadership is, by itself, inadequate. There is too much information to be evaluated so that leadership processes could extend indefinitely, delaying implementation of multicultural and social justice initiatives, which may prove costly in the context of the competitive marketplace of higher education and student welfare.

Although it is possible to become lost in a flood of information, it is not inevitable. A balance between the industrial (top-down) perspective and the ecological perspective is necessary for producing effective adaptation (Wielkiewicz and Stelzner 2005, 331). Too much structure can inhibit adaptation, whereas a focus on "process" to the exclusion of structure or hierarchy can cause disintegration because it is possible to discuss a problem forever without taking any action. The more skill organizational leaders bring to the task of balancing the tension between industrial and ecological processes, the more effective the organization will be. One way to balance the process of reaching consensus and the implementation of decisions is for organizational leaders to create time-limited dialogues and implement a decision in the organization that fully accounts for the input of organizational members. Of course, positional leaders who make decisions with no input from organization members are also destined for failure, because no individual can evaluate all the relevant information; they need the help of other organization members. In addition, involvement from others leads to more organizational commitment to the decision. This is the opposite extreme to pursuing the process excessively. Neither extreme works. Instead, the decision-making process and implementation ideally strike a balance between process and pragmatism.

Multicultural and social justice initiatives are as complex as any issues faced by academic institutions. Therefore, being successful at making change on any campus requires that organizational members from a variety of backgrounds and perspectives influence leadership processes. Furthermore, most minoritized groups have been excluded from decision-making processes, which must be changed to account for their input. This is particularly critical when positional leaders enjoy privileged, majority identities and thus may experience blind spots and biases about the needs of minoritized members of their campus communities. An additional challenge is resistance to change as some do not see any need for intervention or programming. These individuals should be targeted for involvement in the process which can reduce resistance. The result of such a diversity of perspectives is that reaching consensus on the nature of multicultural organizational change is an exceedingly complex task, and those involved are likely to be overwhelmed by the conflicting inputs and massive amounts of information. This is where individuals may need help to reach consensus and make concrete programmatic proposals. Imposition of deadlines and executive decisions may be needed. Reminders to all involved that a perfect plan is impossible and that a balance between process and implementation of policy will take the institution in the desired direction.

As organizational members struggle to reach consensus, it may be helpful to assure individuals that change is not written in stone. Change efforts are certain to have flaws and problems and that attempting to anticipate every contingency is not realistic. Instead, the initiative must be designed to be flexible and self-correcting. This flexibility is accomplished by building in feedback loops (see Premise 4) that provide the information needed to make changes that improve the program. Responsiveness to diverse feedback is particularly important for colleges and universities that aim to pursue transformative inclusion (Hinton 2017, 2), which posits that inclusion requires an ongoing process of community formation and deconstruction of oppressive structures that may change over time and in response to shifting institutional composition.

PREMISE 3: LEADERSHIP OCCURS IN A WEB OF INTERDEPENDENT SOCIAL AND BIOLOGICAL SYSTEMS

All organizations exist within an interdependent web of social and biological systems. For example, all educational organizations need to be concerned with the potential impact of climate change (e.g., Wielkiewicz 2016) which is part of the biological systems in which institutions exist. All higher education institutions may be required to give priority to lowering their carbon footprint, which could take money away from other priorities. The regulatory system has created numerous requirements for academic institutions, such as maintaining privacy of student records and accommodating students with disabilities. "Net neutrality," the idea that the Internet should be a free and open-source of information has recently come under attack; this could create serious issues for institutions as they store more and more academic materials on distant servers. Moreover, the current sociopolitical arena features divisive racial and gendered rhetoric along with a 25 percent uptick in hate crimes at all colleges and universities in 2016 (Bauman 2018). In sum, no organization exists as an isolated system; it is located within a network of interrelated systems that affect it in profound ways.

Writing from a developmental perspective, Bronfenbrenner (1977, 514–515) identified four major systems (microsystem, mesosystem, exosystem, and macrosystem) that affect the development of all individuals. Neville and Mobley (2001, 473) further proposed an ecological model of individual counseling that describes the dynamic structure of the systems, which provides a context for understanding individuals. The American Psychological Association (APA 2017, 9) adapted Bronfenbrenner's ecological model to provide structure for the most recent version of the Association's *Multicultural Guidelines*. The APA model replaces Bronfenbrenner's terms with numbered levels. We believe these models provide a good starting point for consideration of academic environments because it helps us understand multidimensional change from an ecological perspective.

The microsystem for an academic institution consists of the living and learning environments of the faculty, staff, and administrators. As Neville and Mobley (2001, 474) point out, there are several counseling-related characteristics of the microsystem, such as cultural competence of service providers, local organizations such as a Black Student Association, academic departments, especially in the areas of cultural studies, student counseling services, and so forth. One of the main goals of academic institutions is to make the microsystem as culturally competent, diverse, respectful, and accepting as possible. However, the academic campus is not an isolated system; it has its own systemic context influencing the individual and the microsystem. The APA guidelines (2017, 10) emphasize the interaction between clients and clinicians, students and educators, and participants and researchers, with each having an impact on the other and their identities. Multiple intersecting identities and a wide range of variation exist within any social identity group, and so these interactions illustrate the way that all ecological systems operate. Educators not only teach their students but they also learn from them, and out of that learning comes a changed interaction between student and educator.

Level 2 surrounds the individual and is labeled the community, school, and family context in the APA (2017, 10) model. These are the components of the ecology with which the individual is regularly in contact. In Bronfenbrenner's (1977, 515) model, this is called the mesosystem. As one moves away from the individual toward the more distant systems, Neville and Mobley (2001, 472) focus on the general system of health care that influences the structure and rules of counseling services. From an academic perspective, the mesosystem of an academic institution may be composed of accrediting organizations, the high schools that feed students to the higher education system, the continuing influences of the family system on the individual and the academic institution, and so on.

The exosystem or Level 3 in the APA guidelines (2017, 11) is composed of the various systems at the local, state, and federal levels, including medical systems, legal systems, the mental health systems, and educational systems. Guideline 5 (APA, 2017) states that practitioners "aspire to recognize and understand historical and contemporary experiences with power, privilege, and oppression" (4). This includes "disparities of law enforcement, administration of criminal justice, educational, mental health, and other systems" (4). Not all forms of oppression come from Level 3; however, when oppression and disparities emanate from institutions, these structures become entrenched and difficult to change. For this reason, all higher education professionals need to be aware of the context that surrounds the students with whom they interact individually.

At the outer layer of systems is the macrosystem, or Level 4, the larger societal context. The description of the macrosystem by Neville and Mobley (2001, 475) is very relevant to educational institutions. White privilege, gender bias, stereotyping, immigration law, and numerous other social phenomena are all part of the macrosystem. Level 4 (APA 2017, 11) also adds human rights concerns to the larger societal context. Through this contextual lens, creating a multicultural microsystem on campus may be a frustrating exercise if graduating students cannot find social justice once they leave the campus. Similarly, successfully recruiting diverse faculty and staff members to campus is useless if they feel isolated, discriminated against, and miserable while trying to live off campus. Thus, Neville and Mobley add the "social structures of class, race, gender, and sexual identity" (473) to the construct of the macrosystem. It is extremely important to acknowledge the existence of these systemic influences and perhaps take steps to help students and employees combat or eliminate those that are most harmful. Organizations must examine and minimize the ways in which they may unintentionally be perpetuating or recreating these systems of oppression through institutionalized policies, procedures, and practices. Intervention could lead to action at the institutional, local, national, or international level. Neville and Mobley (2001, 476) also point out that groups experiencing prejudice or bias will be affected individually in many ways, such as having little trust in the "system." Thus, efforts to create a multicultural campus must deal with this reality.

We argue that including people from marginalized groups into the organizational "system" of leadership and governance is crucial. This is where feedback loops and representation are crucially important. Instead of pitting individuals against the system, a diversity of individuals should be included within the systems of power. Moreover, change will be facilitated by organizations that create an empowering setting wherein individuals who have traditionally been marginalized are empowered to enact change.

The purpose of examining the ecological systems within which all of us exist is not to provide a travel map. The purpose is to indicate the complexity of ecological systems. Everyone exists within this layered system, but the influence of each layer and each component of each layer will vary from person to person. Thus, these layers provide a rough outline that needs to be completed differently for everyone. For example, some people are profoundly influenced by their concerns for the environment, especially the potential impact of climate change (Level 4), and this concern, in turn, impacts how all the other layers interact to create the person's identity. Others may have experienced poverty or domestic violence or familial opioid abuse. The important takeaway is that any person exists within a complex ecological system and that understanding that ecosystem can contribute toward understanding the person and how to intervene to improve life for everyone. Moreover, extending this model to higher education, it is similarly important to recognize the complex ecosystems in which colleges and universities exist in order to create campus communities where all can be included and thrive.

PREMISE 4: THE RICHNESS AND VARIABILITY OF FEEDBACK LOOPS THAT INFLUENCE LEADERSHIP PROCESSES DETERMINES THE ADAPTABILITY OF THE ORGANIZATION

Organizational adaptability is determined by the richness and variability of feedback loops allowed to influence leadership processes. Feedback loops are the mechanism through which adaptation occurs. The more that an organization responds to its relevant feedback loops, the more adaptive it will be. This characteristic of the ecological model is a critical element of successful multicultural programming. Without adequate feedback loops along the way, progress toward a diverse and inclusive campus climate is almost certain to become stalled or regress.

What is a feedback loop? A feedback loop is best explained through examples. A common feedback loop with which almost everyone is familiar is a thermostat. A thermostat keeps the temperature of a house or apartment within a comfortable range by constantly monitoring the temperature. When the temperature falls below the preset range, the heater comes on which raises the temperature. When the temperature returns to the preset comfort range, the heater turns off. Room temperature is maintained at a comfortable level through the operation of the feedback loop: information comes into the system about the temperature, which controls the heater, maintaining temperature within a comfortable range. Temperature information provides feedback to the system, which indicates whether more heat is needed. There is a constant cycle of incoming information, response to the information, and reassessment of the state of the system. A feedback loop could be called a "feedback-action-loop" to emphasize the importance of the action that occurs in response to the feedback. Thus, the sequence of events is that feedback is received by the organization, action is taken to address the feedback, and then additional feedback is obtained to determine whether the action was successful and/or more action is needed.

Another example will help to bring the concept into focus within the context of higher education. Imagine an educational institution in the early stages of a shift toward multicultural change that has recruited a first-year class consisting of many minoritized individuals. Focus groups indicate that most of the minoritized individuals are dissatisfied with the campus climate. In response to this feedback, the institution recruits a group of new faculty from minoritized groups. In turn, institutional researchers find that satisfaction of minoritized students rises. In one sense, this feedback loop has been completed. However, the presence of both faculty and students from minoritized groups has now created a shift in the campus climate and another round of feedback reveals other sources of dissatisfaction that need to be addressed. For example, Reid (2010, 137) found evidence that minoritized faculty, especially black and Asian faculty, received lower course evaluations than white faculty. Similarly, Price-Williams and Maätita (2019, 96) argued that minoritized women faculty members experience excessive demands for scholarly output, while being assigned to numerous committees and having excessive numbers of advisees. These organizational citizenship behaviors then go unrecognized and create difficulties in tenure and promotion decisions. If bias exists in the way minoritized faculty are evaluated for retention and tenure, another issue that requires action has been identified. Thus, the cycle of feedback-action-reassess continues.

A study by Mayhew, Grunwald, and Dey (2005) further illustrates the complexity of feedback loops in this context. They surveyed students at a large, predominantly white, US Midwestern university. The major dependent variable was a three-item scale that measured the extent to which the institution had "achieved a positive climate for diversity" (399). Characteristics that students perceived as helpful included a public institutional commitment to diversity, faculty commitment to incorporate multiculturalism into their instruction and curriculum, interaction with diverse peers and faculty, taking diversity courses, and involvement in cocurricular activities. However, an interesting finding was that institutional efforts to promote a multicultural climate might make students inclined to critically evaluate such efforts and become highly critical of flaws and inconsistencies. This could present a challenge to many institutions; that is, to recognize that "feedback" is not a "feedback loop." Just because an institution seeks comments from students or any other group about diversity initiatives, this does not constitute a feedback loop. Furthermore, it is important not to confuse a verbal reaction or comment with a feedback loop. A verbal response does not qualify as a component of a completed feedback loop unless there is some action to address the problem. Empty promises such as "we will look into that" or fake empathy "that must be difficult for you" that is not followed by intervention to prevent future occurrences is inviting even more negative feedback. A feedback loop consists of receiving feedback, taking action to address the issues, and then conducting another round of feedback to determine if things have improved. Merely inviting feedback and verbally responding to it is *not* a feedback loop.

The complexity and number of feedback loops to which an academic organization must respond makes the process extremely complex. Potential sources of information to which an academic institution must respond if it is to adapt and remain a viable and successful organization include students, faculty, staff, administrators, parents, the population of high school students who may apply to the institution, regulatory agencies, accrediting agencies, donors, employers, the climate, and others. An essential element of multicultural change is to design feedback loops that inform the organization about how the intervention is working and how it can be improved. The mindset is that no intervention or program is perfect. Therefore, one of the main goals of those who implement a program should be to find its flaws and correct them. This is accomplished by deliberately creating feedback loops. One way to monitor a program is to conduct focus groups and surveys as part of an ongoing, sustained process of institutional assessment.

PREMISE 5: A TENSION EXISTS BETWEEN THE NEED FOR HUMAN AND SOCIAL DIVERSITY AND SINGLE-MINDED PURSUIT OF ORGANIZATIONAL GOALS AND OBJECTIVES

Adaptability and diversity are inseparable. Diversity is the material out of which adaptability emerges (Klingsporn 1973, 441–447). If, for example, all the people on a campus were from the white majority culture, what would be the source of ideas for recruiting and retaining students from minoritized cultures? On the other hand, listening to every single voice on a diverse campus could create such a cacophony of input that discussion continues without end, and decisions about new policies and procedures that could create a more welcoming community for minoritized students and faculty are never made. Diversity leads to adaptability, but in an organizational context, too much diversity of thought, opinion, and policies can leave the organization floundering without a clear direction. Thus, Wielkiewicz and Stelzner (2005, 334) see a need to balance the tension between diversity and pursuit of common goals and objectives. Too much of either diversity or single-mindedness places the organization in a precarious position.

How does this apply to multicultural programming on campus? Imagine two contrasting approaches to multicultural programming. On the one hand, an institution could implement a multicultural program with a packaged set of faculty, administrator, and student workshops with the goal of maintaining a high percentage of participation. This represents the single-minded pursuit of goals and objectives. This could be a winning strategy in an unchanging environment and a program that has demonstrated success. On the other hand, an institution could approach multicultural programming in a completely unstructured way, responding to campus needs as they are identified and creating multiple feedback loops to measure success and identify new issues. This approach is likely to produce a confusing array of interventions with little stability and little thematic content. In fact, constantly responding to feedback can cause the processes to get out of control, as variation increases exponentially. A balanced approach lies somewhere in between these two extremes. Multicultural programming should have some stability across time, so its impact can be evaluated and understood. At the same time, the program should be subjected to feedback loops and modified using a flexible approach that responds to important issues, but where sound judgment is applied to differentiate the important issues from the trivial ones.

Diverse groups of organizational members contribute to organizational adaptability. This idea comes directly from ecological principles (Capra 1996; Klingsporn 1973, 441–447). The more diversity within a system, the more adaptable it will be because variability enhances the ability of the system to generate a wide range of adaptive strategies. For example, if enrollments are in decline, a diverse student body and a multicultural orientation might provide the ability to recruit diverse groups of students. Similarly, students who have graduated from institutions with a high degree of diversity are prepared for a variety of occupational contexts. Diversity improves adaptation in any context. However, there is an important but neglected issue regarding diversity and feedback loops. While it is crucial to diversify the voices included in these loops, it is worth noting that simply *including* those voices is not enough. Inclusion must be combined with action.

In a review and analysis of terminology commonly used in higher education, including diversity and inclusion, Drazenovich, Rodriguez, and

Mercedes (2017, 215) emphasized the importance of attending to the role of power and engaging in self-reflection. In particular, with regard to inclusion, they highlight that inclusive pedagogy or education cannot be strictly about interventions targeted for marginalized students; crucially, it must also be about meaningful self-reflection about one's own social location in systems of power and oppression, and examination of the effect on our interactions and our classrooms. Furthermore, they highlighted that inclusion is commonly framed as being about identifying groups of people who are excluded or marginalized and working to assimilate them into preexisting institutional norms, stating, "We are only expanding the boundaries of who we are, and whom we will allow to fit in to 'us'; we are not fundamentally shifting who we are . . . we need to guard against using it in any way that renders power differentials invisible" (30). Moreover, inclusion sometimes connotes images of creating a platform for people who have exclusive views, so the authors stated "if we want institutions that deconstruct oppressive norms, we will need to say so" (31).

We have heard anecdotal reports from people of color observing that new multicultural initiatives on campuses are doing things that they have been talking about and suggesting to leadership for years. This creates a bittersweet situation. While they are glad to see the organization has the will to act, they understandably feel some resentment that there is so much enthusiasm for these efforts now when this was lacking in the past. Therefore, the inclusion of diverse voices is not enough. There must be a genuine investment in collaborative leadership lest those voices stop speaking up or leave entirely. In other words, the voices must not only be heard, action must be taken to reflect the feedback. Otherwise, the request for feedback is not genuine. Organizational leadership can address these issues by never issuing feigned requests for feedback. Positional leaders need to acknowledge that they are giving up command and control when they seek feedback. Adaptation emerges from genuinely *responding* to feedback, not merely requesting it. The organization must be open to change in response to feedback.

PREMISE 6: LEADERSHIP PROCESSES ARE EVALUATED IN TERMS OF HOW ADAPTIVELY THE ORGANIZATION RESPONDS TO ITS LONG-TERM CHALLENGES

Heifetz (1994, 8; Sparks 2002, 44–46) identified a type of problem faced by organizations called "adaptive challenges." Adaptive challenges are emerging out of our current environment and have never been encountered previously, so strategies for coping with them do not exist; they must be developed by the organization. Climate change is an example of an adaptive challenge. Humans have never faced this problem. Therefore, new strategies for coping with and mitigating climate change are required. Similarly, educational institutions must respond to an ever-changing environment, so they can meet the needs of students. The need for a multicultural, social justice approach to education emerges out of the shifting demographics of the U.S. population, internationalization of business and commerce, serving diverse groups of students, and other trends. The response of educational organizations to these long-term trends will ultimately determine whether they remain successful in the future. Thus, enrollments for the current semester are not as important as adjusting to future population trends and societal needs. Leadership processes are successful to the extent that the organization can adjust and adapt to the future.

SUMMARY

Taken together, the following premises that comprise this model will guide a recursive, dynamic approach to institutional change within the complex ecological context of higher education:

- Premise 1: Leadership is an Emergent Process
- Premise 2: Effective Leadership Consists of Finding a Balance Between the Industrial and Ecological Approaches to Leadership
- Premise 3: Leadership Occurs in a Web of Interdependent Social and Biological Systems
- Premise 4: The Richness and Variability of Feedback Loops That Influence Leadership Processes Determines the Adaptability of the Organization
- Premise 5: A Tension Exists Between the Need for Human and Social Diversity and Single-minded Pursuit of Organizational Goals and Objectives
- Premise 6: Leadership Processes are Evaluated in Terms of How Adaptively the Organization Responds to its Long-Term Challenges

The Mellon Inclusion Research Initiative described in this volume may serve as a helpful illustration of the key elements of this ecological leadership model. While this inclusion effort was initiated by a positional leader, namely by the college president, along with leadership from multiple faculty grant administrators, it embraced a flexible, emergent leadership approach that distributed decision-making and change efforts across the institutional ecosystem. For instance, by offering a call for proposals to the campus community, we were able to engage a broad coalition of change-makers that included faculty, staff, and student leaders on over ten research teams from departments and units across the campuses. This allowed for a rich diversity of perspectives that enabled adaptability as we collectively pursued the goal of transformative inclusion on our campuses. Our inquiry-based approach to inclusion facilitated the creation of meaningful feedback loops, allowing for deep examinations of factors that promote or inhibit inclusion in varied departments and student populations. Many of these research projects involved gathering in-depth perspectives and lived experiences of minoritized student groups on campus via qualitative and quantitative research; thus, centering the feedback of individuals often marginalized in leadership processes. These research findings were then used to inform subsequent inclusion initiatives by project leaders and communicated to a group of campus partners (including a diverse collection of campus leaders) to inform future interventions, including a second wave of grant-supported research projects and program implementation. Thus, consistent with an ecological leadership approach, the Mellon Inclusion Research Initiative produced a recursive process of action, feedback, and change.

CONCLUSION

Through this extension of Wielkiewicz and Stelzner's (2005) ecological framework for leadership, we describe processes that will aid other higher education professionals in creating effective institutional change. This approach emphasizes the centrality of ecological principles of interdependence among organizational leaders and multiple stakeholders, open systems with an emphasis on feedback loops, and cycling of resources which involves broadly engaging stakeholders across the organization. We emphasize the systemic context in which change must take place and argue that an extension of this theoretical model to the domain of higher education will help professionals create more diverse and inclusive colleges and universities.

REFERENCES

Allen, Kathleen E., Stephen P. Stelzner, and Richard Wielkiewicz. 1999. "The Ecology of Leadership: Adapting to the Challenges of a Changing World." *Journal of Leadership and Organizational Studies* 5 (2): 62–82. doi:10.1177/107179199900500207.

American Psychological Association. 2017. "Multicultural Guidelines: An Ecological Approach to Context, Identity, an Intersectionality." https://www.apa.org/about/policy/multicultural-guidelines.pdf.

Bauman, Dan. 2018. "After 2016 Election, Campus Hate Crimes Seemed to Lump. Now the Data Confirm it." *The Chronicle of Higher Education* 64 (25): A18+.

Bronfenbrenner, Urie. 1977. "Toward an Experimental Ecology of Human Development." *American Psychologist* 32 (7): 513–531. doi:10.1037/0003-066x.32.7.513.

Buenger, Victoria, Richard L. Draft, Edward J. Conlon, and Jeffery Austin. 1996. "Competing Values in Organizations: Contextual Influences and Structural Consequences." *Organization Science* 7 (5): 557–576. doi:10.1287/orsc.7.5.557.

Capra, Fritjof. 1996. *The Web of Life.* New York: Anchor Books.

Chin, Jean Lau, and Joseph E. Trimble. 2015. *Diversity and Leadership.* Thousand Oaks, CA: SAGE.

Colarelli, Stephen. M. 1998. "Psychological Interventions in Organizations: An Evolutionary Perspective." *American Psychologist* 53 (9): 1044–1056. doi:10.1037/0003-066x.53.9.1044.

Drazenovich, Dana, Terri L. Rodriguez, and Anna Mercedes. 2017. "How Far Can Inclusion Take Us? Framing the Narrative for Transforming Our Community." *Headwaters* 30 (1): 211–222.

Heifetz, Ronald A. 1994. *Leadership Without Easy Answers.* Cambridge, MA: Belknap Press of Harvard University Press.

Hinton, Mary Dana. 2016. "CSB Inclusion Ecosystem." Transcript of CSB Inclusion Ecosystem. Retrieved from: https://prezi.com/uk0pinierufu/csb-inclusion-ecosy stem/.

Hinton, Mary Dana. 2017. *Becoming Community.* Unpublished grant proposal manuscript funded by the Andrew W. Mellon Foundation.

Hinton, Mary Dana, and Michael Hemesath. 2017. "An Introduction on the Mellon Grant." *Headwaters* 30 (1): 6–63.

Kelly, James G., Ann Marie Ryan, B. Eileen Altman, and Stephen P. Stelzner. 2000. "Understanding and Changing Social Systems: An Ecological View." In *Handbook of Community Psychology,* edited by Julian Rappaport & Edward Seidman, pp. 133–159. Kluwer Academic Publishers.

Klingsporn, M. J. 1973. "The Significance of Variability." *Behavioral Science* 18 (6): 441–447. doi:10.1002/bs.3830180607.

Kotter, John P. 1996. *Leading Change.* Boston, MA: Harvard Business School Press.

Mayhew, Matthew J., Heidi E. Grunwald, and Eric L. Dey. 2005. "Curriculum Matters: Creating a Positive Climate for Diversity from the Student Perspective." *Research in Higher Education* 46 (4): 389–412. doi:10.1007/s11162-005-2967-0.

Neville, Helen A., and Michael Mobley. 2001. "Social Identities in Contexts: An Ecological Model of Multicultural Counseling Psychology Processes." *Counseling Psychologist* 29 (4): 471–486. doi:10.1177/0011000001294001.

Pope, Raechele L., Amy L. Reynolds, and John A. Mueller. 2014. *Creating Multicultural Change on Campus.* San Francisco: Jossey-Bass.

Price-Williams, Shelley, and Florence Maätita. 2019. "Critical Examination of Tokenism and Demands of Organizational Citizenship Behavior Among Faculty Women of Color." In *Navigating Micro-Aggressions Toward Women in Higher Education,* edited by T. Ursula, pp. 96–121. Hershey, PA: IGI, Inc.

Quinn, Robert E. 1988. *Beyond Rational Management.* San Francisco: Jossey-Bass.

Quinn, Robert E., and John Rohrbaugh. 1983. "A Spatial Model of Effectiveness Criteria: Towards a Competing Values Approach to Organizational Analysis." *Management Science* 29 (3): 363–377. doi:10.1287/mnsc.29.3.363.

Reid, Landon D. 2010. "The Role of Perceived Race and Gender in the Evaluation of College Teaching on RateMyProfessors.com." *Journal of Diversity in Higher Education* 3 (3): 137–152. doi:10.1037/a0019865.

Rost, J. C. 1997. "Moving from Individual to Relationship: A Postindustrial Paradigm of Leadership." *The Journal of Leadership Studies* 4 (4): 3–16. doi:10.1177/107179199700400402.

Sparks, D. 2002. "Bringing the Spirit of Invention to Leadership [An interview with Ronald Heifetz]." *Journal of Staff Development* 23 (2): 44–46.

Stelzner, Stephen. P., and Richard M. Wielkiewicz. 2015. "Chapter 3: Understanding Ecological Systems." In *Community Psychology: Foundations for Practice,* edited by Susan M. Wolfe and Victoria C. Scott, pp. 63–112. Thousand Oaks, CA: Sage.

Wielkiewicz, Richard M. 2016. *Sustainability and Psychology* (2nd edition). St. Cloud, MN: Main Event Press.

Wielkiewicz, Richard M., and Stephen P. Stelzner. 2005. "An Ecological Perspective on Leadership Theory, Research, and Practice." *Review of General Psychology* 9 (4): 326–341. doi:10.1037/1089-2680.9.4.326.

Chapter 2

It Takes a Community

Everyone Is Responsible for Creating a Food Secure Campus

Emily K. Heying and Jonathan Nash

Obtaining a college education is considered by some to be just another stepping stone to success. But what if one gets to college and cannot survive due to lack of basic needs? There is a myth that exists surrounding higher education costs: "If students can afford college tuition, they can afford basic needs, like food." Thanks to recent research and advocacy, institutions of higher education are beginning to realize that many college students do not have equitable access to food. As professors at liberal arts institutions, we witness the stark reality of many students who cross the finish line to get to college, only to realize they are behind in the next race to complete college. Food and water are basic human needs. When students sacrifice access to food for other requirements to survive college, the risks and potential consequences can be devastating.

DEFINING FOOD INSECURITY

Food insecurity is defined as the limited or uncertain availability of nutritionally adequate and safe foods or limited or uncertain "ability to acquire acceptable foods in socially acceptable ways" (United States Department of Agriculture 2019). On the contrary, food security means that all household members can access enough food for an active, healthy life. Food secure individuals have ready availability of nutritious, safe foods, and can access those foods in socially acceptable ways (USDA 2019). Affordability, transportation, and physical limitations are potential barriers to food security in the general population.

The consequences of food insecurity are well established in the scholarly literature. Food insecure individuals are at higher risk for malnutrition because caloric and nutrient intake are potentially altered. Resulting malnutrition issues can manifest as deficiency (too little) and/or excess (too much). Food insecure individuals may be more likely to consume diets higher in energy-dense and empty calorie foods and beverages because those choices may be more affordable or accessible, depending on the situation (Drewnowski 2010, 187; Darmon and Drewnoski 2015, 648–649). Aside from links to diet and metabolic diseases, food insecurity is also associated with higher risk for psychosocial issues, such as depression and anxiety (Laraia et al. 2006, 181; McLaughlin et al. 2012, 7).

The most widely used instrument to assess food security status in the United States is the USDA Household Food Security Survey Module (HHFSM) (USDA 2012). The instrument is available for free online and validated in a variety of populations. There are different versions of the survey, each varying in the number of questions. In 2018, household food insecurity impacted 11.1 percent of U.S. households. Rates of food insecurity were higher than the national average for several household and demographic groups. Households with children and headed by a single parent, particularly a single woman, had higher rates of food insecurity. Black and Hispanic households also experienced higher prevalence of food insecurity than the national average. Between 2016 and 2018, Alabama, Louisiana, and Mississippi were states with the highest prevalence of very low food security (the most severe) with 6.8 percent, 6.8 percent, and 6.3 percent of households, respectively (U.S. Department of Agriculture Economic Research Service 2018). These states also rank highly for poverty rates in the United States. While most research regarding prevalence and consequences of food insecurity focuses on children, low-income adults, and elderly populations, college students have been overlooked as a food insecurity risk group until the last decade.

ZONING IN ON COLLEGE CAMPUS FOOD INSECURITY

Traditionally aged college students (eighteen to twenty-five years old) are a unique population to study regarding food insecurity. The experience is a time of transition and growing independence for many. College students may develop changes in dietary habits due to dining in campus centers, having more freedom over their food choices, and adjusting to a new lifestyle or schedule (Plotnikoff 2015, 2). Some students may also transition to preparing meals for themselves for the first time, whereas other students are already familiar with these skills. Living situations of college students vary based on type and location of institution, resources, and preference.

There is no one framework to describe the overall college experience because institutions vary so widely. For example, a student attending a large publicly funded university in an urban area may live on campus with a meal plan their first year, but in an off-campus apartment the following years. Meanwhile, a student at a liberal arts institution with a much smaller population may find it the norm to live in on-campus housing all four years with some variation of a campus meal plan.

Like the rest of the population, eating habits affect college students' overall well-being. A 2014 review of forty-nine studies reported that duration in college was the largest contributing factor to weight gain among this young-adult age group. While first-year students gain weight on average, this rapid period of change does not contribute as intensely to weight change or status as the overall duration of college (Fedewa 2014, 649). According to the spring 2019 American College of Health survey of students at sixty-five institutions, approximately 70 percent of college students self-reported consuming two or less servings of fruits and vegetables per day. Additionally, 37.6 percent of college students reported a body mass index (BMI) classified as overweight or obese (American College Health Association 2019, 14).

One of the most prominent research efforts investigating food insecurity among college students is from the Hope Center, a research lab led by Dr. Sara Goldrick-Rab at Temple University. Goldrick-Rab's "Real College" project has surveyed over 167,000 college students from both two-year and four-year institutions between 2015 and 2018. In their 2019 annual report (from surveys administered in 2018), approximately 42 percent of respondents from four-year colleges reported low or very low security. From the HHFSM survey, the two questions students most commonly responded "yes" to were: "I couldn't afford to eat balanced meals," and "I worried I would run out of food before I could buy more." Respondents who identified as black, African American, or Latinx experienced higher rates of food insecurity than white, Asian, or Native American respondents (Goldrick-Rab 2019, 12–14).

In addition to lower dietary quality and higher malnutrition risk, food insecurity during college is associated with lower academic achievement and poorer mental health, both of which may have long-term implications. Numerous studies identify correlations linking food insecurity with lower grade point averages throughout college (Patton-Lopez 2014, 212). A 2018 study in the California public university system revealed that poorer mental health indicators, such as feelings of depression and anxiety, were more prevalent in food insecure student participants. Furthermore, this study demonstrated that poor mental health stemming from food insecurity can contribute to lower academic achievement (Martinez 2018, 6–7).

Although scholars' awareness of food insecurity among college students is increasing, specific data on liberal arts institutions is limited. Private institutions made up less than 25 percent of colleges represented in the Hope Center study and colleges in rural areas or townships made up less than 2 percent of colleges represented. Our study complements the existing literature on college food insecurity by examining a liberal arts college for women and a liberal arts university for men, both located in rural Minnesota. Our data indicate that food insecurity at liberal arts institutions mirrors trends scholars have identified at larger, public institutions frequently situated in urban areas.

OUR STUDY—OVERVIEW AND METHODS

Our interest in college students' food insecurity developed during conversations around a cafeteria table. At our weekly "lunch club," a colleague expressed concern about a student's story. During the week after spring break, our colleague met with a first-year male student for a routine advising appointment. When asked, did you do anything fun over break? The student replied, "I was able to go to McDonald's!" Upon asking more questions, our colleague learned that this student did not have his own car on campus and stayed on campus during spring break. From campus, there is extremely limited transportation to the nearby town. The student's highlight of spring break was finding someone with a car and going to McDonald's for a meal. It seemed that after every break, more stories like these were exchanged among concerned faculty. Meanwhile, scholars' awareness of food insecurity on college campuses was growing, yet our institutions had no data on the topic.

We felt that our institutions, a rural, liberal arts college for women and university for men existing on two campuses offered a unique opportunity to research food insecurity prevalence, causes, and best actions for supporting students who need more equitable access to food. The two primary objectives of this study were to 1) determine the prevalence of food insecurity among students at a rural, private liberal arts college; and 2) determine what factors increase risk for students to experience food insecurity.

Our joint institutions of higher education are mid-sized Catholic and Benedictine residential liberal arts institutions, a college for women and a university for men that share one academic program, in the rural Midwest United States. Although the institutions share a common academic program, they have different presidents, boards of trustees, dining services, student development structures, and residential life offices. The institutions are located approximately five miles apart and are connected by institutional buses that regularly shuttle students between campuses when classes are in session. One campus is located in a small town, while the other is in a rural township that is not within walking distance of commercial businesses or food access.

Although the institutions are a historically white college and university, in recent years, the undergraduate students have become increasingly racially, ethnically, economically, and geographically diverse. For instance, in the fall of 2019, nearly 80 percent of students at both institutions identified as "white." According to the institutions' Office of Institutional Planning and Research, "Hispanic" students were the largest "American Minority Group" on each campus; 8.4 percent of the student population at the college and 7.7 percent of the undergraduate student population at the university. Although in the fall of 2019, 78.7 percent of undergraduate students came from in-state, more and more students were coming from distant states making it expensive and difficult to travel home for short holiday breaks during the semester. The number of students applying for needs-based financial aid has increased in recent years to approximately 80 percent to 83 percent of undergraduates during the 2017–2018 academic year. Most students live in on-campus housing. Typically, first- and second-year students live in traditional dormitory-style residences with no private kitchen facilities. Most third- and fourth-year students live in apartment-style residences that vary in kitchen access. Both institutions offer meal plans for purchase each semester. These meal plans consist of "punches" which can be redeemed for meals at the cafeteria-style dining centers on either campus. A student can also redeem a "punch" for certain meals at the ready-to-eat and grill-style dining facilities. Most meal plans include "flex" dollars, which are provided as a lump sum at the beginning of each semester and can be spent at any dining establishment on either campus. Students can add more flex dollars to their account throughout the semester.

Campus dining opportunities, especially during breaks, differ between the two institutions. For longer breaks, university dining services operate the campus cafeteria-style dining center with limited hours, while college culinary services close their cafeteria-style dining facility. At the college, the retail dining facilities are open over the lunch and dinner hour for limited service. There is a shuttle between campuses two to three times per day during breaks.

To study food security among undergraduate students in this unique two-campus context, we used cross-sectional research methods. Inclusion criteria for participants were eighteen to twenty-four years of age, enrolled at one of the joint institutions. After institutional review board approval, a link to a detailed survey was e-mailed to all students within the college's and university's e-mail systems. The survey inquired about a variety of factors that included, but were not limited to food security, demographics, financial status, living situation, academic achievement, and perceived stress. Informed consent was provided on the first page of the survey, and participants were informed that by checking the consent box, their responses would be used in the study. An incentive of a gift card drawing for ten $20 VISA gift cards was used to increase participation. Responses were collected during the last two weeks of the semester. The first data collection was completed in April 2018. After the first data collection, the survey was revised to add questions inquiring about meal plan selections, flex dollar and employment earnings spent, and perceived stress. We administered the revised survey during the last two weeks of the fall 2018 semester.

Food security was assessed using the six-item Household Food Security Survey Module (HHFSM). We chose this variation of the survey because it provides more information than the two-item survey and the ten-item survey included questions not applicable to much of the student population. The HHFSM was presented twice in the survey. First, participants responded to the HHFSM in relation to their experiences thirty days prior to completing the survey. Then, participants repeated the HHFSM questions and responded in relation to their experiences pertaining to the entire academic year. The responses were scored according to the USDA guidelines. A score of 0–1 classified someone as having high or marginal food security. Scores of 2–4 signified low food security, and 5–6 indicated very low food security. We used the perceived stress scale (PSS), a validated tool, to assess perceived stress among participants. The remaining questions on the survey inquired about demographics, financial status, living situations, and perceived health and dietary habits. Frequencies of food security status and other information from the survey were calculated. SPSS was used to determine correlations, differences among groups, and other necessary statistical applications.

Approximately 16–17 percent of the student population who received the initial recruitment e-mail responded to each of our surveys in spring and fall 2018. This is higher than the response rates of many published studies. We attribute this to our recruitment methods and incentives. In addition to sending an initial e-mail to the institutions' student population, we asked faculty and staff to notify students about the study as well. Our thought was that students may be more willing to participate if they receive the information from a known faculty or staff member rather than a stranger. Additionally, students could be entered to randomly receive a $20 VISA gift card for participation, which may have encouraged students to participate because the gift card could be spent at a variety of locations on or off campus.

Food Insecurity at the Institutions—Results of Our First Survey

The initial study in spring 2018 had 603 responses. After removing twenty-five responses—from graduate students, study abroad students, duplicates, and respondents who did not indicate gender—we used 578 responses for

Table 2.1 HHFSM Scores from Survey Respondents by Year and Gender (mean ± SD) Spring 2018 (Total *n* = 576)

Class Year	Female (n = 408)	Male (n = 168)
1	0.85 ± 1.32	1.84 ± 2.12
2	0.83 ± 1.46	2.10 ± 2.17
3	2.62 ± 2.22	2.69 ± 2.40
4	2.60 ± 2.36	2.04 ± 2.09

data analysis. A total of 408 respondents (71 percent) were women enrolled at the college, and 168 respondents (29 percent) were undergraduate men enrolled at the university. Respondents were distributed relatively equally among class year. A similar response was received to the survey in fall 2018.

Female first- and second-year students reported the lowest HHFSM scores on average, 0.85 ± 1.32 and 0.83 ± 1.46, respectively (table 2.1).

These HHFSM scores would translate to food secure status. The average HHFSM score for third- and fourth-year females and all males, regardless of year, fell into a low food security grouping.

Twenty-five percent of total participants (*n* = 145) reported low food security and 17 percent (*n* = 100) reported very low food security in the thirty days prior to the survey, which was the last month of the semester (table 2.2).

Similarly, 23 percent (*n* = 132) and 15 percent (*n* = 86) of participants reported low food security and very low food security during the past academic year as a whole (data not shown). These overall food security scores made clear that the food insecurity anecdotes that faculty and student development colleagues heard from students were representative of a larger problem that institutional leaders could no longer ignore.

Food insecurity impacted students at disproportionate rates. Only 33 percent of participants of color were food secure, compared to 62 percent of white participants who were food secure. Similarly, first-generation participants reported lower food security compared to non-first-generation participants: only 47 percent of first-generation students were food secure (data not shown). These findings mirror larger studies focused primarily at urban, public institutions, such as those by the Hope Center, which saw first-generation students as well as black and Latinx students reporting lower food security

Table 2.2 Percentage of Student Respondents Classified by Reported Food Security Status in Spring 2018 (*n* = 578)

Reported Food Security Status From HFFSM	Percentage Students of Color (n)	Percentage White Students (n)	Percentage All Respondents (n)
Food secure	33 (31)	62 (302)	58 (333)
Low food Security	32 (30)	24 (115)	25 (145)
Very low food Security	35 (33)	14 (67)	17 (100)
Total	100 (94)	100 (484)	100 (578)

than non-first-generation students and white students. The data indicate that food insecurity is a significant challenge for many students who attend private liberal arts institutions.

ISSUES THAT EXACERBATE FOOD INSECURITY AT OUR INSTITUTIONS—BREAKS AND HOLIDAYS

Initial data indicate that food insecurity prevalence was not uniform across gender, year in school, or ethnicity. In addition to demographic characteristics, we asked students about other aspects of campus life (such as meal plan information and travel habits during breaks) to better determine root causes of food insecurity during our second survey in fall 2018. Ultimately, one of the largest risk factors for food insecurity was staying on campus over school breaks. Students who stayed on campus over the week-long spring break the previous month had significantly higher HFSSM scores (3.13 $\pm$ 2.14) than those who did not (1.78$\pm$ 2.11), indicating lower food security ($p < 0.0001$). Additionally, our survey briefly asked students about their experiences staying on campus during breaks. Responses regarding food access during breaks generally fit into three themes.

1) Limited hours and options provided by campus dining facilities were a barrier.
2) Limited transportation between the two campuses and to outside facilities.
3) Students were required to use their "flex" dollars to pay for food at campus dining facilities during breaks. Students could not use a meal punch, which was separate.

Responses to open-ended questions helped us better understand the qualitative dimensions of our data and how students experienced the three themes listed above. One student stated:

> During my four years here, I've often felt stranded during breaks. While this year I have a car and live off campus with a fully equipped kitchen, the past years have been awful. The shorter breaks tend to be the ones where students have even less options. My first year, I remember that during long weekend, everything was closed down. I ate only ramen and oatmeal for three days because that is all I had within my room. After that, I tried to plan better with what is in my room for breaks. It was still often a struggle, especially if I didn't plan well.

During breaks, students felt stranded and abandoned in a food desert. Being on campus during breaks led to isolation, loneliness, and anxiety. Many students found eating on campus during breaks to be stressful because their meal plans operated differently than when classes were in session. Although members of residential life helped individual students, many students perceived life on campus during breaks to be antithetical to the institutions' professed "community values." Another student wrote:

> During spring break specifically, McGlynn's was the only place open on campus and we were required to pay with flex, but I was completely out so my RD paid for me the whole week instead, otherwise I wouldn't have eaten at all. This was a stressful struggle for me, I couldn't imagine being international. For a school to have so much encouragement for our international students to come here in the first place, this school is also extremely inconsiderate of their needs including housing and food options.

The two-campus environment with limited food options over break remains difficult for students to navigate. The university campus dining center is open during breaks, but transportation from the college campus is irregular and rare. Meanwhile, the college dining center is closed, and two retail outlets remain open for extremely limited hours. The directors of the university's dining services and the college's culinary services explained that finding a balance between dining opportunities and student use is challenging. During breaks, college retail options operate at limited capacity because of infrequent use during previous years. When reviewing usage, sales and use were limited, even at typical peak meal hours, resulting in diminished hours of operations during breaks to save money due to lack of use. After reviewing our study's data, the directors of dining and culinary services publicized operating hours more prominently and other administrators worked to improve transportation between campuses during breaks. Other institutions that have multiple campuses may experience similar increases in food insecurity when breaks occur during the semester.

Our study also highlights several other themes that may exacerbate food insecurity on college campuses. First, students' confusion or misunderstandings regarding meal plans may lead to greater food insecurity toward the end of semesters when students' plans run low or are exhausted. Second, students with limited cooking skills or access to cooking supplies increase food insecurity on campus. Third, students with dietary restrictions—cultural, religious, or medical—may find few appropriate dining options on campus, which may lead to increased hunger.

ISSUES THAT EXACERBATE FOOD INSECURITY AT OUR INSTITUTIONS—UTILIZING MEAL PLAN OPTIONS THROUGHOUT THE YEAR

Two themes that emerged as confusions within meal plans were the cost and timing of meal plan usage. Many students found it difficult to budget their "flex" dollars and "block" meals for the entire semester. In addition, students who stayed on campus during breaks did not realize that their meal plan would operate differently than when classes are in session. These problems might be addressed by hosting targeted sessions to help students learn about their meal plans and how to use them most effectively. Alternatively, the meal plans could be revised to make them less confusing and to make misunderstandings less common.

Our data indicate that students choose smaller meal plans as they age and move to residences with greater access to cooking facilities and food storage. Many students are eager to move to smaller meal plans because they are less expensive. Some students, however, may overestimate their ability to obtain food and prepare meals for themselves. Additionally, students may not realize the amount of time needed to prepare meals. It is important to offer students cooking classes—in-person or via video—that highlight basic culinary skills and quick, inexpensive, and easy meals. Likewise, dormitories and other living spaces should include kitchens and basic kitchen supplies, such as refrigerators, stoves, pots, and pans.

ISSUES THAT EXACERBATE FOOD INSECURITY AT OUR INSTITUTIONS—DIETARY RESTRICTIONS

Students with dietary restrictions were unsatisfied with campus dining options. Students with food allergies or intolerances found it difficult to find variety in foods that were safe to eat. One student remarked, "Labeling allergens would go a LONG way to me eating more in campus dining halls." Often mentioning that the only food that they felt was safe was the salad bar or a Mongolian grill where students build their own vegetable and meat bowl. Ingredients in all food options should be clearly and accurately stated on all online menus and cafeteria labels. Several students reported that often in the "all you can eat" dining centers, the protein options often already have sauce on the top of the food item. Lactose-intolerant and gluten-free students commented that if the sauce would be presented on the side for students to add themselves, the protein would be safe to consume. Other students had cultural dietary restrictions. International students stated that the lack of international cuisine is an issue, while Muslim students wished to see more pork-free meat options, particularly during breakfast hours. Dining Services and Culinary Services employ dietitians who can help students with dietary restrictions more effectively navigate campus dining options. Likewise, the nutrition club has discussed filming short PSA-like videos to post on the institutional website in the hope of helping students with dietary restrictions see that there are more food options than they realize in the college and university cafeterias.

INSTITUTION-SPECIFIC FOOD INSECURITY

Although there were common themes on each campus, risk factors and potential causes of food insecurity differed between the two institutions. Broadly, third- and fourth-year college participants experienced lower food security than their first- and second-year counterparts. One contributing factor may be that first- and second-year students at the college are required to have an unlimited meal plan. This meal plan allows students to enter the all-you-can-eat dining centers as frequently as they wish. If the student wants to consume a meal at a campus-food retail outlet, such as an on-the-go salad or sandwich, they can use one of their unlimited meals at those outlets. The spring semester 2018 data did not include responses regarding meal plans. However, the qualitative responses from third- and fourth-year students regarding meal plans indicated that many of these students chose a less expensive reduced meal plan. We adjusted the survey before the next data collection in the fall of 2018 to specifically ask participants which meal plan they currently use. An overwhelming majority of third- and fourth-year students were on meal plans that provided a set number of meals per semester (between 25 and 200).

Although an unlimited meal plan reduces the risk for food insecurity, it is expensive. Incoming third-year students choose smaller meal plans because they are less expensive. The smaller meal plans do not provide enough meals to cover three meals per day each week. These students might see the cheaper cost as the deciding factor without planning how they will supplement other meals not covered by the meal plan. Students may not realize that supplementing a smaller meal plan entails using more of their flex dollars at food outlets on campus or having to shop for groceries. Additionally, student-living situations and cooking or storage space can limit meal plan supplementation. Most third- and fourth-year students who live on campus reside in apartment-style housing with a full kitchen, refrigerator, and freezer shared with three to five roommates. Even though kitchen facilities are present for these students, time and cooking knowledge can be limiting factors even if monetary resources are available to purchase groceries to prepare food independently.

Our university students experience food insecurity at higher rates, potentially due to meal plan offerings, location of the campus, and lack of ability to independently prepare meals. Unlike first- and second-year participants enrolled in the college, first and second-year university students are not required to purchase an unlimited meal plan and may opt for a smaller meal plan that is less expensive. At the time of data collection (2018–2019 academic year) first- and second-year university students were automatically enrolled in a block meal plan that provided 160 meals per semester and $250 in flex dollars. If a student wished to upgrade to an unlimited plan for $300 more, the student must login to an online account to switch the meal plan. The block meal plan and flex dollars do not provide enough to cover three meals per day, seven days per week.

University first- and second-year students typically live in residence halls without private kitchens. From our data collection, all but one first- or second-year participant indicated they had a mini-fridge and microwave in their dorm room. However, the small fridge provides little food storage when shared with a roommate. Most residence halls have one community kitchen, but it is rare that students have the necessary equipment to prepare meals. Between the block meal plan's shortage of meals and students' limited ability to prepare meals, it is easy to understand why food insecurity is more prevalent among our first- and second-year university students than their college counterparts. However, the university students do not upgrade to the unlimited plan for at least two reasons. First, students may not know how to switch their meal plan. Second, students may not have the immediate funds to cover the upgrade cost to an unlimited meal plan.

MOVING FORWARD—SPRING 2019 AND BEYOND

After we analyzed data from the first two semesters of data collection, we presented the findings to as many on-campus stakeholders as possible. We sought audiences with the college's student development office, the university's student development office, the college's residential life office, the university's residential life office, academic affairs, the university's dining services, the college's culinary services, the university's student government, and the college's student government. We scheduled meetings to clarify how these departments viewed food insecurity among students, learned from examples they had witnessed, and learned about efforts they were making to support food insecure students.

Student Development and Residential Life Offices

Initially, student development at the college established a small emergency fund to help students with basic needs emergencies in short-term situations. Additionally, the student development and residential life offices at the college created and shared a few first steps to better identify and support food insecure students over break periods. The first action item was to better identify students staying on campus over breaks and holidays with concerns regarding food access. Student development implemented a plan using an existing form that students complete when staying on campus over breaks. The form was changed to include a checkbox statement "I am concerned about my access to food over break." When a student checked that box, her form is automatically sent to the assistant dean of students for a confidential follow-up conversation. According to the assistant dean of students, in the follow-up conversations most students asked about the transportation schedule between campuses, operating hours of dining facilities during breaks, and how their meal plan would work. For students with limited financial resources, the assistant dean of students could use money from an emergency fund to purchase a small amount of groceries for the student. The student development staff also recommended community resources, such as the local food shelf, as an option if appropriate.

Student development also began to share food-assistance information and resources with students. The college's assistant dean of students created a food assistance webpage as a resource for students. The webpage is located as a link on the student development website for the college and university. The food assistance page includes links to contact student development when a student has concerns, as well as community resources for support. The community resource most available to students is the community food shelf. The webpage also provides information regarding participation in the supplemental nutrition assistance program (SNAP), the nationwide federally funded food assistance.

Culinary Services and Dining Services

Dining services at both institutions increased promotion of dining center hours during breaks via e-mail and physical posters around campus. The promotion of altered hours during breaks is also increased the week before the break begins. Prior to Thanksgiving break in fall 2019, college culinary services collaborated with student development to create freezer-meal options for students staying over break and limited access to food. Meals were packed in food-safe environments by culinary staff and placed in community freezers

University dining services collaborated with us to present to the university board of trustees subcommittee on student development. Starting in fall 2020, our university students will now be assigned an unlimited (continuous) meal plan, instead of a block meal plan with a fixed number of meals, if they are living in a residence hall. This is an important outcome because it may decrease the number of first-year university students who exhaust their meal plans by the end of the semester. The meal plan assignment is not required, and students can use an online portal to downgrade the meal plan to the block plan with 160 meal passes and 250 flex dollars for the semester.

International and Intercultural Student Services

Our International and Intercultural Student Services office continues to sponsor off-campus shopping trips to a nearby shopping mall and grocery store for campus breaks that occur over national holidays and also during the week-long winter break. During winter break, there are two shopping trips that occur—once at the beginning of break and another halfway through.

Challenges Moving Forward

When the awareness of an issue such as food security grows on campus, more people want to be involved. While the growing awareness and interest toward the cause is appreciated, it grew increasingly difficult to generate a cohesive response and plan to move forward. It was difficult to keep everyone on the same page regarding accuracy of data. We decided to form a working group with individuals from varying departments on the campuses—student development offices, dining and culinary services, residence life offices, student senates, and faculty. The goal of this group was to enhance communication, streamline data sharing, and coordinate joint-actions toward creating food-secure institutions.

One of the most significant challenges lies with the fact that the risk factors for food insecurity differ among the two campuses due to location. The town where the college is located and where those students predominantly reside has convenience stores and a small co-op with grocery service within walking distance of campus and a grocery store approximately one mile away. Meanwhile, the university campus is located approximately five miles from that town in a rural township. There are no off-campus food resources within walking distance.

Another barrier to achieving food security for all students is access to community resources. At the time of publication, the local food shelf is only available to town residents—this includes any student who may live off campus in our town and the college students living on campus. However, the location where our university students live on campus is in a different zone for food shelf access. Their designated food shelf is in a small town a few miles in the opposite direction than the college campus. That location for a food shelf may not be accessible to most food-insecure students at the university who do not have the necessary transportation to get there.

Another challenge is access to financial resources. As heavily tuition-dependent institutions, facing declining enrollments and revenue shortfalls that are projected to be exacerbated by the COVID-19 pandemic, it is difficult to finance food-security initiatives, or any initiatives, through institutional funding streams. There is a need to identify alternative, sustainable funding streams to ensure that all students at the institutions remain food secure.

CREATING INSTITUTIONAL CHANGE TO SUPPORT FOOD INSECURE STUDENTS

Supporting students who are high-risk for food insecurity is not easy and does not occur overnight. Finding appropriate resources to best aid students may vary, depending on the circumstances and institutional contexts. A solution for one student may not be in the best interest of another. Likewise, a food pantry might fill a hole for one campus, but not be sustainable on another. Furthermore, addressing food insecurity, a topic that elicits stigmatization and shame, is especially tricky.

The first step in supporting equitable food access on college campuses is to determine if any information exists. If data does exist, consider when the information was collected. In our case, no data existed regarding food insecurity status of students. In order to create meaningful solutions, researchers must first identify how many students are impacted as well as why and how they experience food insecurity.

When embarking on data collection, there is a lot of background study and preparation that must occur. Often, the best initial resources to determine the general landscape of food insecurity are research studies or official food security reports from institutions similar to yours. Doing a background literature search was beneficial to us, especially because many research studies included questions and factors that contribute to food insecurity we had never considered.

We suggest forming a research team with at least one or two individuals with experience in quantitative and qualitative data collection. For us, having two researchers in different fields (natural science and humanities) broadened the input into research design and data collection. We found that the easiest way to collect data anonymously from students for initial information on food security was by constructing a survey and disseminating through a mass e-mail to students.

It takes a community of many stakeholders to bring a college campus alive. Students are at the center, and although they spend a great deal of time in the classroom with faculty, their food environment remains outside of academics. We realized early on in our study that although we interact with students frequently as faculty, food insecurity needs to be addressed from multiple angles. Our study revealed that food insecurity among students exists—this means that not only do the institutions need to support existing food insecure students but establish measures to create a food secure environment in the first place. Creating a food secure environment entails continuously examining access to food preparation spaces and supplies in residence halls, meal plan options, dining service offerings, dining service hours of operations, as well as students' access to financial resources. One of the greatest concerns when brainstorming solutions is the possibility of unsustainable action and further exacerbating the consequences of food insecurity down the road. In return, resources are finite and likely change from year to year.

Food insecurity is a problem throughout higher education. Since solutions to food insecurity are context specific, we recommend studying your own campus context and using a validated survey to identify the scope of the problem. Then, establishing a working group of campus stakeholders with direct exposure to student food insecurity allows multiple perspectives to exchange ideas, concerns, and build a collaborative effort to tackle the issue. The working group should be provided clear goals and each member of the group given clear tasks. Our group, though started recently, has laid the groundwork for addressing pertinent current concerns, while brainstorming for future solutions simultaneously. Although slowly and sometimes hesitantly, we are taking steps to implement long-term solutions that will guarantee that no student goes hungry while studying, working, and living at our college and university.

REFERENCES

American College Health Association. 2019. *American College Health Association-National College Health Assessment II: Reference Group Executive Summary Spring 2019*. Silver Spring, MD: American College Health Association. Accessed March 9, 2020. https://www.acha.org/documents/ncha/NCHA-II_SPRING_2019 _US_REFERENCE_GROUP_EXECUTIVE_SUMMARY.pdf.

Committee on Examination of the Adequacy of Food Resources and SNAP Allotments; Food and Nutrition Board; Committee on National Statistics; Institute of Medicine; National Research Council; J. A. Caswell, A. L. Yaktine (eds.) 2013. "Individual, Household, and Environmental Factors Affecting Food Choices and Access." In *Supplemental Nutrition Assistance Program: Examining the Evidence to Define Benefit Adequacy*. Washington, DC: National Academies Press. Accessed March 9, 2020. https://www.ncbi.nlm.nih.gov/books/NBK206912/.

Darmon, Nicole and Adam Drewnowski. 2015. "Contribution of Food Prices and Diet Cost to Socioeconomic Disparities in Diet Quality and Health: A Systematic Review and Analysis." *Nutrition Reviews* 73 (10): 643–660. doi:10.1093/nutrit/nuv027.

Drewnowski, Adam. 2010. "The Cost of US Foods as Related to Their Nutritive Value." *American Journal of Clinical Nutrition* 92 (5): 1181–1188.

Fedewa, Michael V., Bhibha M. Das, Ellen M. Evans, and Rod K. Dishman. 2014. "Change in Weight and Adiposity in College Students: A Systematic Review and Meta-Analysis." *American Journal of Preventive Medicine* 47 (5): 641–652.

Goldrick-Rab, Sara, Christine Baker-Smith, Vanessa Coca, Elizabeth Looker, and Tiffani Williams. 2019. *College and University Basic Needs Insecurity: A National #Real College Survey Report*. Philadelphia: The Hope Center. Accessed March 9, 2020. https://hope4college.com/wp-content/uploads/2019/04/HOPE_realcollege _National_report_digital.pdf.

Laraia, Barbara A., Anna Maria Siega-Riz, Craig Gunderson, and Nancy Dole. 2006. "Psychosocial Factors and Socioeconomic Indicators are Associated with Household Food Insecurity among Pregnant Women." *Journal of Nutrition* 136 (1): 177–182.

Martinez, Suzanna M., Edward A. Frongillo, Cindy Leung, and Lorrene Ritchie. 2018. "No Food for Thought: Food Insecurity Is Related to Poor Mental Health and Lower Academic Performance among Students in California's Public University System." *Journal of Health Psychology* 1–10. doi:10.1177/1359105318783028.

McLaughlin, Katie A., Jennifer Greif Green, Margarita Alegría, E. Jane Costello, Michael J. Gruber, Nancy A. Sampson, and Ronald C. Kessler. 2012. "Food Insecurity and Mental Disorders in a National Sample of U.S. Adolescents." *Journal of the American Academy of Child and Adolescent Psychiatry* 51 (12): 1293–1303. doi:10.1016/j.jaac.2012.09.009.

Patton-Lopez, Megan M., Daniel F. Lopez-Cevallos, Doris I. Cancel-Tirado, and Leticia Vazquez. 2014. "Prevalence and Correlates of Food Insecurity Among Students Attending a Midsize Rural University in Oregon." *Journal of Nutrition Education and Behavior* 46 (3): 209–214. doi:10.1016/j.jneb.2013.10.007.

Plotnikoff, Ronald C., S. A. Costigan, R. L. Williams, M. J. Hutchesson, S. G. Kennedy, S. L. Robards, J. Allen, C. E. Collins, R. Callister, and J. Germov. 2015. "Effectiveness of Interventions Targeting Physical Activity, Nutrition and Healthy Weight for University and College Students: A Systematic Review and Meta-Analysis." *International Journal of Behavioral Nutrition* 12 (1): 1–10. doi:10.1186/s12966-015-0203-7.

United States Department of Agriculture (USDA). 2012. "U.S. Household Food Security Survey Module: Three-Stage Design, With Screeners." Accessed June 7, 2020. https://www.ers.usda.gov/media/8271/hh2012.pdf.

United States Department of Agriculture (USDA). 2019. "Food Security in the U.S., Measurement." Accessed Feb. 22, 2020. https://www.ers.usda.gov/topics/food-nut rition-assistance/food-security-in-the-us/measurement.aspx.

United States Department of Agriculture Economic Research Service. 2018. "Food Security Status of U.S. Households in 2018." Accessed March 9, 2020. https://ww w.ers.usda.gov/topics/food-nutrition-assistance/food-security-in-the-us/key-stat istics-graphics.aspx#foodsecure.

Chapter 3

Transportation Accessibility and Its Relation to Students' Sense of Belonging and Inclusivity on Campus

Robert A. Kachelski, Amanda Macht Jantzer, and Emily J. Booth

Campus transportation accessibility is a frequently overlooked aspect of inclusion at colleges and universities that disproportionately impacts minoritized students and their sense of belonging.[1] A sense of belonging is an important factor in the success of college students because a strong sense of belonging can promote the growth of healthy relationships, increase student participation in extracurricular or cocurricular activities, and facilitate active learning. A lack of transportation options for college students can negatively influence their sense of belonging, as it can interfere with their ability to complete day-to-day tasks, access affordable necessities, or attend social events. Important experiential learning opportunities, such as internships, service learning, and volunteering, can also be very difficult to participate in without access to off-campus transportation. Thus, we argue that transportation accessibility needs to be addressed to create an inclusive campus with an improved students' sense of belonging. In this chapter, we share our research and rationale as a potential model for other institutions similarly struggling with transportation access and campus inclusion. Together, we hope to create more accessible institutions of higher education so that all students may feel that they belong and may thrive.

Often, higher education professionals readily acknowledge that a lack of transportation options at a rural college or university campus is an inconvenience, but they rarely identify it as a problem that can have a detrimental impact on their ability to achieve important aspects of their institutional missions. However, for any institution that strives to build an inclusive community of students with diverse backgrounds who all feel that they belong, we argue that transportation accessibility is fundamentally tied to this goal and deserves more attention. In particular, when viewed through the important lens of campus inclusion, we encourage consideration of the following questions: Who tends to experience transportation challenges on college campuses? Which opportunities are denied to those students that others enjoy? How does that impact students' sense of belonging? In the pages that follow, we share how we explored these questions on our campuses and offer suggestions for translating such research into action. First, we begin with a review of the literature on belongingness and on transportation accessibility on college campuses to provide context for our research and action.

SENSE OF BELONGING

Psychologists have long argued that belonging is a fundamental need among humans. In Maslow's (1954) famous hierarchy, belongingness needs are viewed as essential to human well-being, becoming a main force motivating behavior after physiological needs (e.g., food, water, sleep, etc.) and safety needs have been satisfied. For individuals lacking a sense of belonging, feelings of loneliness and alienation may interfere with efforts toward self-enhancement and achievement (16–20). Similarly, after an extensive review of the literature, Baumeister and Leary (1995, 497) stated that the evidence supports the conclusion that "the need to belong is a powerful, fundamental, and extremely pervasive motivation." Their review showed that creating and maintaining social bonds is a high priority, and that concerns about belonging affect the way people think about themselves, others, and the situations and events in their environment. In addition, lack of social attachments and a sense of belonging is associated with a host of negative outcomes in terms of physical and mental health, adjustment, and well-being.

A sense of belonging is important to promote good mental health, a feeling of acceptance, and individual success or achievement. With regard to college students, Strayhorn (2018, 4) stated that a "sense of belonging refers to students' perceived social support on campus, a feeling or sensation of connectedness, and the experience of mattering or feeling cared about, accepted, respected, valued by, and important to the campus community or others on campus such as faculty, staff, and peers." This is especially important for college-aged students due to their stressful environment and the influential point in their development that frequently involves defining themselves as individuals, building careers, and exploring passions. Interactions that promote a strong sense of belonging can instill a higher sense of satisfaction that allows for a better college experience as well as a higher level of retention.

Conversely, a college that fails to give students a sense of belonging inhibits personal growth and educational achievement (Strayhorn, 2018, 17–23).

Means and Pyne (2017, 908–909) argue that instilling a sense of belonging is crucial throughout the first-year experience of college students. Moving to any new place involves a great deal of uncertainty and is accompanied by anxiety about fitting in. However, when that new place is a college or university, students are also often apprehensive about their ability to meet academic expectations and challenges. In their first year, students can begin to feel more comfortable by making new friends and becoming involved in extracurricular activities and student organizations. Although interactions among peers are instrumental in achieving a sense of belonging, they are not the only important interactions. It is also important that students build positive relationships with staff members and with their instructors so that they feel they are able to approach them for guidance or assistance when they are struggling. These relationships with staff and faculty members help students to succeed by instilling a sense of belonging and support (Means and Pyne 2017, 920–922).

In their research on sense of belonging among first-year college students, Hoffman et al. (2002, 237) found that quality relationships with both peers and faculty members were instrumental in helping students to become "more resilient and more comfortable in the university environment." Many of the first-year students in their study reported being concerned about meeting the academic expectations of college, and managing the stress surrounding the academic workload was one of their major challenges. An important finding reported by Hoffman et al. was that "the development of 'interpersonal ties,' on which a student could rely to provide tangible aid, guidance, and feedback about academic matters and which provided students with a sense of being cared for and of being a member of a network of mutual obligation, enhanced their coping abilities and increased their personal comfort around social and academic matters" (237).

Minoritized students may struggle more with securing a sense of belonging, particularly on college campuses that have limited diversity. In their study of the development of a sense of belonging among first-year students, Vaccaro and Newman (2016, 932–933) found that a lack of diversity on campus can make minoritized students feel isolated, uncomfortable, and out of place. These students reported that they often felt they could not be their authentic selves on campus, although student organizations designed for particular social identity groups sometimes helped to foster a sense of belonging if students were able to make real connections with others within the organizations while being their authentic selves (Vaccaro and Newman 2016, 934–936). According to Museus, Yi, and Saelua (2018, 468–470), a lack of diversity can create a learning environment that does not contain elements relevant to minoritized students' cultural background and identities, and they may feel pressure to conform to the culture of majority on their campus. If students feel that they are not understood and valued due to differences in race, ethnicity, or culture, they are likely to have a lower sense of belonging than those who are surrounded by others who share these characteristics. Institutional support structures that effectively respond to the needs of diverse student populations can help to increase the sense of belonging among minoritized students, which is important because sense of belonging is tied to student persistence and degree completion (Museus, Yi, and Saelua 2018, 468–469).

College students from low-income families may find it harder to develop a sense of belonging than their more affluent peers. In one study, Ostrove and Long (2007, 379–381) found that "social-class background was strongly related to a sense of belonging at college, which in turn predicted social and academic adjustment to college, quality of experience at college, and academic performance." In addition, the social interactions of low-income students can be impacted by their need to work in order to afford college (Means and Pyne 2017, 909). Developing close relationships and a sense of belonging may be more difficult for low-income students because a disproportionate amount of their time is spent working rather than interacting with peers or faculty, engaging in social activities, or participating in extracurricular and leadership activities. Means and Pyne (2017, 909) argue that low-income students are also likely to have a lower sense of belonging if their instructors have an expectation of experiences such as enrollment in advanced courses in high school, studying and traveling abroad, or other privileges that were not available or accessible to them in the way they are to higher-income students. Intersectionality is important to consider here as well, since many low-income students are also first-generation college students, students of color, or out-of-state students, making their development of a sense of belonging on campus more challenging.

As we explore in the next sections, low-income students, out-of-state students, and international students are less likely to have a car on campus, making transportation access a particular challenge for them. Given that these students are also less likely to attend college with a preexisting social network that could assist them in countering these difficulties, the inability to fulfill social needs may result in a lower sense of belonging. When a college or university is not located in a relatively large city, access to a range of transportation options is often required for students not only to be able to attend off-campus social events but also to have access to basic needs such as affordable groceries and specialized medical care. This is especially a challenge for students at institutions located in rural areas that do not have public transportation available. In addition, students may need to hold a job off campus in order to pay for tuition or living expenses and thus require transportation to an offsite work location. Students also typically require transportation options for various activities related to their academic programs, such as internships, service learning, and clinical hours needed for specialized training. Therefore, transportation accessibility can have a significant impact on students' sense of belonging as well as their ability to achieve their academic goals.

TRANSPORTATION ACCESSIBILITY
ON COLLEGE CAMPUSES

Despite anecdotal reports that a range of transportation barriers commonly confront students on many rural college campuses, there is a relatively limited research literature on transportation accessibility for college students. However, we were able to identify several relevant studies. For example, Daggett and Gutowski (2003, vi) conducted a national survey of twenty-three universities and transit agencies across the United States. The authors noted, "Authorities at universities are beginning to understand that, like it or not, they are in the transportation business alongside their municipal counterparts" (1). They found that many universities could improve their master planning related to aspects of transportation, particularly with regard to transportation services, technologies, facilities, and coordination with community transportation authorities (37). Moreover, they found that only 39 percent of universities reported providing financial support for student use of transportation services (25). This leaves many students who cannot afford off-campus transportation in a predicament. In managing such transportation concerns, Daggett and Gutowski (2003, 29) argued that universities and the communities in which they are embedded have a range of transit options and that it is crucial to set goals in order to tailor transportation services to meet campus and community needs, while embracing ongoing performance assessment.

Some of the research in this area has focused primarily on transportation access to college campuses in larger, metropolitan areas. For instance, Allen and Farber (2018) highlighted the importance of spending time on campus for college student success, and they identified transportation barriers to doing so for students in large cities. More specifically, they conducted survey research with 2,011 students enrolled at seven campuses in urban areas in Canada to examine how transportation barriers constrain on-campus engagement and participation, including class attendance (176–177). Examining the results, Allen and Farber (2018, 180) found that the length of time needed for commutes and the number of hours of employment per week significantly impacted such student travel and campus participation. Students who reported that they had to travel farther distances and required more travel time were less likely to come to campus. Such students are therefore less likely to participate in academic and extracurricular activities, constraining their success. Recommended solutions revolved around providing more affordable transit options, improved scheduling of transportation options, and making campus housing more affordable.

Other research has focused on access issues for particular student populations, such as community college students and international students. For instance, Rankin, Katsinas, and Hardy (2010) conducted a review of literature about accessibility and retention issues for community college students, drawing upon a 2008 survey by the first author of a national sample of chief executive officers and chief academic officers at community colleges. They found that accessible transportation for students was a consistent problem (213–216). Challenges included lack of adequate public transportation (particularly in rural locations), lack of reliable personal vehicles, and ineffective ride-sharing programs. They reported that a lack of transportation often leads to retention issues, such as students missing class or dropping out. The authors recommended potential remedies such as considering public transportation timetables when scheduling classes, leveraging social networking to create ride-share programs, and offering classes online or at satellite campuses.

Similarly, Poyrazli and Grahame (2007, 28–45) conducted qualitative focus group research on adjustment barriers in a sample of fifteen international students. With regard to transportation, international students in the focus groups reported the challenges they faced upon arrival in the United States. Students urgently needed transportation in order to obtain items, including important documents for identification. They noted that documents such as social security cards are needed to buy or rent a car, but transportation to obtain such materials was often difficult to access. Students also expressed frustration with not being informed prior to arrival that public transportation was not widely available, and that tuition, vehicle, and insurance costs frequently made car ownership prohibitive. Poyrazli and Grahame (2007) observed that "the well-being of international students at this campus is influenced by its physical location in conjunction with the lack of an important resource (transportation) that might help ameliorate the effects of the campus's relative isolation. This isolation contributes to the difficulty international students have in establishing social support systems both with the campus community and even with co-ethnics in the broader community" (39). The authors advised professionals in higher education, particularly those in rural settings who may not have broad access to public transportation, to consider the needs of international students within an ecological framework that attends to physical and contextual demands. They also offered recommendations about possible interventions, including communicating transportation realities to students in advance of arrival, adding airport pick-up transportation, offering a shuttle service (especially during the week of arrival so that students can access basic needs) and in the long-term, offering a regular shuttle to important locations such as supermarkets.

A MODEL FOR EXAMINING CAMPUS TRANSPORTATION CHALLENGES

While informative, the existing research literature captures only some of the transportation challenges we are experiencing at our institutions. Students on our campuses have recently published editorials in the student newspaper highlighting how lack of transportation has hindered success in academic programs and calling for more transportation options (Servin and Thao 2019). This echoes the call for action that our third author, Emily Booth, gathered from conversations with key stakeholders across our campuses during spring 2019. Although many long-standing efforts by individuals and departments at our institutions have been made to address barriers to transportation between our town and larger regional cities, our campuses and the towns in which they are embedded exist in a transportation desert. This problem not only influences student accessibility and inclusion but also impacts the broader community. The introduction of public transportation to connect our rural community with a larger nearby city would introduce an easier, more accessible, affordable, and sustainable way for members of our communities to seek employment, to pursue educational opportunities, to enjoy reactional activities, and to flourish.

In order to help students who need transportation assistance to meet academic requirements (e.g., student teaching, service learning, and clinicals, etc.), a variety of strategies have been created by various offices and departments on campus. However, these solutions have been largely piecemeal and do not adequately meet student needs. For instance, the general education curriculum at our institutions has an experiential learning requirement that can be completed through service-learning experiences. However, few sites are within walking distance and many students choose to opt out of service learning and complete a research project instead. This is likely due, in part, to students' concerns that service-learning requirements may not be completed without reliable transportation. To address this accessibility issue, our experiential learning office provides a shuttle option; unfortunately, it is an imperfect solution because the shuttle is costly to operate and is only able to stop at ten locations with limited availability. Similarly, carpooling to experiential learning opportunities could raise liability concerns, and such options are less reliable than a public transportation system.

With regard to extracurricular opportunities and basic needs (e.g., afford-able groceries, personal care supplies, speciality health care), the institutions provide weekend busing to a large grocery store and mall in a nearby city in an attempt to expand transportation accessibility. While this is a partial solution, it does not adequately serve all students. The limited availability of this insti-tution-provided transportation means that students need to have the ability to block off an extended period of time on weekends in order to take advantage of it. Moreover, this transportation option fails to serve the broader commu-nity beyond campus. Furthermore, some offices are not open on the weekend or have limited weekend hours that do not coincide with the bus schedule. Therefore, transportation options are needed during the week as well.

Rental vehicles are also available for use on our campuses and are meant to promote opportunity, sustainability, and accessibility outside of campus. However, this transportation resource is similarly inadequate in addressing student need. While convenient, this is an expensive option, accessible only to those students who have driver's licenses and sufficient personal financial resources available. This exclusivity of transportation availability creates an equity gap in our campus community as it allows only those with the financial means to obtain a car of their own or regularly rent a car the opportunity to apply for off-campus jobs or internships. This may in turn constrain available career opportunities upon graduation.

In essence, the current system is not adequately serving students, pro-moting community involvement, and ensuring student safety and success. Transportation challenges are further exacerbated for out-of-state and interna-tional students due to constrained support networks. In contrast, based upon internal data gathered from our experiential learning office, our in-state stu-dents are more likely to have a car on campus than out-of-state or international students. Many in-state students arrive knowing people who also came from their high school or a nearby city, allowing them to more readily connect in some way. Such networking allows in-state students more access to transporta-tion to larger cities for cheaper groceries, social/recreational activities, or other needs such as affordable clothing and school supplies. For out-of-state and international students, the lack of these available networks presents a social barrier that leads to a lack of inclusivity, equity, and opportunity. In sum, this range of transportation challenges constrains our ability to create an inclusive and equitable community and may also hinder students' sense of belonging.

RESEARCH ON TRANSPORTATION ACCESSIBILITY

In order to better understand how serious the transportation challenges were for students at our joint, rural, liberal arts institutions, we conducted a survey in the spring of 2019. In addition, we wanted to determine if students from underrepresented groups reported more problems with transportation to off-campus locations than students from majority groups, and if there was a relationship between these transportation problems and feeling a sense of belonging at our institutions. A total of 350 students completed our anonymous online survey. In general, the sample represented the demographics of the student body fairly well, except that men and international students were underrepresented in the sample.

The transportation survey included questions pertaining to student's car ownership or access to a vehicle on campus, availability of off-campus transportation options for different purposes, and desire to travel off campus. We also investigated how often students required transportation to a regional metropolitan area (including the airport) and how often they relied on various methods of transportation to get there. We also included an open-ended item asking students to add any comments regarding transportation needs for our students.

To measure students' sense of belonging on campus, we included in the survey the Psychological Sense of School Membership (PSSM) Scale (Goodenow 1993). This seventeen-item scale measured belongingness and included items such as "Sometimes I feel as if I don't belong here" and "It is hard for people like me to be accepted here." Students responded using a six-point scale ranging from *strongly disagree* to *strongly agree*. For each participant, we calculated an average score on the seventeen items, after reverse-scoring some items so that higher scores indicated a greater sense of belonging at our institutions. We used average scores rather than total scores because some students did not respond to all items in the scale. Students also provided demographic information that included their gender, race/ethnicity, estimated annual family income, and home state prior to attending college.

SURVEY RESULTS

When thinking about transportation challenges for students, it is useful to start by determining the percentage of students who have their own cars on campus, because that one factor can alleviate most of the transportation problems students experience. If they have their own cars, students can go shopping where and when it is most convenient, easily go to restaurants and social events with their friends, get to a job, internship, or service-learning opportunity without issues, and so on. Of the students who completed our survey, approximately 55 percent reported that they currently had their own car on campus.

However, we found that car ownership on campus was heavily dependent on race, family income, and what state students were from. The percentage of students with their own car on campus was significantly higher for white students (61 percent) than for students of color (25 percent). Regarding family income, students whose estimated annual family income was above $35,000 were significantly more likely to have their own car on campus (59 percent) than students whose estimated family income was below $35,000 (28 percent). Students from in-state were significantly more likely to have a car on campus (62 percent) than students from out of state (29 percent).

For students who do not have their own car on campus (roughly 45 percent in our survey), some of their transportation challenges can be overcome if they have a friend or family member who is willing to let them borrow their car. In our survey, of the students who did not have their own car on campus, approximately 57 percent said that they had a friend or family member who let them borrow their car. Again, however, this percentage was largely dependent on race, family income, and what state students were from. For example, of the students who did not have their own car on campus, the percentage who had a friend or family member who let them borrow their car was significantly higher for white students (71 percent), than for students of color (26 percent). Students whose estimated annual family income was above $35,000 were significantly more likely to have a friend or family member who let them borrow their car (66 percent) than students whose estimated family income was below $35,000 (23 percent). Finally, students from in state were significantly more likely to have a friend or family member who let them borrow their car (69 percent) than students from out of state (34 percent).

The contrast becomes even more stark when looking at the combined impact of not having a car on campus and not being able to borrow a car from a friend or family member. In our survey, only 11 percent of white students had no access to a car, either their own or one they could borrow, whereas the percentage was 58 percent for students of color. For students whose estimated annual family income was above $35,000, only 13 percent had no access to a car compared to 60 percent of those whose estimated family income was below $35,000. Only 12 percent of students from in state reported no access to a car compared to 47 percent of students from out of state. These findings highlight the importance of attending to intersectionality when examining transportation accessibility on campus.

Given these inequities in ready access to cars on campus based on race, family income, and what state students were from, it is not surprising that students' responses to specific questions about off-campus transportation options differed based on some of these same variables. Table 3.1 presents the percentage of students *without cars on campus* who *disagreed* or *strongly disagreed* with specific statements about transportation accessibility. These

Table 3.1   Percentage of Students in Each Group Who *Disagreed* or *Strongly Disagreed* with Each Item Listed

	In-State Students (%)	Out-of-State Students (%)	International Students (%)	White Students (%)	Students of Color (%)
There are enough off-campus transportation options.	74	93	64	76	85
Transportation is readily available for me to access affordable groceries.	66	85	55	72	73
Transportation is readily available for me to access culturally specific items such as food, personal care items, and so forth.	64	85	55	69	73
Transportation is readily available for me to take part in off-campus social activities such as going to the movies, the mall, restaurants, and so forth.	64	81	82	72	78
Transportation is readily available for me to get to a job or internship.	55	72	64	52	76
Transportation is readily available for me to participate in service learning and volunteer opportunities.	45	53	46	41	59

Table created by the authors.

data show not only that most students identified problems with accessibility but also that students of color and out-of-state students reported more transportation challenges than white students and in-state students.

Although these data represent only the views of students without cars on campus, the majority of students identified significant transportation challenges, regardless of whether they had a car on campus. For example, one student wrote, "It would be very difficult to live in apartment housing without access to a car, or without roommates who have one, just in getting access to groceries. Fortunately, I have a car, but I don't know what I'd do without it or access to one." Another said, "I am fortunate to have a vehicle . . . however, I have many friends who are out-of-state or international students who have been in difficult and expensive positions because of transportation difficulties." For students without cars on campus, the lack of transportation options can be extremely frustrating. One student wrote, "I have not been able to get a new prescription for my glasses because I cannot get myself to [the doctor's office] at a convenient time. I have not gotten a haircut since summer because I could never get myself [there] at a convenient time . . . I can't go home either because of how expensive it is. I feel stuck and I can't do much about it." Another put it simply: "Transportation here is awful. I feel marooned on campus."

Experiencing these transportation challenges may be related to students' sense of belonging at our institutions, so we examined students' PSSM scores to look for differences among groups and correlations with survey items asking about transportation issues. An independent samples *t*-test showed that there was a significant difference between white students and students of color in their average PSSM scores. White students had significantly higher PSSM scores than students of color. Furthermore, the results of a one-way ANOVA showed that students' PSSM scores differed significantly based on their estimated annual family income. Post hoc tests using Tukey's HSD showed that the three groups of students whose estimated annual family income was less than $50,000 had significantly lower PSSM scores than the three groups of students whose estimated annual family income was $50,000 or more. None of the other differences between groups were statistically significant. The average PSSM scores for the different income groups are shown in figure 3.1 below.

In order to determine whether students' sense of belonging was related to the transportation challenges they experienced, we correlated their PSSM scores with their responses to survey items asking about transportation challenges. One significant negative correlation showed that students with lower PSSM scores (lower sense of belonging) tended to more frequently want to go to a nearby city or other places off campus but couldn't because they had no way to get there. There were also significant positive correlations showing that students with lower PSSM scores tended to disagree more than students with higher PSSM scores that (a) there were enough off-campus transportation options, (b) transportation was readily available for them to access

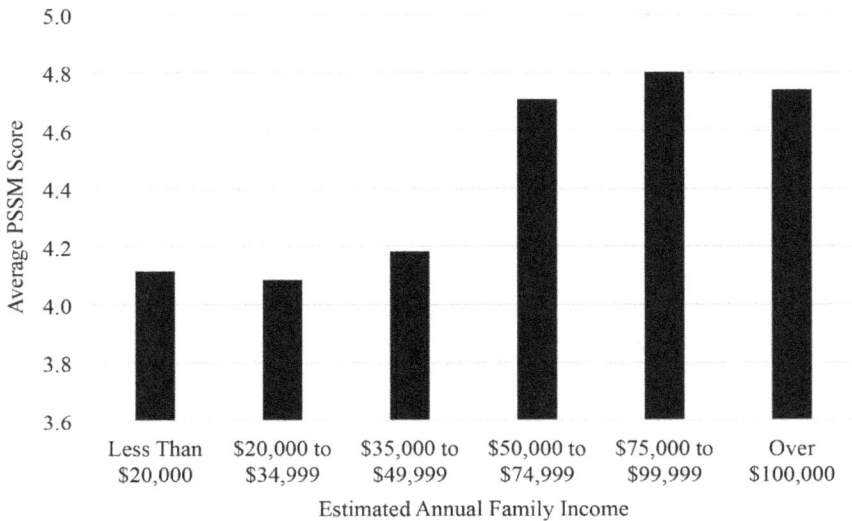

Figure 3.1   The figure shows students' average scores on the Psychological Sense of School Membership (PSSM) scale as a function of their estimated annual family income. Students whose estimated annual family income was less than $50,000 had significantly lower scores than students whose estimated annual family income was $50,000 or more. Figure created by the authors.

culturally specific items, and (c) transportation was readily available for them to take part in off-campus social activities.

In sum, according to our research, transportation inaccessibility is a challenge for too many students and disproportionately impacts students of color, low-income students, and out-of-state students. Students of color and low-income students also report having a significantly lower sense of belonging on our campuses. Our results show that there is a significant correlation between sense of belonging and access to transportation options for students. Thus, we argue that transportation accessibility is an inclusion issue that needs to be addressed in order to create a more inclusive community where more of our students can feel that they belong and can thrive.

EXPLORING POTENTIAL SOLUTIONS

As part of our survey, we included some items designed to explore potential solutions to some of the transportation challenges faced by students. Students strongly supported the creation of a ride-sharing app, with students of color, out-of-state students, and international students showing especially strong support. As another potential solution, most students said they would take advantage of a public transport system from campus to a local city if one were available. Again, the percentages were especially high for students of color, out-of-state students, and international students. As a potential solution to the challenge of traveling to a metropolitan area affordably, most students said they would take advantage of a high-speed commuter line if it were extended to a local city. Students of color were especially likely to say they would take advantage of this option.

Beyond the scope of our campus research, we learned that in and around our state, both private and public colleges and universities are finding ways to improve transportation accessibility for their students. Institutions are approaching transportation challenges with varied approaches. For example, some local institutions have contracted companies that provide transportation to students, sometimes at a low cost. Such institutions pay to have services travel to their campuses to provide rides for students. More commonly, many other regional institutions are using technology to provide carpooling options to their students. Many use a ride-sharing app or online ride-sharing boards for both students and employees. Some also provide incentives for individuals using the ride-share resources frequently, such as earning points or 50 percent off a parking pass. Riders can use these resources to look for or offer rides, discuss meeting locations, and negotiate payments. While such programs are unlikely to solve the complex breadth of campus transportation access problems, they may provide partial relief for campus community members struggling on their own to find adequate transportation to meet their personal and academic needs.

RECOMMENDATIONS

In sum, we found that transportation accessibility is a multifaceted challenge on our campuses that requires a range of responses. Gathering quantitative and qualitative data on transportation barriers was pivotal in allowing us to more fully explore and understand the nature of these issues and how they are linked to issues of exclusion in our campus community. More specifically, our data helped us understand, in a more nuanced way, which groups of students are disproportionately impacted by transportation inaccessibility and how this relates to a reduced sense of belonging. While we grapple with these findings and seek solutions, we recognize that these challenges are not unique to our institutions but may be a commonly unacknowledged inclusion issue for many colleges and universities. Therefore, we encourage other professionals in higher education to similarly examine barriers to transportation accessibility through the lens of inclusion on their own campuses.

We recommend that others embrace a similar inquiry-based approach to this issue by posing meaningful research questions and gathering quantitative and qualitative data. Not only will these data assist campus professionals in better understanding the issue of transportation accessibility on their campuses, but we also argue that when it comes to crafting actionable solutions, data speak. That is, campus administrators and local authorities must be convinced of *and be able to document* unmet needs in order to allocate resources. Therefore, conducting research on the unique transportation barriers that exist on a college campus is critical, followed by communicating these findings to initiate new discussions and collaborations among campus and community leaders. For instance, we have been sharing our research findings that demonstrate unmet need with faculty, staff, and student leaders on campus, as well as city and regional transportation leaders, to spur discussion about ways to expand public transportation options to our community.

Creating a working group with representatives from multiple stakeholder groups also addresses institutional barriers, given that transportation often is not the sole domain of a particular individual or office on college campuses. We have also found that sharing these research findings has helped all stakeholders more clearly grasp the nature and extent of the problem. In many cases, we have observed institutional awareness-raising that has occurred among students and campus personnel who have been privileged to enjoy easy access to transportation and were not aware of the difficult transportation barriers impacting students who did not share their privilege. Thus, dissemination of research results helped stakeholders highlight individual and institutional blind spots. Moreover, dissemination of our results has helped reframe campus transportation barriers as an equity and inclusion issue, which has resulted in an increased sense of shared urgency for change. We strongly encourage other higher education professionals to gather data, create a working group of stakeholders, and begin exploring various strategies for addressing the unique transportation challenges impacting their campus communities. For instance, working groups may explore varied transportation options, providers, and costs, such as adoption of ride-sharing programs, coordination across campus departments to pool resources, and expansion of public transportation.

Finally, as we explore potential solutions on our campuses, we are also attending to those options that will be well received by our students, particularly by our students of color, out-of-state students, and international students. We are aided in this effort not only by information gathered through our student surveys but also by engaging student researchers, student participants, and student senators in our efforts. To anyone undertaking similar efforts, we stress the importance of ensuring that student voices are represented in this process. Given that students are the ones most impacted, they must also have more than just token input to guard against faculty and administrators driving initiatives that may not be well tailored to student needs. Importantly, student involvement in solution generation also elicits buy-in from the student body that will improve the success of pilot programs and other change initiatives. In sum, we hope that this research and our recommendations will be helpful in energizing attempts to address transportation challenges not only on our campuses but also in other campus communities that struggle with limited access to adequate public and private transportation resources.

CONCLUSION

Based upon our research and campus advocacy, we argue that lack of transportation access is an underacknowledged issue and that institutional commitments to addressing these challenges can increase inclusiveness and a sense of belonging among minoritized students, not just on our campuses but at others as well. We call upon leaders across institutions of higher education to address this underacknowledged basic need. Using our work as a model, we hope campus and community stakeholders will gather data about transportation barriers on their own campuses and work collaboratively to develop solutions. Importantly, this step will help create more inclusive campuses where more students may feel that they belong. Moreover, more broad-based attention to this issue will help build a more robust literature on transportation access in higher education. In summation, viewed through the lens of inclusion, there is an urgent need to enact workable transportation solutions on our campuses and others if we intend to more fully enhance the retention, success, and sense of belonging of minoritized students at colleges and universities.

NOTE

1. Acknowledgment: We express our thanks to Kori Friedges, Claire Gammon-Deering, Drew Lodermeier, and Xia Vang for their research assistance and writing support.

REFERENCES

Allen, Jeff and Steven Farber. 2018. "How Time-Use and Transportation Barriers Limit On-Campus Participation of University Students." *Travel Behaviour and Society* 13: 174–182. doi:10.1016/j.tbs.2018.08.003.

Baumeister, Roy F. and Mark R. Leary. 1995. "The Need to Belong: Desire for Interpersonal Attachments as a Fundamental Human Motivation." *Psychological Bulletin* 117 (3): 497–529. doi:10.1037/0033-2909.117.3.497.

Daggett, John, and Richard Gutkowski. 2003. "University Transportation Survey: Transportation in University Communities." *Transportation Research Record* 1835 (1): 42–49. doi:10.3141/1835-06.

Goodenow, Carol. 1993. "The Psychological Sense of School Membership Among Adolescents: Scale Development and Educational Correlates." *Psychology in the Schools* 30 (1): 79–90. doi:10.1002/1520-6807(199301)30:1<79::AID-PITS2310 300113>3.0.CO;2-X.

Hoffman, Marybeth, Jayne Richmond, Jennifer Morrow, and Kandice Salomone. 2002. "Investigating 'Sense of Belonging' in First-Year College Students." *Journal of College Student Retention: Research, Theory and Practice* 4 (3): 227–256. doi:10.2190/DRYC-CXQ9-JQ8V-HT4V.

Maslow, Abraham. 1954. *Motivation and Personality*. New York: Harpers.

Means, Darris and Kimberly Pyne. 2017. "Finding My Way: Perceptions of Institutional Support and Belonging in Low-Income, First-Generation, First-Year College Students." *Journal of College Student Development* 58 (6): 907–924. doi:10.1353/csd.2017.0071.

Museus, Samuel D., Varaxy Yi, and Natasha Saelua. 2018. "How Culturally Engaging Campus Environments Influence Sense of Belonging in College: An Examination of Differences Between White Students and Students of Color." *Journal of Diversity in Higher Education* 11 (4): 467–483. doi:10.1037/dhe0000069.

Ostrove, Joan M., and Susan M. Long. 2007. "Social Class and Belonging: Implications for College Adjustment." *The Review of Higher Education* 30 (4): 363–389. doi:10.1353/rhe.2007.0028.

Poyrazli, Senel and Kamini M. Grahame. 2007. "Barriers to Adjustment: Needs of International Students within a Semi-Urban Campus Community." *Journal of Instructional Psychology* 34 (1): 28–45.

Rankin, Kristie R., Stephen G. Katsinas, and David E. Hardy. 2010. "Community College Retention and Access Issues: A View from the Field." *Journal of College Student Retention: Research, Theory and Practice* 12 (2): 211–223. doi:10.2190/CS.12.2.e.

Servin, Vanessa and Shoua Thao. 2019. "Academic Transportation Options are Lacking." *The Record,* May 2, 2019. https://csbsjurecord.com/2019/05/opinion -academic-transportation-options-are-lacking/.

Strayhorn, Terrell. 2018. *College Students' Sense of Belonging: A Key to Educational Success for All Students*. New York: Routledge.

Vaccaro, Annemarie and Barbara M. Newman. 2016. "Development of a Sense of Belonging for Privileged and Minoritized Students: An Emergent Model." *Journal of College Student Development* 57 (8): 925–942. doi:10.1353/csd.2016.

Chapter 4

Mobilizing a Prejudice and Discrimination Class to Address Inclusion on Campus

Collaborative Research on Institutional Policies and Practices

Pamela L. Bacon, Amanda Macht Jantzer, and Jennifer S. Kramer

In order to create inclusive campus communities, colleges and universities need to identify and change institutionalized policies and practices that discriminate against marginalized students. Usually, such research is conducted by faculty members, staff, and administrators. However, because the examination of discriminatory practices falls within many academic disciplines such as psychology, sociology, and communication, students enrolled in courses on discrimination and prejudice who have received research training can make important contributions to an institution's understanding of institutionalized discrimination. Our aim in this chapter is to share an innovative approach, designed by a cross-disciplinary team of scholars, to teach students in a prejudice and discrimination class to use focus group methodologies to examine important questions regarding institutionalized exclusion of students from marginalized social groups. The students in the class were guided through the qualitative research process from design to dissemination to examine how institutional policies and practices may create differential treatment of marginalized students on our campuses. Moreover, we emphasize how the course design spurred students to translate their research findings into action. We illustrate how the results of this research, centering marginalized student voices, provide campus leaders with data about issues that need to be addressed and changed at an institutional level. We position this innovative classroom approach to student-engaged research within the context of a larger institutional inclusion effort. Finally, we share suggestions about how this approach may serve as a model for other institutions who are similarly striving to create more inclusive campus communities.

Our institutions are historically predominantly white campuses that emphasize the importance of community among faculty, staff, students, and alums. The feeling of community, or inclusion, is stressed as central to students' experiences. Research suggests that such feelings are vital to student success; college students' feelings of inclusion and sense of belonging are important predictors of persistence (e.g., Hausmann, Schofield, and Woods 2007, 803) and well-being (e.g., Gummadam, Pittman, and Ioffe 2016, 300; Pittman and Richmond 2008, 354). Marginalized college students, particularly those from historically underrepresented social identity groups, often report lower levels of belonging than majority students on college campuses (Vaccaro and Newman 2016, 926) which is the case at our institutions where students of color and students from other marginalized groups have reported feeling excluded from the community (Hinton 2017, 4).

Over the past five years, our institutions have been engaging more intensively in multicultural organizational development (MCOD; Pope, Reynolds, and Muller 2014, 21) work by identifying and dismantling ways in which the system is promoting inequity and oppression (Pope et al. 2014, 21). The institutions are best described as being at stage four of the change process, the affirming system, in which the institution actively tries to increase diversity and eliminate discrimination but does not examine or change its institutional policies or practices. The institution is committed to creating a nondiscriminatory organization, but many of the policies and practices had not been reexamined in light of increasing enrollment of students from marginalized social identity groups. This project attempted to help move the institution to the redefining system stage by gathering feedback about institutional policies and practices that created inequity and exclusion from members of marginalized student groups who had experienced those barriers. By making these changes, the institutions will also promote transformative inclusion by ensuring that each member of the community "is transformed and made better by inclusion" (Becoming Community 2018; Hinton 2017).

In order to pursue these goals, the purpose of this project was to work collaboratively with students in a prejudice and discrimination class and conduct focus group research to identify institutional policies and practices that (a) discriminate against marginalized students and (b) inhibit multicultural institutional change (Pope et al. 2014). To ensure that the research projects would be meaningful to students and would result in multicultural change at our institutions, the findings and recommendations from the students were shared with institutional leaders and campus stakeholders during a public presentation and as part of a larger campus inclusion initiative.

FRAMEWORK FOR EXAMINING INSTITUTIONAL POLICIES AND PRACTICES

This effort was guided by a theory of MCOD that argues that in order for institutions and organizations to experience multicultural change, the focus should be on changing the system, rather than merely changing individuals within the organization (Pope et al. 2014, 21). In other words, if an institution identifies inequity and oppression in the organization, the response should not be to focus organizational change efforts solely on changing people's attitudes through diversity training, but instead to identify and dismantle ways in which the system is promoting inequity and oppression (Pope et al. 2014, 21). Therefore, this project focused on identifying institutional policies and practices that led students from marginalized groups to feel excluded, in order to best identify ways to create a more inclusive campus.

CONDUCTING INCLUSION RESEARCH IN THE CLASSROOM

While the issues of prejudice and discrimination are addressed to some degree in courses across many fields in liberal arts curriculums, it may more rarely be the explicit focus of in-depth examination in a course. Similarly, the first author, Bacon teaches social psychology courses and frequently found that her students complete the discrimination unit feeling hopeless about their ability to combat the prejudice and discrimination marginalized groups face on a daily basis. There simply is not enough time in a traditional social psychology class to give the topics of stereotyping, prejudice, and discrimination adequate examination. Therefore, Bacon developed and taught the prejudice and discrimination course to create the time to explore both the injustices faced by marginalized groups and also how to advocate for the equitable treatment and inclusion of members of marginalized groups using empirical evidence. Because conducting research is a high-impact practice and because students were likely to be particularly passionate about the ways in which the institutions' policies and practices harm their fellow peers, Bacon decided to incorporate the research into the course to make students coresearchers. Conducting inclusion research as a major component of the course benefited both the students and the instructor.

The prejudice and discrimination course was designed so that students neither needed a background in psychology nor experience conducting research. That made the course accessible to every student on campus and resulted in a course that had students from a variety of majors, including a number of students who were neither psychology majors nor minors. Bacon actively recruited students through the institutional Intercultural and International Student Services office in order to alert students from marginalized groups to the opportunity to participate in a class that would examine the experiences of marginalized students on campus. Likely because of the course focus on the experiences of marginalized students and the active recruiting by Bacon, the students in the class represented a variety of marginalized groups and was one of the most racially and ethnically diverse groups Bacon ever had taught in a psychology class. Having students in the class who identified with a number of the marginalized groups our class planned to interview brought important perspectives to our classroom discussion and research planning, particularly because focus group research is most effective when the interviewer identifies as a member of the social group under study.

Honoring the voices of those marginalized on our campuses is at the heart of standpoint theory, which prioritizes their experiences instead of viewing them through the lens of those in power, who may simply not be able to see the injustices because of their privileged positions or may have a vested interest in maintaining existing power structures (Wood 2005, 62). Being a member of at least one marginalized group is a necessary factor to earning a standpoint, but the key to embodying a standpoint is critiquing the dominant power structure (Allen 1998, 577). The research through this course provided a space for our marginalized students, both as researchers and participants, to claim their standpoint in order to help influence needed change and help the campuses truly move toward embodied inclusivity, wherein we are living the multicultural system intrinsically working for our entire population, rather than having to be reminded to do so, or fix mistakes after the fact.

In order to work with students with a wide variety of academic backgrounds, ample class time was devoted to teaching the foundational psychological concepts and relevant research methodology. Rather than focusing on learning terms from the textbook, the class focused on self-reflection, personal growth, empathy for marginalized groups, developing community, awareness of current events, and using psychological research to advocate for change on campus. The following learning goals were the foundation for the development of the course:

1. Understand that our own experience in the world is shaped by our level of privilege and that others' experiences are shaped by their level of privilege.

2. Critically evaluate real-world situations for evidence of prejudice and discrimination.
3. Develop empathy for members of marginalized groups.
4. Advocate for the equitable treatment and inclusion of members of marginalized groups.

From the very first day of class, students were aware that they would be conducting focus groups and ultimately presenting their findings and recommendations to campus stakeholders. They took this task seriously and were mindful throughout the semester that they needed to do their best work in order to honor the participants who took time out of their schedules to share deeply personal experiences of marginalization and also to demonstrate to campus leaders that students can be the voice of change. Providing the students with an immersive scholarly experience capitalizes on the high-impact teaching practices of undergraduate research and collaborative assignments and projects (AAC&U 2013), which has a positive impact on learning. Because students were learning about the theories and research necessary to conduct their research, their work was grounded in the literature rather than on their own assumptions or biases. In particular, students used the excellent textbook by Mary Kite and Bernard Whitley Jr. (2016) entitled *Psychology of Prejudice and Discrimination* (3rd ed.) to learn about the essential concepts of stereotyping, prejudice, and discrimination; how psychologists study discrimination and prejudice; types of discrimination (including institutionalized discrimination); the impact of prejudice and discrimination on various marginalized group members; and other topics grounded in social psychological research. In addition to the textbook, students read articles about the social-contextual model of prejudice (Murphy, Kroeper, and Ozier 2018), as well as microaggressions experienced by both LGBTQ+ college students (Platt and Lenzen 2013) and by college students of color (Harwood et al. 2015). Finally, students read two chapters from Pope, Reynolds, and Mueller's *Creating Multicultural Change on Campus* (2014): "Multicultural Organization Development" and "Multicultural Change in Practice." Students had the opportunity to meet with Dr. Reynolds to discuss her work on Multicultural Organization Development and also to get her feedback on their focus group projects, which were under development at the time of the meeting. Finally, students worked in their focus group teams to identify published research on the experiences of members of their marginalized group at other institutions.

In order to focus on the values-based learning outcomes, students were required to engage in self-reflection and wrestle with emotional topics, both in class and online. To prepare students for these challenging topics, the second day of class was spent developing class engagement guidelines. Students were asked to work in groups to generate a list of community expectations that the class will follow both in the classroom interactions and the online discussions. Students then took turns sharing the items from their lists, explaining each addition. Bacon typed up a running list of all of the ideas and grouped ideas when appropriate. The class reviewed the list and voted on the items. The final list included expectations for active participation, being welcoming and inclusive, avoiding dominating the conversation, taking chances during difficult discussions, and also forgiving people (both others and themselves) who make mistakes. This spirit of openness and willingness to take risks allowed the students to have important in-class discussions about challenging topics. In order to continue the conversation and to allow people opportunities to edit their reflections before sharing, students were expected to complete online discussions in which they expanded on ideas discussed in class and reacted to each other's posts.

Building upon this foundation, over the course of the semester, students also became more actively involved in their campus community. One way that Bacon encouraged students' campus involvement was by requiring that students attend a cultural or diversity-related event and share their experience and reflections with the class. Although some of these events directly related to the topic of prejudice and discrimination, many events exposed students to cultural practices and experiences outside of their own cultures. Many students reported that this was the first time they had attended a cultural event on campus and they planned to continue to attend such events in the future.

Students benefited from conducting inclusion research in the classroom. Students learned a valuable research method skill used in many industries, particularly ones who desire in-depth understanding of customers' experiences and/or work with policy or behavior change for a population. Students learned how to facilitate potentially difficult conversations and gain empathy building skills while learning of their participants' experiences, which can translate into improved interviewing skills as well. Finally, as will be highlighted below in some student feedback, they were able to see course material come to life in the form of their participants' lived experiences and experience agency helping to create change from working with cultural insiders. As revealed in the comments presented later in this chapter, students reported that they were much more aware of issues on campus and were learning how to be advocates in their own spheres of influence as a result of this research experience. Students also benefited from the interdisciplinary approach to the research project. Having a communication professor teach students about focus group research helped students see the commonalities across disciplines as well as the important contributions of various disciplines.

Conducting inclusion research in the classroom also benefited the instructor. Bacon modeled inclusive research practices by allowing access to any student who was interested to conducting the research project simply by signing up for the class. Students didn't need to have a specific academic background or earn certain grades to work on the project. Because the research teams were embedded in the classroom, Bacon didn't need to find extra out of class times to meet with student researchers. As a faculty member at a liberal arts college, the top priority is always teaching, which makes it difficult to work on research. By making the research part of teaching, Bacon prioritized it and was ultimately much more productive than she would have been if she offered a research group experience in addition to her regular course load. The research also had a time-limited framework that ensured that the project was completed within the allotted time, which rarely happens with research Bacon conducts on her own. Because this research was clearly needed to address pressing issues on campus, the students and Bacon were motivated by a sense of urgency to keep pressing forward, even when they encountered challenges. This type of inclusive, collaborative research that benefits both students and faculty could be replicated broadly and across disciplines.

TEACHING AND RESEARCH METHODOLOGY

This project was a cross-disciplinary effort that evolved through collaboration among psychology and communication faculty. The course was taught by a social psychologist (Bacon) who worked in close consultation with a multicultural counseling psychologist (Jantzer) and a communication professor whose research focuses on stigma and discrimination (Kramer). The teaching and research methodology particularly drew upon the health communication literature. More specifically, the culture-centered approach (CCA) to health communication which highlights how imperative it is to let the words of cultural insider's guide change. Traditionally, a hierarchy/funding agency dictates what is best for a population; however, this approach rarely results in significant change (Jamil and Dutta 2012). "The CCA suggests that to understand what really matters to an individual, one needs to 'begin by creating spaces for those voices [that have been] systematically silenced through our [the dominant experts'] expertise and elitism'" (Dutta 2008, 45 as cited in Jamil and Dutta 2012, 370). Critical to facilitating successful change is that "the CCA attempts to deconstruct the taken-for-granted attitudes and assumptions of the dominant knowledge base and tries to co-construct meanings and discursive spaces from the perspectives of cultural insiders. Essential to the creation of such spaces is the fostering of a bottom-up structure for articulating experiences and meanings" (Jamil and Dutta 2012, 371). Intricately intertwined in this process is uncovering the inequities which cultural insiders experience and must be addressed in order for systemic change to occur. The strategy to use focus groups for this class project was a means to give voice to cultural insiders within a system that often ignores or diminishes those voices, even if unknowingly.

Several scholars emphasize that when trying to understand the lived experience of those who are marginalized, focus groups are a preferred method in order to create a sense of comfort (Curry 2015; Ulin, Robinson, and Tolley 2004, 93) and a means to elicit rich narratives from hard to reach populations (Barbour 2010, 330, 333). On our campuses, while the groups included for this study are growing, they are still in the minority, and singling them out for one-on-one interviews may have created anxiety. What's more, focus groups tend to generate more information, as participants typically build upon each other's contributions (Ulin et al. 2004, 89). The benefit of having students conduct the focus groups is that, typically, participants are more likely to share more information when the facilitator most closely matches them, as this creates a sense of comfort (Madriz 2000). Because psychology students have limited qualitative research training, one component of this course was to teach students about these important methodologies. In order for students to facilitate the focus groups, they needed to be trained. First, during the summer preceding the course, the third author, Kramer trained the other two faculty members involved in this project, as well as others interested in using focus group methodology and analysis (for more on focus group methodology, see Ulin et al. 2004). Then, early in the semester of the prejudice and discrimination course, Kramer trained students during two class periods. The first class period consisted of helping students understand the value of qualitative research, specifically focus groups, as well as many of the nuts and bolts of conducting focus groups: developing research questions, the roles of facilitators, length of focus groups, ideal number of participants and their recruitment, incentives for participation, need for institutional review board (IRB) approval, key aspects of the focus group guide (facilitators' script for the focus group), and benefits and challenges of different types of questions. To help students feel more comfortable with conducting focus groups, it is best if they practice the focus group guide with sample participants from the class in order to identify questions that need rewording, missing questions, and to provide tips to facilitators on asking follow-up questions. The latter is particularly difficult for undergraduates when facilitating a focus group as they are both trying to pay close attention to their participants' answers, as well as be prepared to address any confusion or problems, and then be able to move participants on to the next question topic. As a result, they often miss opportunities for asking critical follow-up questions needed for garnering examples. Having the student researchers participate in a sample focus group is also beneficial since few have participated in one prior and this experience gives them insight into how they may want to adjust their focus group guide to keep participants engaged while encouraging all to have a conversation together rather than a facilitator peppering the participants with rote questions.

As a result, during the second class session, Kramer led students through practice focus groups where they played the roles of facilitators and participants, including some enacting difficult participants. During this process, we discussed how best to handle challenging participants in an actual focus group. At this point, students showed excitement and anxiety about what they needed to do and asked many questions about how to handle difficult participants. Their concerns were eased some by assurances that they were much more adept at channeling challenging participants than any actual participant their trainer had ever seen. The challenges from participants students are actually likely to face include small distracting side conversations, using cell phones, and one or two participants answering more often than others. All of these issues are easily addressed in the focus group guide which includes setting the ground rules of the focus group beforehand including asking participants to refrain from side conversations and using phones and clarifying that if something becomes distracting, you will kindly ask them not to continue doing the distracting behavior. You want them to know that you are not "yelling" at them, but rather, want to be able to pay close attention to what everyone is saying. Likewise, while reviewing the ground rules, the facilitator should let participants know that if some are quieter, they will be asked specifically for their input because the group is interested in hearing everyone's experiences.

As the students were learning about conducting focus groups, they also identified which groups they wanted to interview for our project. Students spent time speaking with friends and peers about issues of inclusion to identify potential groups. As the students narrowed down the list, Bacon invited a panel of campus experts to talk with students about the experiences of the marginalized student groups they worked with on a regular basis. The director and assistant director of the Intercultural and International Student Services office came to talk about the experiences of international students and students of color, the former chair of the Gender Studies department talked about the experiences of LGBTQ+ students, and the co-director of the Becoming Community grant talked about the issues facing low-income college students, first-generation college students, and students with mental health issues.

Bacon broke the class up into smaller research teams so that all students would have the opportunity to actively participate in the project. Students grouped into teams of five to seven based on interest and an attempt to spread out the group membership evenly. In retrospect, Bacon wishes she had limited the group size to a maximum of five students, as the group of seven experienced some diffusion of responsibility among group members.

The small group approach allowed the class to examine a larger number of social identity groups, but it also meant that we needed to recruit participants for five different focus groups and Bacon had to supervise five projects. Despite the challenges of working with such a large number of groups, Bacon thought that it was worth it to hear about the experiences of a variety of marginalized groups and to provide students with more responsibility and autonomy related to their specific project. It also allowed us to identify common issues that impacted multiple social identity groups, thereby adding weight to the issue. After considering a variety of social identity groups at our institutions, the students identified five groups they wanted to focus on: domestic students of color, international students, first-generation college students, low-income students, and LGBTQ+ students. These groups were selected by the students because they believed, based upon anecdotal reports, that there was a pressing need to better understand and attend to the needs of these students marginalized on our campuses. Additionally, we were able to find published research on college students related to each social identity group.

Many of the past studies on marginalized student groups had focused on the impact of peer interactions on members of those social groups. However, given the call by the Inclusion Research Initiative to focus on ways that the institutions inhibit inclusion, the class focused on college policies and practices that cause exclusion and discrimination on campus and to suggest ways to address those policies and practices. Based on our research focus, the following research questions were used for all of the groups:

1. What are the institutional policies and practices of CSB/SJU that marginalize and/or discriminate against (LGBTQ+ students/low-income students/ first-generation college students/ domestic students of color/ international students) on our campuses?
2. What could be done to improve these policies and practices on campus to create a more inclusive community?

Because the students all used the same main research questions, the IRB allowed Bacon to submit a single proposal that explained why five different groups of students would be recruited and why some of the follow-up questions were different depending upon the specific group. Despite this streamlined approach to the IRB proposal, it was still a time-consuming process. Bacon wanted the students in the class to help develop the questions and select the groups. Unfortunately, Bacon learned that the students were not ready to develop effective research questions, and eventually constructed the research questions for the students. Thus, we recommend that others interested in replicating this process provide the research questions and complete the IRB form prior to the start of the semester, so the approval process does not slow down the projects.

Due to the delay in the IRB approval, the students were recruiting and running their focus groups near the end of the semester. Students recruited participants by tabling in common spaces, sending e-mails to clubs, and asking the Intercultural and International Student Services office to promote the study. We recruited between eight and twelve participants for each focus group. We had received IRB approval to video record and audio record each session, which was invaluable to us as we ended up having to code directly from the videos rather than creating transcripts because of time constraints.

During each focus group, a student conducted the session while some or all of the rest of the researchers helped with recording, taking notes, and asking follow-up questions if needed. However, prior to the start of the session, Bacon would arrive about thirty minutes early to start setting up the room, ensure that the food was delivered and paid for, and help provide the researchers with the informed consent forms, scripts, nametags, and other materials needed during the session. Although the students may have been fine without the help from Bacon, most were quite relieved to have her in the room to help set things up and to welcome the participants. Bacon modeled how to enthusiastically thank participants for volunteering for the study and to encourage participant to eat food. As soon as the study was ready to begin, Bacon left the room and waited in a nearby location in case the researchers had issues during the session. After the study had ended, Bacon would return to help take down the equipment and gather all materials. Bacon would also make sure to talk with the team about issues that arose, main themes that emerged, and to remind the researchers to write down their observations when they got home. To ensure the focus groups were held at times that worked for participants, the meetings were often in the evening, making for long days for Bacon and students. This is another consideration to keep in mind when determining how many focus group projects should be conducted by the students in the class.

Prior to analyzing the results, students were also trained in how to conduct thematic analysis of their focus group transcripts as outlined by Baxter and Babbie (2004, Ch. 16) and Ulin et al. (2004, Ch. 6). For this process, each student individually identified repeating themes inductively followed by a code sorting process in which students compared and revised themes until agreement was met. Students should be given ideally a week (although Kramer's students have done it in shorter time periods when necessary) to individually analyze transcripts for themes and create a thematic document. These individual thematic documents should be shared on the course website, and the professor should become familiar with them. Students then should be given a class period (two if the class is only an hour or less) to begin code sorting in their groups. Starting the code sort process in class is essential so that the professor is present to answer questions as students get stuck. Providing novice students enough time to struggle with the analysis process is critical in that it is the most difficult part of such a study. In order to assist students in understanding this process, if the professor has access to transcripts from a different study, it is useful to have students first go through the thematic analysis process with this data so that students have time to work closely with the professor to ask questions and get frustrated with material that is not attached to their grade. An example of a glitch Kramer discovered in a prior course during the practice analysis session was that students were counting a two-page example from a participant as multiple examples which then would constitute a theme. While this was a great extended example, it was not a theme across participants in the study.

STUDENTS' REFLECTIONS ON THE CLASS

Students had a variety of opportunities to reflect on the impact of their work both during the online discussion posts and also in a series of reflection papers meant to address the values-based learning outcomes of the course. Although the students had spent a semester learning about prejudice and discrimination, hearing examples from their peers was upsetting and surprising for many. Students also were alarmed that marginalized students felt that they had to make the best of unfair situations. One student wrote:

> It was really disheartening to hear the stories from our international students in the focus group. On top of this, most of the students have adopted an attitude of ambivalence towards these injustices. Students explained that it was difficult to face these challenges, but they just accepted it as the way this school works. That piece really saddened me. Ultimately, I have seen a really big change in myself and how I view international students throughout this semester. I have gone from not really thinking about their experience to being passionate about making changes to our institutions to ensure they have the same opportunities to a good college experience as domestic students.

Students also reported that the experience caused them to examine their own behavior to create a more inclusive campus. One student wrote:

> I have been making sure that since I heard about the microaggressions and prejudice our LGBTQ+ participants described that I catch myself or point out to others how they could be hurting someone else with their remarks. I am not

saying that I completely understand how people in the LGBTQ+ community feel about the prejudice against them, but I am starting to see how something that seems harmless to me could be extremely hurtful to others.

Students also reported feeling inspired by the work of the class and felt a calling to fight injustice in their sphere of influence. One student wrote:

Taking this class has changed my perspective on our campuses and society as a whole. I no longer have my closed-minded ways. I no longer believe that no one wants to see change around this campus because I had a classroom full of people that do. I have learned the most from my professor, the members of my focus group, and the participants in our focus group. They have taught me that we are no longer going to be "conditioned" to look past the microaggressions, prejudice, and discrimination that come along with being marginalized, but that we are going to fight for what is right.

Other students saw a disconnect between the institutional rhetoric of inclusion and the experiences of marginalized students on campus and hoped that their research would lead to changes on campus, as can be seen in the following two comments. One student wrote:

I am really hopeful that the students in this class combined with the research we have done are going to make an actual impact on our campuses. I think that our schools have done a really good job of taking the first steps towards making us a multicultural institution, but I think we are able to make them realize that there are more steps we need to take. Right now, our school is doing a lot of bragging about all the different cultures on our campuses, but, as we've learned, simply being aware of these various cultures does not mean that everyone feels like [our college] is a place where they feel they are treated fairly and equally.

And another student wrote,

Overall, the final presentations were an eye-opener for me about this institution. Just hearing the voices of those that were interviewed, there are big issues here on these campuses that we need to address. I am disappointed at the fact that this institution really stresses a lot on diversity and creating a community but yet, these discriminations are occurring daily even as we speak. I hope that with these presentations, we were able to grab the attention of those who attended and hopefully they will take actions from our suggestions and help be the voices of those who have been silenced.

Finally, students valued learning how to use qualitative research to dismantle oppressive policies and practices in the future. One student shared:

> I've also developed many skills from this course. The lectures on how to conduct focus groups will extend to my life, especially when connecting to others and trying to learn their stories. Our project, how we conducted research, and then tried to make change based off it, will be very helpful to me. Not only am I proud that this class might make a change on campus past the end of the semester, being part of such a comprehensive project makes me more confident to pursue similar things in the future. By walking through all the steps, I now have a better idea of what it takes and how to successfully conduct such work. I hope to conduct both research (maybe less academically than in a college setting) and implement structural changes in the future. I've gotten a taste of how that would be done.

OUTCOMES

This course produced a range of positive outcomes, including more empathy for members of marginalized groups coupled with a desire to engage in advocacy to change systems of oppression. Students repeatedly translated their learning into action both in the required research project and in their everyday lives. Midway through the semester, students in the class identified a need to make faculty and staff aware of microaggressions, so during one class period we hosted a microaggressions workshop based on the work by Plous (2000). Bacon facilitated the workshop by presenting introductory information about microaggressions and then two student volunteers conducted a role-play to model how to effectively respond and disrupt a microaggression that targeted the LGBTQ+ community. The audience was then provided with a series of scenarios depicting microaggressions targeting a range of marginalized groups, some of which reflected real-life student experiences on campus. Faculty and staff then engaged in an experiential role-playing exercise, practicing how to respond to the microaggression scenarios with each group of audience members paired with a student from the class, who acted as a coach. This workshop was very well attended by a broad cross section of faculty, staff, and administrators and received the highest ratings from the audience of any of the inclusion workshops offered in fall 2018. Overwhelmingly, attendees found the experiential aspect of this workshop to be useful and illuminating and particularly valued the student coaching. Moreover, students were energized and inspired by their experience actually implementing needed change (i.e., improving faculty and staff training around microaggressions) on our campuses as a part of their course experience. This project was an example of the benefits of working with students as collaborators; without their leadership on this issue, we would not have conducted that highly effective session.

At the end of the semester, one of the most important elements of the project was sharing the results with the campus community. In order to urge the campus community to reexamine policies and practices that were not inclusive, the findings and recommendations that grew out of the focus groups were presented at a public forum with policy makers in attendance. This public presentation to stakeholders in positions of power communicated to research participants that we were committed to making positive change on campus and communicated to the larger campus community that we need to reexamine how policies and practices can have unintended negative consequences on our students.

In order to ensure that the event was well attended, Bacon sent individual invitations to campus leaders and also announced the event in a campus-wide e-mail. The event was also linked to an end of the semester meeting for key stakeholders in a large campus inclusion initiative. The presentation, held during the students' final exam period, was attended by numerous faculty, staff, and administrators. In order to keep the presentation within the allotted time period, the students were required to make brief presentations of no more than eight minutes per group, with each group member contributing to the presentation. Bacon served as the timekeeper and ensured that the event ended on time. A video recording of the presentation was requested by faculty who could not attend the event, thereby increasing the audience.

During the presentation, the students identified a number of behaviors involving faculty and staff that caused students to feel unwelcome and discriminated against. These examples, drawn from the words of the participants, were powerful. The students also identified policies that had unintended impact on students, such as policies regarding class registration. By presenting all of the findings in one session, it became easier to identify institutional policies and practices that impacted a large number of social identity groups. For example, the lack of transportation into the nearby city impacted students of color, international students, low-income college students, and first-generation students.

In addition to making presentations, each group developed a three to four-page policy brief. The policy brief was divided into introduction, methodology, key findings, and recommendations sections, along with references. Students were told that the policy brief needed to be visually appealing yet professional. The introduction section discussed background information on the marginalized group interviewed by the researchers. In particular, demographic information from the school was required. Next, the introduction identified key issues identified in the research literature as impacting college students from their particular marginalized group to build a case that the challenges facing marginalized students on our campus were also issues across the country. Students were encouraged to examine research on retention rates among members of their marginalized group. In addition to the detailed guidelines, students were given an example of a published policy brief focusing on how policies impact walking and bicycling in cities.

After the class was over, the policy briefs and the video of the presentation have been assigned to students in two different communication classes in spring 2019 and spring 2020 as background material for their own discussions and projects on issues of inclusion. One of the policy briefs is being used to advocate for a new resource center on campus. Also, a number of policy changes on campus have been based on the results of the focus group projects. Positioned within the context of the Mellon Inclusion Research Initiative, this work also informed strategic action plans created as part of larger inclusion efforts at the institutions. Former students have gone on to participate in the Student Senate, including taking on leadership roles in which they have advocated for dismantling racism in the wake of the protests following the brutal murder of George Floyd, and have worked to support these campus changes through their participation in student clubs and postgraduation advocacy work.

RECOMMENDATIONS

Reflecting upon the course, we can identify many recommendations to share with other faculty members interested in this approach to inclusion research. The first recommendation is to develop and adopt a strict timeline that will allow students to have adequate time to transcribe and analyze their data. Be sure that the focus groups are held before major holidays so that participants will have the time and energy to volunteer. Prioritize submitting the IRB proposal early, perhaps even submitting it and receiving approval before the semester starts. If the students want to add questions, those questions can be submitted as requested changes to the IRB, which tends to have a quicker turn-around time.

The second recommendation is to give students the appropriate level of autonomy. Although the instructor could have students develop additional questions, it is best if the instructor writes the central questions for the project both so the IRB proposal can be submitted prior to the class and also so the instructor does not have to reject students' contributions if they do not meet the goals of the project. For example, the students in the class enjoyed working on questions, but the questions were often not at all related to the goal of the project. As an alternative, particularly if you have multiple groups, we recommend that instructors develop general research questions that will allow students to gather similar data across the groups.

Third, we recommend limiting the number of focus groups to three in one semester. Although students in this course were excited to have more options, it did create much more work for the instructor of the course. For instance, she had to check in with five groups each class period, and near the end of the semester she had to schedule meetings with all of the groups to discuss their results, presentation, and policy brief drafts. It also meant that students were often competing for research participants. Of course, having large research teams also has drawbacks, so offering the course with a low cap may help this issue.

The fourth recommendation is that the instructor needs a strong hand in the recruitment phase. In other words, the students should take the lead in recruitment, but the instructor needs to stay well informed of the progress and be ready to step in to help recruitment efforts. To that end as well, recruitment should be done through snowball sampling (more commonly known as word of mouth) so that you may secure enough participants for the focus groups. Having approval for the projects early in the semester also would allow for more time to recruit participants.

Finally, we recommend making the final project meaningful by having the students present to campus leaders who could act on the recommendations. Students were excited to make a difference on campus and to contribute to transformational inclusion through their work. A number of the participants in the focus group contacted Bacon to ask if they could take the prejudice and discrimination class or other classes that would allow them to conduct inclusion research on campus. This response is notable, as many of the participants initially expressed hesitation to participate in our project because they felt that their contributions to past inclusion research had not led to any changes.

CONCLUSION

Based upon our experience with this effort, we conclude that working with students to conduct inclusion research in a class is not only beneficial to students and instructors, but it is also an effective way to contribute to MCOD in institutions of higher education. More specifically, such efforts may advance organizational progress in the redefining system stage of the MCOD model (Pope et al. 2014, 25) by prompting deeper examination of barriers to inclusion and spur action to dismantle such barriers by changing oppressive institutional policies and procedures. This approach to student-engaged classroom research centers the voices of marginalized students, translates research into action, and may be adapted for a variety of courses across disciplines. We hope that this work may thus serve as a model for others who strive to apply high-impact practices in course design to not only benefit students' learning but also to create more inclusive campus communities.

REFERENCES

Allen, Brenda. J. 1998. "Black Womanhood and Feminist Standpoints." *Management Communication Quarterly* 11 (4): 575–586. doi:10.1177/0893318998114004.

American Association of Colleges and Universities (AAC&U). 2013. "High-Impact Educational Practices: A Brief Overview." http://www.aacu.org/leap/hip.cfm.

Barbour, Rosaline S. 2010. "Focus Groups." In *The Sage Handbook of Qualitative Methods in Health Research,* edited by Ivy Bourgeault, Robert Dingwall, and Raymond de Vries, pp. 327–352. Thousand Oaks, CA: SAGE.

Baxter, Leslie A. and Earle R Babbie. 2004. *The Basics of Communication Research.* Belmont: Wadsworth/Thomson Learning.

Becoming Community. "What is Transformative Inclusion?" YouTube video, 5:02. Oct. 12, 2018. https://youtu.be/i83U0mwcmFg.

Curry, Leslie. 2015. "Fundamentals of Qualitative Research Methods: Focus Groups (Module 4)." YouTube video, 21:36. https://www.youtube.com/watch?v=cCA Pz14yjd4.

Gummadam, Praveena, Laura D. Pittman, and Micah Ioffe. 2016. "School Belonging, Ethnic Identity, and Psychological Adjustment Among Ethnic Minority College Students." *Journal of Experimental Education* 84 (2): 289–306. doi:10.1080/0022 0973.2015.1048844.

Harwood, Stacy Ann, Shinwoo Choi, Moises Orozco, Margaret Browne Huntt, and Ruby Mendenhall. 2015. "Racial Microaggressions at the University of Illinois at Urbana-Champaign: Voices of Students of Color in the Classroom." University of Illinois: Urbana-Champaign.

Hausmann, Leslie R. M., Janet Ward Schofield, and Rochelle L. Woods. 2007. "Sense of Belonging as a Predictor of Intentions to Persist Among African American and White First-year College Students." *Research in Higher Education* 48 (7): 803–839. doi:10.1007/s11162-007-9052-9.

Hinton, Mary Dana. 2017. *Becoming Community.* Unpublished grant proposal manuscript funded by the Andrew W. Mellon Foundation.

Jamil, Raihan, and Mohan J. Dutta. 2008. "A Culture-Centered Exploration of Health: Constructions From Rural Bangladesh." *Health Communication* 27, (4): 369–79.

Kite, Mary, and Bernard Whitley. 2016. *Psychology of Prejudice and Discrimination.* 3rd edition. New York: Routledge.

Madriz, Esther. 2000. "Focus Groups in Feminist Research." In *The Handbook of Qualitative Research* (2nd edition), edited by Norman K. Denzin & Yvonna S. Lincoln, pp. 835–850. Thousand Oaks, CA: SAGE.

Murphy, Mary C., Kathryn M. Kroeper, and Elise M. Ozier. 2018. "Prejudiced Places: How Contexts Shape Inequality and How Policy Can Change Them." *Policy Insights from the Behavioral and Brain Sciences* 5 (1): 66–74. doi:10.1177/2372732217748671.

Pittman, Laura D., and Adeya Richmond. 2008. "University Belonging, Friendship Quality, and Psychological Adjustment During the Transition to College." *Journal of Experimental Education* 76 (4): 343–361. doi:10.3200/JEXE.76.4.343-362.

Platt, Lisa F., and Alexandra L. Lenzen. 2013. "Sexual Orientation Microaggressions and the Experience of Sexual Minorities." *Journal of Homosexuality* 60 (7): 1011–1034. doi:10.1080/00918369.2013.774878.

Plous, Scott. 2000. Responding to Overt Displays of Prejudice: A Role-Playing Exercise. *Teaching of Psychology* 27: 198–200.

Pope, Raechele L., Amy L. Reynolds, and John A. Mueller. 2014. *Creating Multicultural Change on Campus*. San Francisco, CA: Jossey-Bass.

Ulin, Priscilla R., Elizabeth T. Robinson, and Elizabeth E. Tolley. 2004. *Qualitative Methods in Public Health: A Field Guide for Applied Research*. San Francisco, CA: Jossey-Bass

Vaccaro, Annemarie, and Barbara M. Newman. 2016. "Development of a Sense of Belonging for Privileged and Minoritized Students: An Emergent Model." *Journal of College Student Development* 57 (8): 925–942. doi:10.1353/csd.2016.0091.

Wood, Julia T. 2005. "Feminist Standpoint Theory and Muted Group Theory: Commonalities and Divergences." *Women and Language* 28 (2): 61–64.

UNDERSTANDING THE EXPERIENCES OF MINORITIZED POPULATIONS ON CAMPUS

Chapter 5

Pathways for Native Student Inclusion

A Framework for Redressing Institutional Injustices

Theodor P. Gordon, Belen Benway, and Claire Winters

Can a university meaningfully redress a legacy of injustice? Our joint institutions were once affiliated with four Native American boarding schools that were part of the United States' attempt to force Native youth to assimilate. This legacy continues to affect Native communities today, including students on our campuses. However, we believe it is possible to redress these injustices through three pathways that acknowledge that the work of redress is never finished. In this chapter, we describe these pathways, which include (1) collaborating with affected Native communities to investigate and share our hidden history, (2) empowering Native and Indigenous students to interview their Native and Indigenous classmates for recommendations to increase inclusivity, and (3) forging partnerships that serve Native communities on their own terms. We conclude with a framework for any university to adapt our pathways to redress past and present injustices.

INVESTIGATING OUR PAST

The Dakota and Anishinaabe[1] people are the original stewards of the land that is now home to our institutions of higher education. Throughout the nineteenth century, a series of treaties and military conflicts forced the Dakota and Anishinaabe from most of their ancestral territories. In 1863, Minnesota authorized scalp bounties on the Dakota people, funding settler militias to systematically murder all Dakota within state limits (Routel 2013). In spite of Minnesota's efforts, some Dakota remained. Others later returned to their homeland. In 1867, a treaty sought to remove all of Minnesota's Anishinaabe to the White Earth Reservation in northwestern Minnesota. Many communities resisted, eventually leading to the creation of six additional reservations across the state.

By the late 1800s, the federal government began a new strategy to eliminate Native communities. Instead of relying exclusively on military force, the United States separated Native youth from their parents to attend boarding schools designed to force assimilation. In 1879, the Carlisle Indian Industrial School was the first to implement this model, under the slogan "kill the Indian, save the man." Throughout the 1880s, Congress expanded this model across the United States and funded hundreds of schools. The Indian Appropriations Bill of 1891 formally authorized the Department of War to require all Native families to send their children to boarding schools. Parents could be denied treaty-entitled food rations, and in some cases, could be imprisoned, for refusing to give up their children (Child 1998, 13; Woolford 2015, 72).

In 1863, sisters from the Order of St. Benedict (OSB) founded a Benedictine monastery in a small, rural town. Three miles away, in 1866, OSB monks founded a Benedictine Abbey. The monastery later founded a college for women and the Abbey founded a university for men. In 1878, OSB opened an Indian Mission to serve a local reservation's existing Catholic population and create new converts. By 1884, OSB secured funding from the federal government to operate four Native American boarding schools modeled after the Carlisle School. This included developing two schools at local reservations as well as two which operated on what are now our joint college and university campuses (McDonald 1957; Barry and Klingeman 1993). At the reservation-based schools, children could visit their home on weekends but could not on weekdays, until the schools converted to day schools in the 1940s. One of these schools closed in the early 1970s. The other continues to operate as a day school without OSB affiliation (Berg 1981, 176; Lindblad 1997, 219). Thousands of Anishinaabe youth attended these schools. Most students at the industrial schools were members of the White Earth Nation.

The monastics who operated OSB's Native American boarding schools each had their own motivations and attitudes about native cultures. Berg's (1981) interviews and archival analysis of the White Earth Mission demonstrate that they often disagreed quite strongly with each other about the value of Anishinaabe culture and whether OSB should be working toward assimilating students or preserving their traditions. Likewise, in Fruth's (1956) interviews former Industrial School students identified monastics who were kind to them. They also identified those who were abusive.

Today at our institutions, most on our campuses have no awareness of these schools, just as many Americans have little knowledge of the federal government's nationwide efforts to force Native assimilation through boarding schools. While there are a handful of historical narratives that describe OSB's schools (Berg 1981; McDonald 1957; Barry and Klingeman 1993; Lindblad 1997; Laliberte 2008), these texts are only accessible to those who would comb our libraries looking for them. The Native communities affected by these schools are intimately aware of their impacts but have not had easy access to any of OSB's archival materials or photographs. The first pathways discussed in this chapter outlines our attempt to investigate the history of OSB's Native American boarding schools as a first step toward raising our campuses' awareness and sharing archival materials with Native communities. Our campus archives house several thousand pages of school records and several hundred photographs documenting these schools. If we are ever to redress our role in the nationwide historical injustice of forced assimilation, we must begin by acknowledging it to ourselves and to the Native communities impacted by it. We are now collaborating with the Tribal Historic Preservation Offices of each affected Native nation to share materials as we find it. We hope to transform our campuses into a community where each member understands our legacy of forced assimilation and appreciates the resilience of the affected Native communities.

INDUSTRIAL SCHOOLS

At our institutions, the industrial schools are the closest to home, having once operated on our campuses. However, we have few archival resources on these schools, which only operated from 1885 to 1896. According to the schools' catalogues, at their peak, the Industrial School at what is now our university had over 150 Anishinaabe students and the Industrial School at the location of our college had over 125. During this time, OSB operated academies and what would later become our university, but the industrial schools had significant presence on both campuses. In 1890, Native youth accounted for approximately 60 percent of students at one of these industrial schools and just under 50 percent at the other. In other words, Native youth were once nearly a majority of students on what became the campuses of our joint college and university.

The few materials that we have include school catalogues that describe the curriculum and list the names of enrolled students. The federal government mandated that the schools use curricula that emphasized manual labor and assimilation (Woolford 2015, 142). Fruth (1956) found that the daily schedule at the industrial schools emphasized manual labor over education, with four hours a day for labor and three hours of class activities. For girls, labor often included cooking, cleaning, and other domestic work. For boys, labor included farming and shop work. Classes included reading, arithmetic, history, and theology. In 1956, Rev. Alban Fruth, OSB conducted interviews with two former Industrial School students. Our archives include his notes from the interviews. In Fruth's notes, one interviewee explained that at the Industrial School, "Discipline was strict, and often boys were severely whipped for mere trifles. . . . The boys were extremely afraid of their teachers because you could never be sure when their tempers would flare up." Another former student described frequent whippings and noted, "The boys were never struck or whipped at home by their parents—the parents would talk to them when they needed correction" (Fruth 1956). Students at the industrial schools frequently attempted to run away (Skjolsvik 1957, 111–123). Others died from disease. Our research team located five burials in the Abbey Cemetery.

As outlined above, our research is uncovering moments in our institutions' histories that are devastating. Our research team believes that our institutions' relationships with Anishinaabe communities do not need to end with the historical traumas inflicted at the boarding school. By taking steps toward redressing these injustices, we can transform our institutions' relationships with Anishaabe communities into ones based on truth and reconciliation. We believe that truth must come before reconciliation, therefore, our first steps focus on identifying archival materials that illuminate the experiences of students at these schools and sharing these materials with the affected Native communities. This labor-intensive effort would not be possible without the contributions of undergraduate student researchers. Including students in this work is important for reasons beyond skill development. In order to achieve our goal of transforming our community into one where all members understand our legacy of forced assimilation and the resilience of Native communities, students must be engaged in the work of investigating our past and sharing our findings. This way, students can become agents of change, while developing professional skills.

The following sections are authored by two undergraduate student researchers who have made invaluable contributions to our research. Both sections are written in first-person to highlight their experiences as researchers working to transform our institutions. In the next section, third author Belen Benway describes her projects digitizing materials from the Industrial and reservation-based schools and her work with our institutions' digital archive, Vivarium.

DIGITAL ARCHIVES

I, Belen Benway, have been working closely on two projects that will help create awareness around our campuses' history and past goal of assimilating Native American youth through boarding schools. The first project that I worked on was digitizing photos of the industrial schools in our institutional archives. My goal for this project was to go through the archives, find the photographs, and try to identify who the children are in the photos and what Anishinaabe tribes they are from. Once I was able to find some identifiers of the children in the photographs, I categorized them by specific tribes.

Our institutions' have four separates archives maintained by our monastery, abbey, college, and university. I focused on collected photographs in the Monastery Archive, which includes photos from the Industrial School that was located at what is now our college, as well as photos from the two schools that were located on reservations. I found individual school photographs, class photos, pictures of the schoolchildren in the classrooms learning, playing, and photos of the buildings and classrooms.

I began by searching through all the photos the archives had and identifying which ones were relevant to this project. After I identified the photos, I worked with archive staff to scan them and categorize them by tribe, date, location, and other features. Fortunately, some of the photos include detailed notes including the names of those in the photos. Once we found out what the student's name was, it was a matter of looking through the catalog to find the fitting tribe. Currently, we have identified over 150 photographs and we keep finding more.

The end goal for this project is sharing these photos with their respective tribes. It's humbling to know that some of these photos haven't been seen in over 100 years, and they are finally now being shared with the relatives of former students. Sharing these photos is a symbol of our school extending respect and taking a first step toward healing.

I feel that our work is especially needed at our institutions to create a more collaborative partnership with the Native communities around us. I started to realize the problem when I was asking around campus and no one knew about our schools' past with the industrial schools. The first step to redress these injustices is acknowledgement. These photos helped to create a picture for us of what being at one of these industrial schools really looked like. My second project helps us to understand what it was like to attend one of these schools.

For my second project, I have been categorizing the articles found on Vivarium, a digital archive operated by our institutions. Our campus newspaper has been digitized and through Vivarium you can now search articles online going all the way back to the 1880s, when the industrial schools were open. However, I not only found articles from the newspaper, but I also found school catalogs from both industrial schools. The school catalogues reveal their curriculum, policies, and a list of student names.

By searching Vivarium, I have already identified over 500 articles that reference the boarding schools or Minnesota's Native communities. To help organize my search results, I created a searchable database that includes the basic information about each article. This database will make it easier for our institutions and for Native communities to quickly find articles that will help us better understand our past.

We have only just begun the process of analyzing these articles, and we have already found some that are quite revealing about our institutions' past relationships with Native communities. For example, one article was about a destructive tornado that hit the university in 1894. The tornado completely ripped through the Industrial School and living quarters. Luckily, school staff were able to wake the boys from their slumber and evacuate them from the building before any lives were lost. Another article reported on two Ojibwe chiefs that visited the industrial schools. According to the article, chiefs Little Wolf and Moonlight came from the Mille Lacs Band of Ojibwe to inspect the Industrial School on December 1, 1889. The article has few details about their visit, but it does show Mille Lacs leadership cared deeply for their youth and OSB granted them permission to visit.

While our archives have few materials on the industrial schools, we have identified over 2,000 pages of materials documenting one of the mission schools. In the next section, second author Claire Winters discusses her analysis of those materials.

MISSION SCHOOL

In searching the Monastery Archive, I, Claire Winters, found a variety of materials that paint a complicated picture of the century-long history of the White Earth Mission School. One of the most valuable items is Sister Carol Berg's (OSB) 1981 doctoral dissertation on the school, which includes surveys and interviews with former teachers and students. In addition to the interview excerpts in her dissertation, the archive contains transcripts of the complete interviews as well as interviews conducted by other OSB sisters. My research would not have been possible without the work of OSB historians and archivists who worked to preserve this history.

Originally intended to be a mixed-gender school that housed both orphans and "day-scholars," the school quickly became a female-only boarding school instead. The school was supported primarily by philanthropic funding and functioned as a boarding school up until 1945. It then functioned as a mixed-gender day school, up until its closing twenty-four years later in the early 1970s. In total, about 2,000 to 3,000 children were enrolled over the school's lifetime, with a large portion of the children being orphans (Berg 1981, vi).

Berg's (1891) analysis found that the school was overwhelmingly staffed by recent immigrants to the United States or first and second-generation immigrants from German, Swiss, or neighboring German-speaking countries. Many assigned to the school were English language learners. Their limited proficiency proved challenging as they worked to instruct Anishinaabe youth in English. In her interview, former student Beatina Vanoss shared that school staff frequently spoke German because it was helpful "when the sisters wanted to keep something a secret from the girls" (Berg 1981, 2). Further complicating matters was a high turnover rate: the monastics that staffed the school commonly stayed less than a decade, and those who stayed longer were very often younger and inexperienced. One could imagine how having a revolving door of sisters serving short terms at the school, with limited teaching experience, and in some cases, limited English, could have created a challenging environment for students.

Despite the mission school being founded through government structures, it quickly found itself relying on outside funding for its continued existence. By the 1890s, the school faced barriers due to a growing preference for military-run boarding schools over religious, with further threats came from rising anti-Catholic sentiment in the United States. By 1900, funding was gone: surplus funds were to be relied on, and it was determined that "the continuance of the school must depend on the charity of the faithful" (Watrin 1978, 7). Most significant to this funding shift was the philanthropy of Saint Katharine Drexel, philanthropist and founder of the Sisters of the Blessed Sacrament, an order dedicated to missionary work among Black and Native populations. Drexel's philanthropy fully funded the expansion of the school, expanding the scale of operations that the missionaries could take on from about 50 students to a maximum of 150.

One key difference between the mission school and other Native American boarding schools was that the mission school had no formal language ban on the Indigenous languages; early letters suggest that there was in fact no real initiative to create one. Carol Berg, OSB (1981, 45–46) suggests that because many in the monastic population experienced "sufficient struggle" with reading and writing in English as their second language, for many the added struggle of policing a third language may have been too much to be worth it. While many former students recall that they were only able to speak little Ojibwe—if any at all—by the end of their time at the school, Ojibwe was spoken by some of the students to keep secrets from the sisters, similar to the sisters speaking German to hide things from the students (Berg 1981, 1).

Many students expressed that the mission school curriculum negatively represented Native identities. Rose Barstow, a former student who attended from 1923 to 1930, recalled an event in fourth grade wherein "[we] were studying a book on colonial history . . . I said, 'these are awful people.' [The teacher] said, 'Why, my girl, you're one of those savages. We came here to civilize you'" (Katz 1996, 265). Rose's experience is corroborated by the experiences of many of the monastics from this time. Sister Mary Degel recalled that "most of the sisters wanted to change the Indians" (Berg 1981, 1). This was furthered by current educational policy in place at the time. The mission school placed a heavy emphasis on patriotism, especially in history class; "the Indians were to be Americans first and Indians second, destined for absorption into the national life" (Berg 1981, 69–70).

Upon arrival, students would receive a mandatory haircut and change of clothes, with the result of "look[ing] like everybody else. I felt really lost" (Katz 1977, 117). While the policy on hair relaxed in later years—if hair was considered too long it was either cut or required to be braided—the ideas of dress largely stayed the same. Students continued to dress alike, in part because they often wore the same things: "Although your parents could bring clothes for you, all clothes were put in a closet and you were given an outfit from a common collection. You didn't wear your own clothes'" (Berg 1982, 3). Beatrice Swanson expressed that there was too much emphasis on discipline and that "some children had no one and needed more mothering—especially the younger ones" (Berg 1982, 2). Further concerns related to assimilation; for instance, many of the values students were taught ended up creating a conflict with the structures of life on the reservation. More specifically, Catholic values had the potential to undermine tribal authority or familial bonds, creating long-term relational problems for students and their families.

During the 1930s, the mission school experienced a shift away from assimilation and toward acculturation (Berg 1981, 71). A greater emphasis was placed on Native culture, with students learning traditional crafts such as "beadwork . . . tapping maple trees, and smoking meat and fish" (Berg 1982, 4) at the mission school; attitudes and curriculum surrounding race became more inclusive. But for many, this process ultimately resulted in walking an uncomfortable line: while aspects of the students' culture were present materially, this often didn't transfer over into the class curriculum. In an interview with Sister Carol Berg, former student Beatrice Swanson, who attended the mission school from 1935 to 1941, expressed, "The mission school training had no room for Indian culture. . . . [T]he sisters should have built up the students' pride in Indianness" (Berg 1982, 2). Berg's interviews with students reveal that many of the monastics still held negative stereotypes, believing that Native youth are less intelligent than white youth and having preference for Native youth with lighter skin (Berg n.d.). Thus, even as the mission school incorporated some aspects of Anishinaabe culture, instructors may have continued to hold racial and cultural biases, perpetuating the school's original goal of suppressing Indigenous identity.

While the full impact of the mission school may never be understood, cofounder of the American Indian Movement Clyde Bellecourt wrote in his autobiography that as a result of abuse at the school, "If you look at my knuckles today, you'll see they all have scars on them" (2016, 16). Our research will never heal the scars inflicted at the mission school, but we can develop collaborations and work toward revealing the truth as a first step toward reconciliation.

Because of our outreach to Tribal Historical Preservation Offices, the Native communities affected by these schools now have a first glimpse at these materials. We are now in the early stages of developing transformative research collaborations. In partnership with White Earth's Tribal Historic Preservation Office, we applied for and received a grant from the Council for Independent Colleges to develop a forum to present our archival research at the White Earth Reservation and hear whatever stories, ideas, or concerns White Earth tribal members may want to share with us. Through this collaboration, our institutions will have the opportunity to be transformed by the perspectives of White Earth tribal members as we work to redress the trauma we once inflicted.

Before proceeding, it is important to note that one reservation-based school that we have not yet investigated has taken important steps to reform itself into an institution truly inclusive of Anishinaabe culture. Beginning in the 1970s, St. Mary's mission school at Red Lake began implementing curricular changes that brought tribal elders into the classroom for language, history, and culture lessons and receiving significant funding from the tribal council. The curriculum is now developed through a collaborative effort that fully incorporates Anishinaabe traditional knowledge and values. While the school is no longer affiliated with OSB, many members of our monastic communities continue to hold strong ties to the reservation (Linblad 1997).

The above discussion only scratches the surface of the complex historical relations between our institutions and the Anishinaabe nations. From the little that we currently know, it is clear that OSB took part in a nationwide effort to force Native communities to assimilate. In many ways, OSB's goals for Native communities aligned with the government's assimilative policies. It is also worth noting that OSB did not implement all of the government's goals, especially Indigenous language suppression. Notwithstanding these exceptions, if there is one lesson to draw from our historical analysis, it is that our institutions have always enrolled Native students and have used education as a tool to force assimilation. The next section examines the experiences of contemporary Native and Indigenous students on our campuses and offers recommendations to increase inclusion.

EXPERIENCES OF CONTEMPORARY NATIVE AND INDIGENOUS STUDENTS AT OUR INSTITUTIONS

Nationwide, Native students have the highest college dropout rate of any ethnic or racial group. Feelings of isolation, macroaggressions, and microaggressions by classmates, and staff, as well as a dearth of representation in curricula are all significant factors in low Native student retention (Patterson and Bulter-Barnes 2015, 2). However, research suggests that institutions can employ best practices to make their campuses more inclusive for Native students, resulting in increased academic performance and retention. These best practices include social interventions, where Native students are connected to each other, often through clubs and student organizations, as well as faculty training to increase Native representation in curricula and decrease microaggressions (Patterson and Bulter-Barnes 2015, 2; Windchief and Joseph 2015, 267).

According to institutional data, we currently have twenty-four students who self-identify as Native. However, the number of Native students might be considerably higher when one includes students who identify with communities that are native to anywhere in North or South America. Outside of the United States, the term Indigenous is more frequently used than the term Native. Our institutional demographic profile does not include data on Indigenous students. If one includes Native and Indigenous students together, as we do, then the total number is likely higher.

Do the nationwide trends of feeling isolated exist at our institutions? Given that our institutions once took part in a nationwide effort to force assimilation through education, we ask, to what extent do our Native and Indigenous students experience inclusion, or isolation on our campuses? Currently, our college and university do not have any student club or organization that represents Native and Indigenous students. And we have not offered any semester-long courses focused on Native American content since spring 2014. All of these factors suggest that our Native and Indigenous students' experiences may unfortunately be similar to the nationwide trends. For further examination, we chose qualitative, open-ended interviews as our method for gathering data on the experiences of our current Native and Indigenous students. This method can bring us the richest data while also collecting student recommendations on how we can make our campuses more inclusive.

Our research design implemented a theoretical and methodological framework developed from Standpoint Theory. In describing this theory, Sandra Harding (2004, 7) explained, "To the extent that an oppressed group's situation is different from that of the dominant group, its dominated situation enables the production of distinctive kinds of knowledge. . . . Thus standpoint theories map how a social and political disadvantage can be turned into an epistemological, scientific, and political advantage." Therefore, our primary method for gathering data was Native/Indigenous students interviewing other Native/Indigenous students. We used this method because Native students know which questions to ask and may be more able to more easily develop the trust and rapport needed for these interviews and the focus group. Two Native and Indigenous students served as our interviewers: Regina Therchik, from a Yupik village on coast of Alaska and Sophie Koloski, who is Indigenous to a Mayan community in Guatemala. During the 2018–2019 academic year, our team interviewed seven Indigenous/Native students. Our analysis of these interviews revealed three themes and common recommendations. All names are pseudonyms and any information that could identify the participants has been redacted. Interviewees were recruited through flyers and word-of-mouth.

THEME 1: ISOLATION

Interviewees reported that they did not know any other Native/Indigenous students. Each felt that they were the only Native/Indigenous student on our campuses. Mikela explained, "[I feel like] a minority among minorities." She recognized the challenges faced by other underrepresented students, but she also saw them as at least having a small cohort of classmates they could identify with. For Mikela, this feeling of being the only Native/Indigenous student became acute when she would share her identity with others. She noted, "Every time that like I do tell people that I am Indigenous, like, people who are like shocked by it, they just like, stare and you could like obviously tell they've like never met an Indigenous person here." She felt she was by herself until connecting with others through the interviews we conducted. Ana expressed a similar feeling of isolation, "I don't think there were any places I felt included as a Native or Indigenous person." Julio noted the intersection of his identities as Hispanic and Native, "I can't even express being Hispanic on campus at times. . . . It would be even harder to express that [Native] side of me." He struggles to feel included as a Hispanic student, so expressing his Native identity would be even more challenging.

Each interviewee shared that they felt as if they were the only Native/Indigenous student at our institutions, but in fact they are not alone. They have Native/Indigenous classmates but had not had the opportunity to meet others who expressed their identity. Often these interviews were the first time they met another Native/Indigenous student—in some cases, the interviewer and interviewee already knew each other but did not know that they shared a common Native/Indigenous identity.

THEME 2: CONCEALED IDENTITIES

Why are our Native/Indigenous students each believing that they are the only one? We found that this common feeling may arise from shared concerns about how classmates, faculty, and staff will respond if they disclose their identity. This leads to a common strategy of carefully selecting who they disclose their identity to. Many only tell close friends. As Ana explained, "I would tell people [about my identity] that I'm close with and I have, for lack of a better word, people who I have the patience to discuss my identity with."

According to Irma, when disclosing a Native or Indigenous identity, "you'll get like ignorant or arrogant questions, um, because I know that a lot of the times people like mean well with the questions. Sometimes they don't, and they really just want to be a jerk." For Irma, disclosing her identity results in either intentionally hurtful or unintentionally ignorant questions. Even when other students were genuinely open to respecting and learning more about Native/Indigenous cultures, those students have no opportunities on our campuses to take classes that focus on Native/Indigenous cultures. When curious and open-minded students learn that Irma is Indigenous, they ask her to explain her culture to them. For Irma this is tiring, "I don't think we should have to always explain ourselves." Like others, her strategy is to limit who she discloses her identity to.

Concerns about disclosing one's identity can also create a double bind. According to Julio, "I don't feel free to express [my Native identity] without getting eyes. There are times where I think 'I don't care, I don't give a fuck right now.' So, I'll just act that way. But I can't do that all the time, because it's draining. Both ways, like if I hold it in, or if I don't, it's emotionally draining both ways." While expressing his identity leads to negative responses from his peers, hiding his identity is "emotionally draining" too. This presents an unfortunate double bind. Both expressing and hiding his identity threaten his emotional well-being.

THEME 3: TOKENIZATION

Disclosing an identity to a professor can be even more fraught. It can alter the dynamic of the classroom and the student's learning experience. Julio explained, "[In class] I feel like I'm being used because I have a different perspective . . . I feel like I'm contributing more than what is being contributed to me. . . . It's frustrating for me to be around that. So, that's why I skip class a lot." For Julio, having a professor call on him to share his perspective leads him to feel the professor sees him as an opportunity for other students to learn about a different culture. This makes Julio feel that more contributions are expected from him than his classmates so that they can learn from him. He explained that skipping class is a strategy he uses to avoid feeling "frustrated" for being "used" this way.

Even keeping their identities hidden does not always protect students from being tokenized. Ana described a scenario where she did not disclose her identity to a professor. However, the professor misidentified her as Mexican and asked her questions based this assumption. She explained, "I remember like being tokenized as fuck in that class . . . he [the professor] basically was like, 'Can you give us a Mexican perspective?' And like oh my god, you've got to be kidding me." She is not Mexican, so she could not provide such a perspective even if she wanted to. Even if the professor knew that she is Native, calling on her to share a Native perspective would have also been tokenization and put her in the position of educating her classmates, which is ultimately the responsibility of the professor.

RECOMMENDATIONS

Interviewees made several recommendations for our institutions to become more inclusive for Native and Indigenous students. One common recommendation was to offer a class focused on Native and Indigenous histories and cultures for the entire semester. Irma explained, "[Our institutions should] have a class specifically designated [about] Native and Indigenous populations. . . . [I]f I had that I'd be more able to express myself, and that would just give me the knowledge that I'm craving to know myself more as an Indigenous person." She is "craving" to learn more about her own culture and for non-Native and Indigenous students to also have that opportunity. Seeing her identity represented in our curricula would help her feel included. She understands why non-Native/Indigenous students are interested in learning about Native and Indigenous cultures and she wants our curriculum—not her—to be responsible for educating them.

Another common recommendation was to offer a club as well as programming on Native and Indigenous cultures. Ana noted, "[Do] they respect my identity? I would also say no because, where are the programs for Native and Indigenous students? Where are the resources for Native and Indigenous students?" She and other interviewees see other students' cultures represented in campus clubs and events. Having a club would provide a space for Native and Indigenous students to come together to talk about their shared interests and concerns. Guillory (2009) found that a primary factor in American Indian and Alaska Native college student persistence is their capacity to give back to Native communities through service. To this end, as we work to implement our interviewees' recommendations, we are also developing Native community partnerships that will ensure that our Native and non-Native students can give back to neighboring Native communities. The following section discusses the final pathways, serving Native communities, which we are just beginning with an emerging partnership with the Mille Lacs Band of Ojibwe.

SERVING YOUTH FROM MILLE LACS

According to Guillory (2009), universities can increase Native and Indigenous student inclusion by providing opportunities to serve Native communities on their own terms. This pathway offers this opportunity while also working to redress our institutions' past role in forced assimilation. However, serving Native communities may be the most challenging pathway. Forming new relationships where there previously were none—or worse, previous relations that were marked by systematic injustice—may take years of careful relationship building. However, we do believe that we have made some important first steps.

In August 2018, I (first author, Theodor Gordon) attended the Native Studies Summer Workshop for Educators, which was hosted by Nay-Ah-Shing (NAS), a tribal school operated by the Mille Lacs Band of Ojibwe. During this workshop, I met their teachers and administrators. We discussed our shared history and ways our institutions could serve NAS students. Mille Lac's Commissioner for Education, Rick St. Germaine, suggested starting a student exchange where NAS students could visit our campuses for activities with our faculty, staff, and students, both inside and outside the classroom. We also discussed opportunities for our students to serve as mentors at Mille Lacs. Because our campuses and NAS are only a seventy-five-minute drive apart, such an exchange seemed feasible. Since fall 2018, our institutions and NAS have each hosted the other three times. Each time, I worked closely with NAS faculty to understand the gifts and needs of their students and the best way that our institutions' resources can enrich their curriculum. Below, I describe a few of our successes as well as the challenges of our partnership.

In my first meetings with NAS, I learned that their strengths include a place-based curriculum that emphasizes outdoor education and sustainability, but college readiness remains a challenge. We discussed how a visit from NAS to our campuses could support and enhance their focus on sustainability while providing their students with a visit to our campus and connections with students, faculty, and staff, that could increase their interest in attending college. Fortunately, our institutions already have an extensive K-12 outdoor education program, called OutdoorU, which connects thousands of students each with Student Naturalists. OutdoorU was a natural place for us to begin and its director, Sarah Gainey, was happy to serve NAS. But before we could begin, NAS faculty suggested that their students would benefit from first meeting me and an OutdoorU Student Naturalist so we could develop rapport. In early October 2018, Student Naturalist Kateri Heymans joined me in visiting middle and high school classrooms at NAS. We arrived with a few activities and a quick introduction to the campuses and OutdoorU. I quickly learned that my experience in front of a college classroom did not translate well to K-12. But Kateri, with her years working with such students through OutdoorU quickly connected with their students. The following week, NAS visited with thirty-two students and eight staff. Several OutdoorU naturalists and students joined us for activities and lunch. The teachers expressed gratitude for their students having such a positive experience on a college campus. One of their social studies teachers told me that he saw some students open up in ways he had never seen before. We agreed to plan more student exchange activities.

We hosted another visit in April 2018, where NAS middle school students connected with two of our Environmental Studies majors who developed exercises for the NAS students to learn about campus solar energy and sustainable farming projects on campus. Meanwhile, NAS juniors and seniors paired up with three of our Native and Indigenous students for a day of mentorship and a tour of the college. Our goal was for NAS students to have space apart from faculty and staff, to learn about the experiences and challenges of our Native and Indigenous students. Third author Belen Benway served as one of the Native/Indigenous student mentors. The following paragraph is her reflection on their visit.

I, Belen Benway, really believe these types of events are important because being a minority at a mostly white, Catholic school can be hard at times. We wanted this to be a chance for prospective students to meet other Indigenous students. We wanted this to showcase our school and its resources as well as to show the prospective students how you can find a small community at college. Throughout the day, we gave them a tour around both campuses and got the chance to connect with them about college. Many of the students that visited either grew up on or around the reservation and want a community of like people at their college, much like where they are now. This project gave the students a chance to meet other Indigenous students and learn more about what their lives would look like if they attended our college or university. This event was a great opportunity to grow our schools' relationship with the surrounding Native communities. Events like these encourage our school to create a more inclusive space, thus working on our collaboration with Native communities on their terms. If we continue these types of events with other tribes, I believe we are taking large steps forward.

PATHWAYS TOWARD REDRESSING INJUSTICE

In summary, our institutions were complicit in a federal policy that significantly disrupted Anishinaabe communities by separating children from their parents with the intent to vanquish native nations through forced assimilation. While OSB did not impose all aspects of federal policy, the trauma imposed by these policies, as well as the abuse inflicted by some staff, cannot be understated. The present-day Native/Indigenous students at our institutions are not subjected to legally enforced assimilation. However, we found that the current campus climate is one in which our interviewees expressed the need to hide their identities. Ignorance by the classmates and professors leads to situations where, at best, disclosing their identity may lead to situations that are "emotionally draining." At worst, it can lead to responses by classmates who "really just want to be a jerk," as Irma said, or professors who will expect the student to teach the class about her or his culture. These concerns lead our Native/Indigenous students to hide their identities to the extent they the each believed that they were the only Native/Indigenous student on our campuses.

While the federal goal of forcing assimilation did not succeed on a national scale—fortunately hundreds of Native nations are still with us today and working toward revitalization—our campus climate creates a de facto enforced assimilation. Native and Indigenous students cannot express their identity because of legitimate fears about negative social and academic consequences. This has led to Native and Indigenous identities on our campuses being effectively invisible while neighboring Native communities experience educational disparities that are, at least in part, the result of the legacy of OSB's Native American boarding schools. By working toward our three pathways (1) collaborating with affected Native communities to investigate and share our hidden history (2) empowering Native and Indigenous students to interview their Native and Indigenous classmates for recommendations to increase inclusivity, and (3) forging partnerships that serve Native communities on their own terms, we are beginning to make important steps toward redressing these past and present injustices. We believe other universities can adapt these pathways toward greater Native and Indigenous student inclusion.

Higher education has always been marked by differences in equality and access. While few universities may have a history of Native American boarding schools, the work of Patterson and Bulter-Barnes (2015), Windchief and Joseph (2015) and others demonstrate that structural biases against Native and Indigenous students are pervasive and widespread. Furthermore, all American institutions of Higher Education exist on the ancestral homelands of displaced Native communities and many directly profited from the removal of Native communities. For example, Lee and Tristan's (2020) recent investigation reveals how the Morrill Act of 1862 displaced Native communities from over 10.7 million acres of their land and transferred it directly to fifty-two land grant universities to develop their campuses and endowments. Every institution of higher education has benefited in one way or another from injustices inflicted against Native communities. Our work demonstrates that making these injustices visible and undertaking work to redress them can lead to greater inclusion that benefits both the institution and the communities it marginalized.

Our focus has been on hidden injustices against Native communities, but these pathways can be applied to increase inclusion for any marginalized group. Each individual pathway has not only its advantages but also its own blind spots. Solely investigating an institutions' past ignores its present and the needs of neighboring communities. However, without an investigation of institutional history, any steps a university takes to address present-day student inequities may be well intentioned but misplaced if they do not account for how such inequities emerged and changed over time. Collaborations that serve neighboring communities can expand the sense of place for current students, but such partnerships require acknowledging the institutions' past relationship (or lack of relationship) with that community. When applied together, each pathway can act as a pillar ensuring that past and present injustices are addressed both on and off campus.

How can other institutions apply our pathways? First, university archives house rich, and often unexplored, narratives of how marginalized communities were treated, or neglected, on campus. For example, one could explore how campus newspapers have represented marginalized groups. Were their articles reporting on activists fighting for greater inclusion? Did campus publications ever deride the marginalized community? When is the first time a campus newspaper mentioned the community? It is equally revealing if campus publications only recently acknowledged a marginalized community, which may have always been present on campus. Enrollment and curriculum records can also yield important data. If the institution collected enrollment data on a particular population, one can track how the population may have grown, or shrunk, over time. If enrollment for that community has never been tracked, they may have always been present but not acknowledged by the institution. From curricular materials, such as course catalogues and syllabi, one can learn when and how students have had the opportunity to learn about any marginalized community.

To better understand the experiences of current students, we find that in-depth interviews, conducted by students who are members of that community, can provide detailed accounts of their experiences. While universities often use surveys to gauge student experiences of inclusion, survey questions may be biased toward the perspective of the administrators who design the survey and may only provide a partial view of student experiences. No one knows the experiences of a given marginalized campus community better than members of that community. By giving community members the capacity to form their own interview questions, when coupled with training in how to interview, the questions asked are more likely to reflect their actual concerns and experiences. Having community members conduct the interviews not only builds much needed interviewer-interviewee rapport in a deeper way than an interview conducted by an outsider, it also empowers community members to take important steps toward improving their university.

Every marginalized community on campus is also present, at least to some extent, in neighboring communities. Providing opportunities to serve these communities off campus can provide students with an opportunity to open students to develop new relationships. Connecting marginalized students with community members who share their identity can ground them with a sense of place and giving back, which can increase retention (Guillory 2009, 16). Such partnerships benefit all students by providing new avenues for service learning and strengthening the university's relationships with the wider community. By combining these pathways, universities can ensure that their work toward inclusion addresses all aspects of social injustice, from past to present, from on campus to the wider community.

NOTE

1. The terms Anishinaabe, Ojibwe, and Chippewa refer to the same Indigenous population. In this chapter, we use the term "Anishinaabe" because it is their ethnonym in their language. Ojibwe and Chippewa are terms developed by European colonizers, and we use them only when citing texts that use them.

REFERENCES

Bellecourt, Clyde. 2016. *The Thunder Before the Storm: The Autobiography of Clyde Bellecourt.* St. Paul, MN: Minnesota Historical Society Press.
Berg, Carol. 1981. *Climbing Learners Hill: Benedictines at White Earth 1875-1945.* Ph.D. Dissertation, History, University of Minnesota.
———. 1982. Interview with Beatrice Swanson. St. Benedict's Monastery Archive.
———. n.d. Interview with Beatina Vanoss. St. Benedict's Monastery Archive.
———. 1982. Interview with Lucetta Doepke and Annette Fairbanks. St. Benedict's Monastery Archive.
———. n.d. Interview with Sister Thea Greiman. St. Benedict's Monastery Archive.
Barry, C. and Klingeman, D. 1993. *Worship and Work: Saint John's Abbey and University 1856-1992.* Collegeville, MN: Liturgical Press.

Child, Brenda. 1988. *Boarding School Seasons: American Indian Families 1900-1940*. Lincoln, NE: University of Nebraska Press.

Fruth, Alban. 1956. Interviews with Former St. John Industrial Students. St. John's Abbey Archives.

Guillory, R. M. 2009. "American Indian/Alaska Native College Student Retention Strategies." *Journal of Developmental Education* 33 (3): 12–38.

Harding, Sandra. 2004. *The Feminist Standpoint Theory Reader: Intellectual and Political Controversies*. East Sussex, UK: Psychology Press.

Katz, Jane. 1977. *I Am the Fire of Time: The Voices of Native American Women*. New York: Dutton.

———. 1996. *Messengers of the Wind: Native American Women Tell Their Stories*. New York: Ballentine Books.

Laliberte, David J. 2008. *Indian Summers: Baseball at Native American Boarding Schools in Minnesota*. M.A. Dissertation. St. Cloud State University.

Lee, Robert and Tristan Ahtone. 2020. "Land-Grab Universities. Expropriated Indigenous Land is the Foundation of the Land-Grant University System." *High Country News* 52 (4): March 30. https://www.hcn.org/issues/52.4/indigenous-affairs-education-land-grab-universities.

Lindblad, Owen OSB. 1997. *Full of Fair Hope*. St. Joseph: St. Joseph's Monastery.

McDonald, Grace. 1957. *With Lamps Burning*. St. Joseph, MN: Saint Benedicts' Priory Press.

Patterson, David A. Silver Wolf (Adelvunegv Waya) and Sheretta T. Bulter-Barnes. 2015. "Impact of the Academic-Social Context on American Indian/Alaska Native Student's Academic Performance." *Washington University Journal of American Indian & Alaska Native Health* 1 (1): Article 3.

Routel, Colette. 2013. "Minnesota Bounties on Dakota Men During the U.S.-Dakota War". *William Mitchell Law Review* 40 (1): 1–77.

Skjolsvik, Olap. 1957. "St. John's Indian Industrial School". *Scriptorium* 16 (1): 111–123.

Watrin, Benno. 1978. *St. Benedict's Mission, White Earth MN, 1878-1978*. Unpublished Manuscript, St. Benedict's Monastery Archive.

Windchief, Sweeney and Darold H. Joseph. 2015. "The Act of Claiming Higher Education as Indigenous Space: American Indian/Alaska Native Examples". *Diaspora, Indigenous, and Minority Education* 9 (4): 267–283. doi:10.1080/15595692.2015.1048853.

Woolford, Andrew. 2015. *The Benevolent Experiment: Indigenous Boarding Schools, Genocide, and Redress in Canada and the United States*. Lincoln, NE: University of Nebraska Press.

Chapter 6

Fostering Religious Inclusion on Campus

Insights from Student Experiences

Megan Sheehan, Chris Conway, Maria Schrupp,
D'Havian Scott, and Rediet Negede Lewi

INTRODUCTION

Burgeoning research on inclusivity and campus climate critically examines experiences of students from underrepresented racial and ethnic groups and analyzes disparities based on gender and sexuality.[1] To further address inclusion on campus, scholars argue that it is vital to also consider religion (Cole and Ahmadi 2010; Furrow et al. 2004; King 2003). At public and secular institutions, religious practices are often overlooked aspects of inclusion and diversity, and discussions of religion are typically avoided (Cole and Ahmadi 2010; Mutakabbir and Nuriddin 2016; Rockenbach et al. 2015). At religiously affiliated institutions, engagement with religion is more prominent; however, research indicates that students who identify with underrepresented religions experience higher rates of attrition and are significantly less likely to graduate from the institution (Astin 1993; Patten and Rice 2009). These students report challenges to integrating into campus culture at religiously affiliated schools (Mayhew et al. 2014). Moreover, there are important intersectional experiences among students from underrepresented religions, with some populations reporting greater challenges to inclusion (Andrade 2006; Mahaffey and Smith 2009; Rockenbach et al. 2015). Religion and religious engagement figure importantly in the identity development of young adults (Cole and Ahmadi 2010; Furrow et al. 2004; King 2003), and the ability to engage freely with religious communities and spiritual practices fosters positive outcomes for students, including academic gains (Mayhew et al. 2014) and increased feelings of acceptance and belonging (Hurtado and Carter 1997). Considerations of religious inclusion must be understood within the context of broader efforts to promote inclusive institutions recognizing the diverse and multifaceted lives of students, faculty, and staff.

This chapter examines the challenges that students from underrepresented religions, denominations, and beliefs face while attending religiously affiliated institutions of higher education. The data analyzed here were collected at two liberal arts colleges located in the Midwest. The schools are steeped in Catholic, Benedictine traditions and invite persons of all faiths into the academic community. While more than half (51 percent) of the students self-identify as Roman Catholic, 30 percent identify with another Christian denomination (including 11 percent of students who identify as Lutheran), 15 percent report no religious affiliation, and the remaining 4 percent include students from diverse religious traditions, including Islam, Judaism, Hinduism, and Buddhism. In this chapter, we present insights drawn from interviews conducted with students from diverse religious backgrounds. Initial findings highlight the ways in which institutionalized norms shape student experiences; the nuanced, flexible, and individualized manner in which students describe their beliefs and identities; and the challenges to fostering open dialogue and an inclusive campus climate. We share both the challenges to religious inclusion that our campuses face as well as our research process in order to provide a model for researchers at other institutions. In doing so, we hope that the important, intersectional, and often underexplored topic of religion will be increasingly incorporated into efforts to make institutions of higher education more welcoming to all students.

BACKGROUND AND LITERATURE REVIEW

On our campuses, students from underrepresented religious traditions identify the incongruity between their own experiences of exclusion and the schools' aspiration to be a welcoming, religiously inclusive community that supports students' spiritual growth. This reveals the many ways in which Christian, particularly Catholic, hegemony and privilege operate on campus. Adams and Joshi define Christian hegemony as "the dominance of Christian observances, holy days, and places of worship without regard for those of non-Christians" (2016, 256). Christian privilege entails the social advantages held by Christians relative to non-Christians in such Christian normative contexts. In this context, the disadvantages and structural barriers (oppression) that students from underrepresented religious traditions experience are immediate and felt deeply, while students from the normative tradition benefit from a privilege that often remains unrecognized (Adams and Joshi 2016). This disconnect reveals the need for studies such as ours. As Young states, "Oppression designates the disadvantage and injustice some people suffer not because a tyrannical power coerces them, but because of the everyday practices of a well-intentioned liberal society" (1990, 41). Without input from students from underrepresented religions, those in privileged positions, even while trying to do right, will fail to address oppressive systems and structures.

The schools' desire to be religiously inclusive communities is rooted in their Catholic, Benedictine identity. The director of campus ministries at another Catholic university, Helen Wolf, argues that "Catholic higher education has a paramount duty to foster and actively cultivate purposeful and substantive interreligious engagement and understanding because interreligious dialogue is a fundamental component of Catholic teaching and intellectual discourse" (2017, 21). In a similar call, the founder of Interfaith Youth Core (IFYC), Eboo Patel, also identifies Catholic colleges as being particularly open and committed to fostering such engagement. He notes, "IFYC has found that Catholic institutions are not only well-equipped to engage in such [interfaith] leadership practices but are consistently on the vanguard of this work" (Patel 2017, 2).

While there is real potential for cultivating religiously inclusive communities at Catholic colleges and universities, there is nevertheless great theological, cultural, and missional diversity among these schools. In research identifying the breadth of Catholic higher education, Morey and Piderit distinguish four types of schools based on mission and campus culture: Catholic Immersion, Catholic Persuasion, Catholic Diaspora, and Catholic Cohort (2006, 3). While no model perfectly captures any school, our institutions most closely align with Catholic Persuasion as they possess a student body that is majority Catholic, a faculty and administration comprised of a significant number of Catholics, a small array of Catholic courses, and a strong nonacademic Catholic culture (Morey and Piderit 2006, 89, see also 63–64). In light of this model, Brecht notes "even when persuasion schools have a majority of Catholic students, the schools do not assume its students have familiarity with Catholic teachings . . . core curricula do the lion's share of the work helping students develop this knowledge and appreciation" (2015, 151–152). At our school, this particular role of the curriculum is established in its vision statement. Here, "the Catholic Intellectual Tradition as guided by the Benedictine principles of colleges' founders" joins "the liberal arts tradition" to serve as grounding principles. In our curriculum, the two required theology courses—an introductory course and an upper level—become the primary loci where student learn about the Catholic tradition. While content varies from course to course, most introductory and upper-level theology courses are centered on the Christian tradition—often with special focus on the Catholic tradition. For Catholic Persuasion schools, this small array of required courses connects the curriculum to the Catholic facet of the mission.

The classroom generally, and theology courses particularly, are logical places to focus a study on religious diversity and inclusion, especially given their embodiment of the institutional and curricular mission. However, student experience is not limited to the classroom, and any critical response necessarily extends beyond course work. Strain et al. (2009) provide a thoughtful critique of Morey and Piderit's (2006) four models. They offer a new model, Catholic Engagement, which emphasizes and engages the pluralism present in the United States, in Catholicism, and especially at their large Catholic university (2009). This model presents pluralism not as a threat to Catholic identity, but instead as "intrinsically positive" (2009, 175). In the words of an administrator, this shift recognizes that "We have kids from so many religions that one of the best things we can do is fortify how the Catholic religion can lead in embracing other religions, creating interfaith dialogue and making sure our kids are appreciative, aware, and articulate of their own values and ethics" (Morey and Piderit 2006, 159; quoted in Strain et al. 2009, 175). In the efforts to foster more inclusive Catholic campuses, actions speak louder than words. Several school administrators might agree with Mark Laboe, a vice president at DePaul University, "It's in our DNA to be open to other religions" (quoted in Zimmerman 2016). Fewer follow through as DePaul did with the kinds of systemic and structural changes necessary for this potential to be actualized: hiring Muslim and Jewish chaplains and providing prayer space. Such potential is present at our institutions and resonates with students from diverse religious identities. Diverse student perspectives, like those illustrated in data presented here, might suggest avenues toward an engagement model (Strain et al. 2009) in which interfaith dialogue assumes a more central role in higher education.

APPROACH AND METHODS

This research grew from student interest in addressing religious inclusivity on campus and developed as a collaborative initiative. As a student, Lewi worked at the campus interfaith center, and there she heard anecdotally from students who voiced feelings of exclusion at the predominantly Catholic colleges and who noted a lack of campus resources to support their spiritual needs. To more systematically examine these student concerns, Lewi pitched this project to a qualitative research methods class taught by Sheehan. Together, Lewi, Schrupp, and Scott designed the research project as a class assignment, and the team worked in collaboration to conduct the research over the subsequent year and a half. Conway, a theologian, and Sheehan, an anthropologist, worked with Lewi to secure a small grant to fund the research as part of an effort centered on fostering a more inclusive campus. The project brought together students and faculty from several disciplines, and data collection, analysis, and write-up continue to be collaborative endeavors. Moreover, the project was also conceived as an applied initiative, embodying a community-based participatory research approach that prioritizes collaboration, seeks to develop community networks, melds research and action, and promotes the reciprocity of knowledge production (c.f. Austin 2004; Austin et al. 2004; Brown and Vega 1996; Minkler and Wallerstein 2003, Waldmeir et al. 2017). Throughout the process, the research team has been in conversation with institutional stakeholders and will share research findings upon completion of the project. Given the interest in fostering a more inclusive campus environment, this research is centered on understanding the experiences of students, particularly those from underrepresented religions, denominations, or beliefs. In this effort, the research team aimed to describe the lived experiences of students from underrepresented religious communities; to detail Catholic students' religious practices on campus and their perspectives on religious inclusivity; to identify how students perceive the campus climate regarding religion; and to document what changes students and staff think would promote an inclusive campus climate. To get a feel for student experiences and to offer students a forum to speak freely about their time on campus, the research team designed a qualitative study built around interviews. As a research method, interviews enable an interpretive perspective on social norms, allowing research participants to identify the connections, relationships, and nuances that they see between particular beliefs, traditions, norms, and behaviors (c.f. Bernard et al. 1986; Schensul and LeCompte 2012; Spradley 2016). In short, interview data gives "a human face to research problems" (Mack et al. 2005, 29). In this case, students interviewed contributed positioned insight on religion, traditions, and beliefs on campus.

Data from semi-structured interviews enables an analysis of salient themes and patterns underlying the barriers to inclusion that students face around religion, faith, and beliefs (Leech 2002; Schensul and LeCompte 2012). For the study, participants were recruited through purposive sampling (Bernard 2018; Patton 1990) carried out both through referrals as well as through an open invitation to all students. A quota sample was applied with the goal of enrolling equal numbers of participants who identify with underrepresented religions, denominations, and beliefs as those who identify in line with the school's affiliation as Catholic.[2] While the population of students who self-identify with an underrepresented religion, faith, or beliefs is limited, Guest et al.'s (2006) research indicates that with just twelve research participants salient themes, issues, and concerns can often be identified.[3] Data collection is ongoing, and the initial data analyzed in this chapter is based on twenty-two semi-structured, hour-long interviews.[4] Of the students interviewed, eight identify as Catholic or note that they were raised Catholic, and fourteen describe diverse religious identities and belief systems, including Christian, Buddhist, agnostic, atheist, Muslim, and Jewish, reflecting within those broad categories distinct denominations, faiths, beliefs, and practices. Participants also represent diversity along the lines of gender, sexuality, race, ethnicity, academic focus, and year in school. As interviews were completed, the audio recordings were transcribed and analyzed. To identify trends and insights among student experiences, the research team utilized a grounded theory approach to data analysis (Bernard et al. 2016; Strauss and Corbin 1994), developing a codebook and coding data for salient themes (DeCuir-Gunby et al. 2011). Insights from the data are detailed in the findings below.

RESEARCH FINDINGS

Structuring Norms—Institutional, Material, Ritual, and Social

Catholic traditions are foundational to the educational institutions and frame student experiences. When asked what expectations they had of the schools, several students interviewed described their first week on campus. The Orientation Mass left an indelible impression, setting a tone for student engagement with religion and the normative Catholic culture. One sophomore, Julie,[5] describes herself as believing in a higher being, but not "adhering to any type of religion." She recounted her first weekend on campus.

> I actually really didn't know [the school was Catholic]. I'm trying to remember when I realized it was a Catholic. I think orientation, ... And then I was like, "Duh, it says Saint" . . . that makes sense now, but I was quite shocked at orientation how they forced us to attend Mass . . . I was quite shocked that they said that you don't need to be religious to attend this institution, but they forced all, all first years . . . to attend Mass regardless of whether you wanted to go.

While most students were aware of the institutions' religious affiliation prior to arriving, the prominence of the first Mass and the perceived expectation of participation in the service was memorable for students interviewed. A Christian student, Stewart, who frequently attends Mass, noted: "I don't remember anyone saying, 'Oh, you don't have to go to this.' . . . it was assumed that everyone would go! I mean, I would have gone anyways, I guess. But I can see how other people would feel discomfort." While the institutions do not oblige students to attend Mass or other religious services— including the one during Orientation—students interviewed reported feeling pressure to attend, often by fellow students, both their cohort and orientation leaders. These examples illustrate the dispersed ways in which the norms of the school are passed along—through new roommates, orientation leaders, residence life employees, and other actors—often in an uncoordinated fashion. This assumption of full participation provides a jarring entry to the assumed norm of Catholicism and Catholic privilege on campus.

Curricular requirements signal school values. For religiously affiliated schools, theology or religious studies courses often indicate a commitment to theological discussions as part of what constitutes a well-rounded graduate. Our schools require students to complete two semester-long theology courses. Students interviewed reported varying perspectives on these courses, and many noted the benefit of taking classes that they otherwise would not have sought out. Stewart commented that the theology course he took on Islam "made me much more open when it comes to religion." Similarly, a senior who was raised Catholic, Laura, noted that her theology courses "made me a little bit more accepting of religion overall, and the role it plays in people's lives, because I was definitely one of those people that cringed anytime religion was brought up." That said, the required nature of the course paired with the largely Christian and Catholic content of the course offerings drew strident critique. Isabel, who described herself as both spiritual and Catholic, noted that she had greatly enjoyed her theology courses even as she voiced a common refrain—an interest in learning about other belief systems:

> While I think that it is really important as a Benedictine school to educate people . . . about the major faith of the monastic community that surrounds us . . . I feel like it is equally important that, whether it be Judaism, . . . Hindu[ism], or [Islam] or Buddh[ism], I think that it's just as important that they educate themselves, on not just the Catholicism surrounding the schools but on a different faith, as that would kind of help educate them both, on whatever their identity is [and] on the other religious groups that they would be studying.

Many students interviewed noted that their theology courses afforded them new insights. However, throughout the interviews—and regardless of students' religious identification—there was a recurring critique of the limited theology options paired with student interest in exploring other religions, comparative approaches, and diverse theological perspectives

In discussing theology courses, students also raised concerns about common barriers to full class participation. Kendra, a student who identifies as Catholic, noted:

> Maybe if you weren't Christian, you were probably set back, because [the professor] ran through the information really quickly with the assumption that students had already experienced this material. And I gather that . . . most people

had experience with the Christian faith. And students who if they were in the class and didn't have Christian faith didn't speak up.

Kendra's comment explicitly references the Christian privilege manifest in some classes. The required theology courses enroll students from a variety of faith backgrounds with disparate prior knowledge on the topic, complicating the delivery of course content and necessitating further consideration of inclusive pedagogy. Moreover, discussions of these courses suggest that they are sites where students experience feeling like the "other" and are reminded of their position as a member of an underrepresented group. Sara, a Muslim student shared:

> I was very opposed to taking my religion class. . . . Because I was very angry and upset that, basically, why isn't this just an Intro to Religious Studies? Why does it have to be Catholicism? And I understand, okay, this is a Catholic school, but I'm pretty sure one of the mission statements here is like inclusivity, diversity, and welcoming all people, blah, blah, blah, and all that.

Students voice interest in expanding the options for discussions about faith, beliefs, and spirituality as a way to make the school curriculum more inclusive to students who do not identify as Catholic, particularly for those who do not identify as Christian. Moreover, student responses highlight the ways in which theology classes are often understood as at odds with inclusivity and diversity, illustrating the challenges of expressing the schools' many values across curricular, institutional, and community facets of university life.

Many of the ways that the institutions embrace their Catholic and Benedictine traditions are overt. Churches figure prominently on the campus, crucifixes hang in some classrooms, the school coat of arms includes the St. John's cross, Masses are offered regularly, monastic community members walk the campuses, and school rituals often start with a recognition of these traditions. Institutional decisions, such as shaping the school calendar, send messages that students understand as embodying the schools' priorities and values. For example, David, a black student who identifies with an underrepresented religion, noted, "The fact that MLK day, wasn't, you know, taken off, . . . yikes! I may not be Catholic, but you guys want me to do Catholic things . . . like, having Good Friday. Up until [school], I've never heard of Good Friday, I've only heard of Easter . . . but MLK Day?"[6] David ended his reflection with a pause of incredulity, and his example illustrates the often-intersectional experiences of religious exclusion, articulated directly as a symbol of the schools' values. In interviews, students noted the ways that institutional decisions, curricular requirements, and the structures of the campuses are understood both as markers of the values of the school and as barriers to full inclusion. The structural ways in which values and behavioral norms are articulated frame how students relate to educational institutions. Student insights point toward the need to identify the multivocal messages embedded not just in institutional communications but also in curricular requirements, scheduling decisions, campus-wide events and activities, and the actions of affiliated personnel.

Personalized Religious Identification

The ways in which students identify are central to understanding religious diversity at our colleges. Interview data reveals that students view religious categories as dynamic and were often hesitant to categorize themselves as adhering strictly to one religion. This was common both for students who identified as Catholic and for those who identified with an underrepresented religion. For example, Isabel, a senior, acknowledged, "I still do identify as Catholic because I do still follow a lot of the traditions of the church and recognize a lot the aspects of that particular faith [. . .] I consider myself overall spiritual as opposed to specifically religious." For Isabel and many other students, personalization and nuance are not fully recognized under the limitations of blanket terms like "Catholic." Additionally, several students noted that their beliefs do not coincide with one particular religion. Julie, a sophomore, shared: "I realized that I don't really align with any of the major religions," adding later "I believe that I am on a spectrum. I really don't adhere to any type of religion." In a similar vein, Laura, who grew up Catholic noted: "When I decided to identify as an atheist, I did realize that I do appreciate a lot the ideas that are brought up in Buddhism." Julie and Laura represent many students who have individualized understandings of religion. College serves as a time of religious exploration, and students report greater independence to consider what religion means to them and the importance it holds in their lives. With this exploration comes religious fluidity. Julie shared, "I do feel comfortable [discussing religion], I just don't know how to explain it in full terms. I don't feel like I'm an atheist, but I don't know what I would call myself. So, I don't talk religion with other people. I don't know. It's just weird. [. . .] But if I don't really know you, [and] we're having a conversation about religion, I will say I identify as Christian." Julie's audience-dependent and fluid discussion of religious identification suggests the ways in which campus climate and perceptions of receptivity figure into how students describe their own practices and how they share with other students.

In addition to avoiding strict categorization, many students expressed the notion that religion and religious practices are highly personal. One senior, Stewart, shared that he spent time in the church "when there was no one," and that "I just like that private space and my own time to pray and to think."

For Stewart, religion does not necessarily need community engagement and can be practiced privately. Similarly, an international student named Jeremy, when asked to describe his religious community on campus, noted: "I'm confident enough in my ideas to be able to practice on my own [. . .] without the need of people around me." The Catholic dominance of the institution may have less influence on these students since their religious practices exist in spaces of solitude. Other students articulated their engagements with religion through lifestyle choices instead of overt practices, again positioning religion as an internal process rather than a community practice. Tom, a student from an underrepresented religion, explained that he practices "sustainability, seeing the light in others, being good just to be good, and identifying that not one religion is, like, more significant than the other." A senior from an underrepresented Christian denomination, Derek, explained that his faith was more "a way of life, a way of being, a way of treating other people" than a religion. These understandings of religion and identification exemplify what Smith describes as Moralistic Therapeutic Deism (2007). The turn away from communal engagement, the nuanced self-identifications, and the emphasis on morality, goodness, and consideration of others are consistent with broader trends documented among teenagers and young adults (Smith 2007), even as they stand in contrast to the dominant norms of the schools.

It is difficult to discern if students from underrepresented religions also define their religious engagements as private because they prefer to practice in solitude or because there is a lack of community and support for their religion on campus. While campus climate is discussed below, several students expressed that the environment on campus made it so that they feel more comfortable practicing in private. Sara, a student who identifies as Muslim, said that religion "doesn't really come up in everyday conversation. It's more like, behind closed door, my personal thing." Stewart, a senior who is from an underrepresented Christian denomination, commented that religion felt "very personal and isolated." The extent to which the campus climate affects religious identification is unclear, yet students report feeling like they cannot openly talk about their religious beliefs with their cohort—necessitating that religion becomes a personal affair. Regardless of the cause, the diverse, multiple, and personal religious identifications highlighted in this research suggest a need for resources that cater toward the individual, and allow for exploration, privacy, and flexibility. Members of underrepresented religions, denominations, and beliefs, as well as Catholic students, show interest in flexible categorizations of religion which allow room for their personal beliefs.

Consistent with national trends (Rockenbach et al. 2015), race, gender, ethnicity, sexual orientation, and socioeconomic status were all mentioned as significant intersectional influences on religious identification and experiences of religion on campus. Jon, a student who identifies as black, agnostic, and atheist, noted that "for the most part, I feel like a lot of the students of color are those who practice different religions. Um, not all of them, but, a . . . a . . . a lot of them." This compounding of identities that do not fit the campus norms can further exacerbate feelings of isolation. Tom explained "I'm [a member of an underrepresented religion], I'm gay, and I'm poor, and I'm also, a student of color. A lot of things typically factor against me within this school." In many cases, religion is just one of several identities that make students feel in the minority. Additionally, students highlighted the ways in which the Catholic affiliation of the institution juxtaposed with other parts of their identities and beliefs. Kendra, a Catholic student, expressed her issues with the patriarchal nature of the Catholic church saying "it's really annoying that all of religion is just so blind. And it's like without the females in the church, there would literally not be a church." Several students brought up the ways that gender and sexuality norms on campus are often understood by students within a Catholic framework, becoming poignant reminders that they or their beliefs lay outside the perceived norms. Senior Alexa also found issue with Catholicism: "This was a religion that was forced on people and like, contributed, like went hand in hand with like slavery and genocide and cultural erasure." For students, religion is often articulated as part of wider institutional structures, and their considered, individualized identities and practices juxtapose with their perceptions of the schools' religious affiliation.

Diverse Experiences of Campus Climate

Students experience the schools' campus climate in diverse ways, mediated by their beliefs, religious affiliations, interest in spiritual questions, and intersectional identities. Overwhelmingly, students noted that the campus norm—sometimes voiced as hegemonic—was that of Catholicism. Students reported that the assumption, unless they have a signal otherwise, is that their fellow students are Catholic. While students often operate under this assumption, they voiced divergent views about how this shades life on campus. Students interviewed were very aware of the ways their positionality impacts their experiences of campus climate. Many of the Catholic and Christian students were quick to note this. For example, Hannah's parents met at the schools, she was raised Catholic, and she now identifies as agnostic. She shared, "I would guess that it's a lot easier to be Catholic here and say that you're Catholic, because most people even if they aren't, they know what that means. . . . But if you practice like something else, . . . then you have to . . . explain yourself." The possibility of having to explain oneself or detail one's beliefs or religious practices in new social settings creates pressure for students from underrepresented religions, denominations, or beliefs.

For many students—regardless of their beliefs—institutional discourse of Benedictine values, like community, hospitality, and justice, are employed as a way of trying to find common ground across differing beliefs. A first-year student, Jane, who identifies as Catholic and participates in campus religious activities, shared: "I think the Catholic identity here tries to make students follow the Benedictine values. And you don't need to be Catholic to follow Benedictine values. But I think a lot of students do try to be good people, and so I think that might have effect on it. [. . .] I think it's just making it available but not forced." Catholic privilege and campus religious norms are understood and experienced by students in very different ways. Some students note that the campus is more open and progressive than their high schools, others comment that religious expectations are just one facet of life at school, while others must grapple with the personal choices that the campus climate frames for their everyday life—highlighting disparities in the lived experience of religion on campus.

The institutional religious affiliation coupled with campus demographics create an assumed norm of Catholic student identity, prompting the erasure of other faiths, traditions, and beliefs, and fostering social pressure to not draw attention to oneself. As Tom described:

> Sadly, the whole truth is, those who do identify as other religions, we're keeping it quiet. So, the only thing that we typically can rely on, is [that] everyone here is Catholic. Because, honestly, I have not met another person who has another belief other than Catholic. And . . . if I do encounter those students, I'm pretty sure they're not going to share it . . . nor am I going to share it with them either. Because we have that assumed belief. I'm definitely uncomfortable sharing it, knowing I'll get judgement from others.

Social norms on campus subtly encourage students to not share their beliefs or religious practices if they are not part of the norm. This hegemonic suppression of discussion about religion, beliefs, and faith is in tension with the institutions' desire to create spaces for spiritual formation. The pressure to not disclose or share their beliefs was voiced by most students interviewed, highlighting a paradoxical reticence to discuss beliefs at institutions with a deep-rooted institutional history of interreligious dialogue.

Even in instances in which students have no direct experience of pushback against stating their beliefs, there is still hesitance to speak openly about religion, faith, and beliefs. Many of the students interviewed reported both casual conversations and class discussions that were off-putting to fostering open dialogue. Isabel critiqued the unstated limits to acceptable conversation: "I know that, as a Catholic-identifying student on this campus, I am in the religious majority group. [And] I've heard comments that have been said derogatorily from people within [the Catholic] faith about others, basically saying if you're on this campus, you need to have a Catholic identity. [. . .] And that if you have opposing religious views, you shouldn't necessarily express your views." She went on to detail her desire both to open campus up for interfaith dialogue and to enable more nuanced and open conversations about "thorny topics," like abortion and gender norms. In general, student responses highlight the assumption of normative Catholic beliefs and how the perception of this norm frequently discourages students from sharing their beliefs. There were, however, exceptions in the data. As Jon shared, "I get some looks from people [when] I say I am an agnostic or I'm an atheist. But for the most part, I feel like a lot of the students here are pretty accepting of other beliefs."

While the schools aim to foster both academic and spiritual formation, students—including Catholic students—overwhelmingly voiced reluctance to speak openly about religion, faith, and beliefs. Julie, a student who identifies as spiritual, noted her reluctance to voice a counterpoint to a class discussion:

I was not able to voice my opinion at that time. I'm not sure why . . . Maybe I felt like I was the only one there . . . I felt like if I said something, . . . I probably would have been like looked at as the atheist [. . .] I feel like it's kind of disrespectful for me to say something and oppose them—if that's what you believe, that's what you believe. So, I also don't want to impose my beliefs on other people.

While Julie's silence came in response to a normative Catholic perspective, interview data suggests that reluctance to discuss religion is a widespread issue. One very active Catholic student, Jane, reflected: "I think [religious topics] are hard conversations. [. . .] especially if people are making new friendships, it's not really a good place to start. Once you get to know people more than you can possibly have those conversations, but they could be really hard to have." The understanding of religion and beliefs as personal and private issues to be shared only selectively, such as when students have already developed strong relationships, was a recurring theme. Additionally, students from underrepresented religions, denominations, and beliefs noted hesitance sharing beliefs and perspectives that ran counter to the norm. As Tom shared, "honestly, I don't feel the need to like tell other people [about my religion]. Mainly because, I kinda feel like the people here, would start questioning me. And then, it will turn into this whole epidemic of an argument saying, 'Well, why are you even here? This a Catholic school, and like well . . .'" In emphasizing why they refrain from bringing up religion and beliefs in casual conversation, students described their own religious or spiritual identification as personal choices, noted the strong assumption that most students are Catholic, voiced hesitance at being judged for their beliefs, and noted that they did not want to prompt debate.

CONCLUSION

I feel like, because the school is very overwhelmingly Catholic—I mean it is more like the majority Catholic—I think people just automatically assume you're religious. [. . .] I definitely think that we like to always talk about these Benedictine values but yet we don't always accept those who are different than us when it comes to religion. We really talk about community at [school] and I just think it's definitely something we can improve on. (Jon, a student who identifies as agnostic)

The greatest challenge to addressing student concerns about barriers to inclusion on our campuses lies in the central tension between the deep-rooted traditions as Catholic institutions and the concurrent interest in fostering inclusive campus, classroom, and community experiences for an increasingly diverse student body. The Catholic identity is a formative part of these institutions. Many students note that Benedictine values, such as justice, hospitality, listening, stewardship, and community, resonate with them, and students discussed how these values afford areas of concordance across different beliefs. As Jon notes, "We really talk about community," positioning this value as an aspirational goal yet to be fully realized. While Benedictine values, like community, are often articulated as common ground, interviews with students also illustrate the ways in which Catholicism is positioned as a hegemonic norm. The student quoted above identifies as agnostic, finds atheism compelling, and was raised in a non-Christian tradition. On campus, Jon notes that "people just automatically assume you're religious" and elaborates to say that he knows that he is often assumed to be part of the norm, regardless of how he actually identifies. This commonly voiced assumption illustrates the centrality of Catholic privilege on campus. When paired with the structural realities of curricular requirements, calendars, and material symbols like crucifixes, the assumption of normative Catholicism exemplifies what Adams and Joshi identify as "religious oppression" (2016) and places an additional burden on students from underrepresented religions. In light of Catholic privilege, assumptions that students are generally Catholic, and the stated reluctance of students to discuss religion, faith, and beliefs, the challenges to creating more religiously inclusive campus environments are many.

In openly acknowledging the Catholic hegemony at our schools, we can begin to move toward dismantling barriers for students from underrepresented religions and beliefs. Our schools are already working toward this goal, mindful of the leadership practices laid out by Patel and his co-authors (2015).[7] For our schools and other religiously affiliated institutions, the Engagement model (Strain et al. 2009) provides an avenue toward greater inclusion of diverse religions and beliefs—one that emphasizes interfaith learning across traditions and creates spaces where all students can share openly and without judgment about their experiences, backgrounds, traditions, and beliefs. It is important to note, however, that good intentions are insufficient and perpetuate rather than transform oppressive structures. Missions may be aspirational, but they also ought to be assessable. In that vein, interview data suggest some tangible avenues, including everything from raising awareness of religious diversity, conducting workshops on inclusive pedagogy, providing specific resources to support student religious practices (transportation, prayer space, dining options, and housing), and fostering more open interfaith conversations. A full report will be provided to the institutions at the conclusion of data collection and analysis in the hope of prompting fuller consideration of religious diversity in institutional policies, programmatic decisions, and academic mission.

For all schools—including public and secular colleges and universities—it is important to be mindful that religion, faith, and beliefs have often been sidelined on campus (Patel 2018a). Patel (2018b) argues that universities can play a unique role as models of religious pluralism, promoting interfaith dialogue and forming students who respectfully engage with others' beliefs in the interest of promoting the common good. Moreover, overlooking religion on campus means that the spiritual needs of students frequently go unsupported (Patel 2018b; Rochenbach et al. 2015b). At institutions like ours, students often experience these exclusions in intersectional ways, with students from underrepresented races, ethnicities, national origins, sexualities, and genders subject to compounded barriers to belonging. Each institution has a unique student body, and we present our research and these initial findings to suggest the utility of a student-centered analysis. Qualitative research holds the potential to better understand religious diversity on campus, student experiences with religion and beliefs, and what services, policies, or changes would support student religious and spiritual practices. In presenting this research, we hope to broaden considerations of diversity and to foster more supportive environments for students to engage with and develop all aspects of their identities—including religion.

While the research findings call us to consider how to foster religious inclusivity at our institutions, the research process also warrants similar consideration. The research presented here was developed by students and carried out under a community-based participatory research (CBPR) model. In CBPR, "Key tenets are to foster collaboration among community members and researchers (including students), engage all in reflective practice and reciprocal learning, build the capacity of community groups to create change, balance research and action, practice inter- and multidisciplinary work, and situate community concerns in a larger context" (Minkler and Wallerstein 2003, 421–422). The concern about religious inclusion examined here was identified by students, and student team members acted both as representatives of the school community and as skilled researchers. In this case, the research team developed organically, with a student member bringing together the faculty partners and identifying critical campus stakeholders. Full student integration in CBPR initiatives demystifies the research process, facilitates the development of valuable research skills, and prepares students for diverse postbaccalaureate careers. In turn, student researchers afford faculty and institutional stakeholders invaluable insight into student perspectives. Interdisciplinary teams facilitate the growth and learning among all team members, as methodological processes and diverse bodies of literature are shared. In short, while CPBR requires considerable time and coordination, it offers a model for making the research process more inclusive. This consideration becomes increasingly important as teams work to address barriers and exclusions at universities. As groups of students, faculty, administrators, and other stakeholders work to make campuses more welcoming to all, research efforts and action plans should reflect the same ethos of inclusivity and collaboration in the search for more equitable institutions of higher education.

NOTES

1. We are deeply grateful to the students who shared their experiences, insights, and opinions in the hopes of making our schools more inclusive. Thank you to Cai Selmo for her participation on the research team. John Merkle's unwavering support for this project was critical to its completion, and we thank the Jay Phillips Center for Interfaith Learning, the Fleischhacker Center for Ethical Leadership in Action, and the Mellon Becoming Community Research, Practice, and Implementation grants for their support. Angela Storey and Ellen Block provided insightful comments on early drafts. Finally, thank you to Amanda Macht Jantzer and Kyhl Lyndgaard for organizing this volume and offering helpful feedback.

2. As detailed below in the findings section, student discussions of religious self-identification, beliefs, and practices were individualized and nuanced, challenging the premise of the quota sample even as they exhibited the diversity in student responses that the research design aimed to capture.

3. Guest et al.'s (2006) research assumes a relatively homogenous group and our research team aimed to recruit as wide a sample as possible, mindful of recognizing the diversity student experiences and cautious of analyzing diverse student data under glossed categories. However, in analyzing the data, the lived experience of Catholic privilege and the barriers it presents for those who identify with other religions, faiths, or beliefs illustrate consistently recurring themes, suggesting that data saturation is possible among a small, diverse sample experiencing similar contexts and external pressures.

4. Data collection was interrupted in March 2020, and the research team aims to complete a total of forty-eight interviews for a more robust data set.

5. All names are pseudonyms. Streamlined versions of how students self-identify in terms of religion, denomination, beliefs, school year, race, and ethnicity are provided for context. In some instances, more general descriptions of religious identification were provided to ensure that students would not be identifiable. The necessity of having to obfuscate analytically useful religious self-identifications further underscores the lack of religious diversity on campus, the pressure that some students face to represent their religion, and the isolation that students from some religions encounter on campus.

6. In response to student activism, in January 2020 Martin Luther King, Jr. Day was observed as a day without classes and with scheduled programming to honor King's memory and the ongoing struggle for racial justice.

7. Our schools have a long history of engagement with students and community members of other faiths, from the presence of the boarding schools detailed in the Gordon, Benway, and Winters chapter to the current ecumenical research institute, interfaith center, and monastic interreligious dialogue group. The latter initiatives are in line with the Engagement model, and yet our data show a disconnect in which such interreligious commitments seemingly fail to trickle down to students' lived experiences. Welcoming students into these existing spaces presents a place to further interfaith dialogue.

REFERENCES

Adams, Maurianne and Khyati Joshi. 2016. "Religious Oppression." In *Teaching for Diversity and Social Justice*, edited by Maurianne Adams and Lee Ann Bell. New York: Routledge, pp. 255–297.

Andrade, Maureen. 2006. "International Student Persistence: Integration or Cultural Integrity?" *Journal of College Student Retention* 8 (1): 57–81. doi:10.2190/9MY5-256H-VFVA-8R8P.

Astin, Alexander. 1993. *What Matters In College? Four Critical Years Revisited*. San Francisco, CA: Jossey-Bass.

Austin, Diane. 2004. "Partnerships, Not Projects! Improving the Environment Through Collaborative Research and Action." *Human Organization* 63 (4): 419–430. doi:10.17730/humo.63.4.v7x1t5mwqfl1xl3v.

Austin, Diane, Edna Mendoza, Michele Kimpel Guzmán, and Alba Jaramillo. 2004. "Partnering for a New Approach: Maquiladoras, Government Agencies, Educational Institutions, Non-Profit Organizations, and Residents in Ambos Nogales." In *Social Costs of Industrial Growth in Northern Mexico*, edited by Kathryn Kopinak. San Diego, CA: University of California, San Diego, Center for U.S.-Mexican Studies, pp. 251–281.

Bernard, H. Russell. 2018. *Research Methods in Cultural Anthropology: Qualitative and Quantitative Approaches*. Lanham, MD: Rowman & Littlefield.

Bernard, H. Russell, Amber Wutich, and Greg Ryan. 2016. *Analyzing Qualitative Data: Systematic Approaches*. Thousand Oaks, CA: SAGE.

Bernard, H. Russell, Pertti J. Pelto, Oswald Werner, James Boster, A. Kimball Romney, Allen Johnson, Carol R. Ember and Alice Kasakoff. 1986. "The Construction of Primary Data in Cultural Anthropology." *Current Anthropology* 27 (4): 382–396.

Brecht, Mara. 2015. "God Talk Across and between the Boundaries of Traditions." *Journal of Catholic Higher Education* 34 (2): 151–172.

Brown, Leland and William Vega. 1996. "A Protocol for Community-Based Research." *American Journal of Preventive Medicine* 12 (4): 4–5.

Cole, Darnell and Shafiqa Ahmadi. 2010. "Reconsidering Campus Diversity: An Examination of Muslim Students' Experiences." *Journal of Higher Education* 81 (2): 121–139. doi:10.1353/jhe.0.0089.

DeCuir-Gunby, Jessica, Patricia Marshall, and Allison McCulloch. 2011. "Developing and Using a Codebook for the Analysis of Interview Data: An Example from a Professional Development Research Project." *Field Methods* 23 (2): 136–155. doi:10.1177/1525822X10388468.

Furrow, James, Pamela King, and Krystal White. 2004. "Religion and Positive Youth Development: Identity, Meaning, and Prosocial Concerns." *Applied Developmental Science* 8 (1): 17–26. doi:10.1207/S1532480XADS0801_3.

Guest, Greg, Arwen Bunce, and Laura Johnson. 2006. "How Many Interviews are Enough? An Experiment with Data Saturation and Variability." *Field Methods* 18 (1): 59–82. doi:10.1177/1525822X05279903.

Hurtado, Sylvia and Deborah Faye Carter. 1997. "Effects of College Transition and Perceptions of the Campus Racial Climate on Latino College Students' Sense of Belonging." *Sociology of Education* 70 (4): 324–345. doi:10.2307/2673270.

King, Pamela. 2003. "Religion and Identity: The Role of Ideological, Social, and Spiritual Contexts." *Applied Developmental Science* 7 (3): 197–204. doi:10.1207/S1532480XADS0703_11.

Leech, Beth L. 2002. "Asking Questions: Techniques for Semi-Structured Interviews." *Political Science and Politics* 35 (4): 665–668. doi:10.1017/S1049096502001129.

Mack, Natasha, Cynthia Woodson, Kathleen MacQueen, Greg Guest, and Emily Namey. 2005. *Qualitative Research Methods: A Data Collector's Field Guide*. Research Triangle, NC: FHI 360.

Mahaffey, Caitlin and Scott Smith. 2009. "Creating Welcoming Campus Environments for Students from Minority Religious Groups." In *Student Engagement in Higher*

Education, edited by Shaun Harper and Stephen Quaye. New York: Routledge, pp. 81–98.

Mayhew, Matthew, Nicholas Bowman, and Alyssa Rockenbach. 2014. "Silencing Whom?: Linking Campus Climates for Religious, Spiritual, and Worldview Diversity to Student Worldviews." *The Journal of Higher Education* 85 (2): 219–242.

Minkler, Meredith and Nina Wallerstein. 2003. "Introduction to Community Based Participatory Research." In *Community-Based Participatory Research for Health*, edited by Meredith Minkler and Nina Wallerstein. San Francisco, CA: Jossey Bass, pp. 5–24.

Morey, Melanie M, and John J Piderit. 2006. *Catholic Higher Education: A Culture in Crisis*. New York: Oxford University Press.

Mutakabbir, Yoruba, and Tariqah Nuriddin. 2016. *Religious Minority Students in Higher Education*. New York: Routledge.

Patel, Eboo. 2018a. "Faith Is the Diversity Issue Ignored by Colleges. Here's Why that Needs to Change." *The Chronicle of Higher Education*, October 29. https://www.chronicle.com/article/Faith-Is-the-Diversity-Issue/244953.

———. 2018b. *Out of Many Faiths: Religious Diversity and the American Promise*. Princeton, NJ: Princeton University Press.

Patel, Eboo, Katie Bringman Baxter, and Noah Silverman. 2015. "Leadership Practices for Interfaith Excellence in Higher Education." *Liberal Education* 101: 1–2.

Patel, Eboo, Noah Silverman, and Kristi Del Vecchio. 2017. "In Our Time: Advancing Interfaith Studies Curricula at Catholic Colleges and Universities." *Engaging Pedagogies in Catholic Higher Education* 3 (1): 1–6. doi:10.18263/2379-920X.1023.

Patton, Michael Q. 1990. *Qualitative Evaluation and Research Methods*. Beverly Hills, CA: SAGE.

Patten, Todd and N. Dwaine Rice. 2008. "Religious Minorities and Persistence at a Systemic Religiously-Affiliated University." *Christian Higher Education* 8 (1): 42–53. doi:10.1080/15363750802349323.

Rockenbach, Alyssa, Matthew Mayhew, and Nicholas Bowman. 2015a. "Perceptions of the Campus Climate for Nonreligious Students." *Journal of College Student Development* 56 (2): 181–186. doi:10.1353/csd.2015.0021.

Rockenbach, Alyssa, Matthew Mayhew, Shauna Morin, Rebecca E. Crandall, and Ben Selznick. 2015b. "Fostering the Pluralism Orientation of College Students through Interfaith Co-curricular Engagement." *The Review of Higher Education* 39 (1): 25–58. doi:10.1353/rhe.2015.0040.

Schensul, Jean, and Margaret D. LeCompte. 2012. *Essential Ethnographic Methods: A Mixed Methods Approach* (Vol. 3). Lanham, MD: Rowman Altamira.

Smith, Christian. 2007. "Moralistic Therapeutic Deism." In *Transforming Traditions for the Next Generations of Jews, Christians, and Muslims*, edited by James L. Heft. New York: Fordham University Press, pp. 55–74.

Spradley, James P. 2016. *The Ethnographic Interview*. Long Grove, IL: Waveland Press.

Strain, Charles R, James Halstead, and Thomas Drexler. 2009. "Engagement with Pluralism: A New Way of Understanding and Fostering a Catholic Culture Within Catholic Universities." *Journal of Catholic Higher Education* 28 (2): 169–186.

Strauss, Anselm, and Juliet Corbin. 1994. "Grounded Theory Methodology." In *Handbook of Qualitative Research*, edited by Norman K. Denzin and Yvonna S. Lincoln. Thousand Oaks, CA: SAGE, pp. 273–285.

Waldmeir, John, John Eby, Samantha Eckrich, and Rebecca Edwards. 2017. "Interfaith Inquiry: Learning from Community-Based Research, Pluralism, and Student-Faculty Collaboration." *Engaging Pedagogies in Catholic Higher Education* 3 (1): 3. doi:10.18263/2379-920X.1017.

Wolf, Helen. 2017. "Peer Ministry: Students Leading Conversations on Interreligious Issues at Catholic Colleges and Universities." *Journal of Catholic Higher Education* 36 (1): 21–40.

Young, Iris Marion. 1990. *Justice and the Politics of Difference*. Princeton Paperbacks. Princeton, N.J.: Princeton University Press.

Zimmerman, C. 2016. "Catholic Colleges Practice and Keep Learning about Interfaith Efforts." *Catholic News Service*. http://catholicphilly.com/2016/02/news/national-news/catholic-colleges-practice-and-keep-learning- about-interfaith-efforts/.

Section C

ADDRESSING ISSUES FACING UNDERREPRESENTED STUDENTS IN VARIED FIELDS OF STUDY

Chapter 7

Taking Stock

An Equity Audit of a Teacher Education Program

Madeleine H. Israelson, Diana Fenton, Catherine M. Bohn-Gettler, Terri L. Rodriguez, Allison Spenader, and Brandyn Woodard

INTRODUCTION

Like many professional preparation programs in higher education, there is an urgent need for the field of teacher education to explore ways to recruit, retain, and graduate preservice teachers from underrepresented backgrounds, specifically U.S. students of color and first-generation college students. This need for an increasingly diverse teaching workforce in the United States is well documented by teacher education scholars (Milner and Howard 2013, 552; Villegas and Davis 2007, 137–138). It is important to align teacher and student demographics to ensure representational equity. The disproportionate representation of white female teachers exists alongside an enduring education debt and persistent gaps in access to opportunities and resources for students of color (Ladson-Billings 2006a, 5).

Our team of teacher educators adapted and utilized an equity audit framework to examine how our program might be transformed to yield better outcomes for underrepresented student groups. Commonly used in K-12 educational settings, an equity audit is a tool to "uncover, understand, and change inequities that are internal to schools" (Skrla et al. 2004, 133). In higher education contexts, an equity audit is a way to raise consciousness and make systemic inequities visible with the goals of improving programmatic changes.

THE NEED FOR INCLUSIVITY IN
TEACHER PREPARATION

According to the most recent available results of the U.S. Department of Education 2015–2016 National Teacher and Principal Survey, of the 3.8 million public elementary and secondary teachers in America, 80 percent are white and 77 percent are female (Taie and Goldring 2017, 3). In 2014, approximately 96 percent of Minnesota public elementary and secondary schoolteachers were white (Minnesota Department of Education (MDE) 2017), yet the state student population is over 30 percent children of color. While K-12 student demographics in Minnesota, as across the country, are changing rapidly, teacher demographics are not (MDE 2017). These descriptive statistics stand in stark contrast to the most recent available demographic information about the 50.3 million elementary and secondary students served by U.S. public schools (table 7.1).

To rectify these issues, in some states, lawmakers have proposed legislation to increase the number of teachers of color (Shockman 2019). Although such recognition of the need for improved teacher diversity is important, ultimately the success of such efforts depends on institutions of higher education encouraging greater recruitment of preservice teachers of color and training all teachers in culturally responsive pedagogy. Studies suggest that when students of color have a teacher of color as part of their academic experience, they are more successful academically (Easton-Brooks 2015, 259). Additionally, research has shown that "[a]all students benefit from being educated by teachers from a variety of different backgrounds, races and ethnic groups, as this experience better prepares them to succeed in an increasingly diverse society" (Casey, Di Carlo, Bond, and Quintero 2015, 1). Research also suggests that preservice teachers of color may hold more complex and advanced views of multicultural education (Castro 2010, 207). Given what we know about the importance of diversifying the teaching force, national

Table 7.1   Racial Demographics of U.S. Public School Teachers and Students, 2015–2016

	Public Elementary and Secondary Teachers[1] (%)	Public Elementary and Secondary Students[2] (%)
White	80.1	48.5
Black	6.7	15.5
Hispanic	8.8	26.6
Asian/Pacific Islander	2.3	5.4
American Indian/Alaskan Native	0.4	1.0
Two or more races	1.4	2.9

accreditation standards for teacher education mandate that teacher education programs "recruit and support completion of high-quality candidates from a broad range of backgrounds and diverse populations . . . [who] reflect the diversity of America's P-12 students" (Council for the Accreditation of Educator Preparation 2013, 8).

We recognize that solely changing demographics of our program may not necessarily change teaching practices or lead to more equitable outcomes, and therefore, this audit focused on the concomitant aims of increasing preservice teacher diversity in our program and fostering the development of culturally relevant and equity literacy-grounded practices in all preservice teachers. Currently, the demographic trends of our teacher education program mirror those of the national teaching workforce. As faculty members and researchers, we consistently seek to more deeply understand our practices in the areas of recruitment, retention, and support of underrepresented preservice teachers for the purpose of contributing to the development of a more inclusive and diverse teaching force. Teacher education cannot continue to solely reflect Euro-American values and perspectives and normalized white culture.

The framework we have adopted for preparing preservice teachers is one that is informed by culturally relevant pedagogy and equity literacy. We purposely ask preservice teachers to demonstrate knowledge, skills, and dispositions for working in multicultural classrooms with diverse students. Our goal is to prepare our preservice teachers to implement culturally relevant pedagogies, and to ground their instruction in equity literacy. Culturally relevant teachers are culturally competent, hold complex views about diversity, and are sociopolitically aware (Ladson-Billings 2006b, 37). In other words, they are aware of the issues around equity and inequity and can create equitable learning experiences for all students, regardless of their students' backgrounds. It includes practices such as student-centered pedagogies, communicating high expectations, keeping a positive view of students and families, understanding that learning occurs within the context of culture, examining curriculum for representation, viewing the teacher as a facilitator, and emphasizing multicultural activities and history.

As faculty and researchers, we have pursued ways in which we can work to improve our own practices and programs to foster equity, both in demographic representation and in culturally relevant pedagogy. Our study evaluated the current state of our department's practices to support inclusive and effective teaching and mentorship for our preservice teachers from underrepresented populations. Further, our work sought the creation of more inclusive environments both in and out of the classroom, specifically for education majors and minors. Lastly, this project led us to reflect on our individual practices, uncovering ways to strengthen our own pedagogical practices that may not have been revealed without work on this project.

EQUITY AUDIT

Our team of researchers looked to the field of public PreK-12 education for methodologies to progress toward our inclusion goals. We determined that a multipronged equity audit might be adapted to our higher education context for our program that prepares K-12 teachers for work in public schools. This is a commonly used approach in PreK-12 educational settings in response to state and federal mandates to ensure demographic equity for public education outcomes. An equity audit is a tool that can be used to identify, explore, and act to dismantle inequities in school settings (Skrla et al. 2004, 133). Skrla et al. (2004, 141) define equity audits as leadership tools that can be used to guide schools in working toward equity and excellence. They involve the use of data to identify, address, and remove inequities that come from within the school itself. Equity audits have a history in civil rights enforcement and are also known as "representivity audits" (Skrla et al. 2004, 138).

Adaptations of the equity audit can be implemented in teacher education to raise consciousness and make systemic inequities visible. Equity audits provide rich opportunities to examine, critique, and ultimately act upon inequities (Groenke 2010, 91). Because many people still believe that factors such as class differences, families, and access to learning opportunities at home are the most reliable predictors of achievement, equity audits carry the potential to disrupt systemic patterns within schools themselves, including the beliefs and practices that reinforce educational inequities (Brown 2006, 704).

Auditing by itself, however, is not enough to create change. What is needed, according to Brown, is a focus on transformative learning that leads to "a new way of seeing" (Brown 2006, 706). Transformative learning involves experience, critical self-reflection, and rational discourse stimulated by people, events, or changes in contexts that challenge a learner's assumption of the world. Although this process may not necessarily lead to change in values or beliefs, examining and identifying their sources can lead to action as values are accepted and justified, revised, or rejected (Brown 2006, 706).

As we have noted, like many professional preparation programs in higher education, it is imperative that the field of teacher education actively seek effective ways to recruit, retain, support, and graduate preservice teachers from underrepresented backgrounds. We realized that not only did we need "a new way of seeing" our program and its outcomes, but we needed to act with a new vision. An equity audit allowed us to collect a number of data points to ascertain the current state of inclusive practices in our program and to utilize these data to plan specific changes geared toward increasing inclusivity. Further, the equity audit approach allowed us to leverage and utilize the research experiences and expertise of each member of the research team.

This chapter describes the design, application, and findings of our departmental equity audit. We will detail how we utilized this tool to engage in careful self-study, to more deeply understand programmatic practices, and to foster the development of a more inclusive and diverse teaching force. First, we describe the process our team utilized for designing our equity audit to leverage the experience and expertise of each member of our research team to meet our overarching objective of transforming our program to yield more positive outcomes for preservice teachers from underrepresented demographic groups. We then describe each data source, including the strategies used for collection and analysis, and summarize the findings from each. Finally, we describe the most significant implications of our study, offering key points for academic departments seeking to collaboratively engage in equity work.

DESIGNING OUR EQUITY AUDIT

The research questions that drove our study emerged from engaged dialogue among faculty in our department and from broader conversations occurring on our campus. Our team met several times initially to craft the research questions that drove our inquiry. We determined that we had several objectives as we engaged in this project, including the following: documenting and deepening our understanding of our current practices through seeking students' voices and perspectives; examining our own individual intercultural knowledge and inclusive pedagogy practices; and identifying specific, evidence-based actionable steps to improve the experiences and outcomes of underrepresented students in our department. With these goals in mind, our study sought to answer the following research questions:

1. How are we recruiting, retaining, and supporting underrepresented students in education? How do the experiences of underrepresented education majors/minors inform improvements in recruiting, retention, and support?
2. How are faculty developing in their knowledge and enactment of inclusive practices?
3. In what specific ways can we improve our program and practices to improve our recruitment, retention, and support for underrepresented students?

To answer these questions, we sought to collect three types of data: data yielding the perspectives of students in our courses and programs, data from our department faculty and instructors to understand our own practices, and data drawn broadly from the institution to provide insight into the sociocultural context of our study. Figure 7.1 illustrates the design of our equity audit structure.

Our research team determined that survey and focus group interview data would afford us the unique perspectives of students during all stages of our program, from the introductory course through induction as a first-year teacher. We collected survey data from all students in our introductory course, whether they chose to continue toward a teaching license in our program or not. We also conducted a series of focus group interviews with students who self-identified as belonging to our underrepresented groups. Through the focus groups, we sought to understand the experiences of those who continued in our program, as well as those who did not.

The second type of data we collected examined the practices and beliefs of the faculty in our department. We invited faculty to complete the Intercultural Development Inventory (IDI) (Hammer, Bennett, and Wiseman 2003, 421) and participate in a group debriefing on the results. The IDI is a tool based on Bennett's Developmental Model of Intercultural Sensitivity (Hammer, Bennett, and Wiseman, 421) and provides both a measurement of interculturality, as well as tools and interventions for moving individuals and groups toward more intercultural mindsets. We also invited department faculty to engage in a syllabus analysis workshop designed to facilitate revision of syllabi to increase inclusivity in the language, content, and design of syllabi.

Finally, our equity audit included collection of data to deepen our understanding of the broader institutional context in which we prepare future teachers. We conducted interviews with three individuals from key offices across campus. These individuals were selectively sampled as staff members actively engaged in the work of supporting students from the specific demographic groups for which the study seeks to improve educational outcomes.

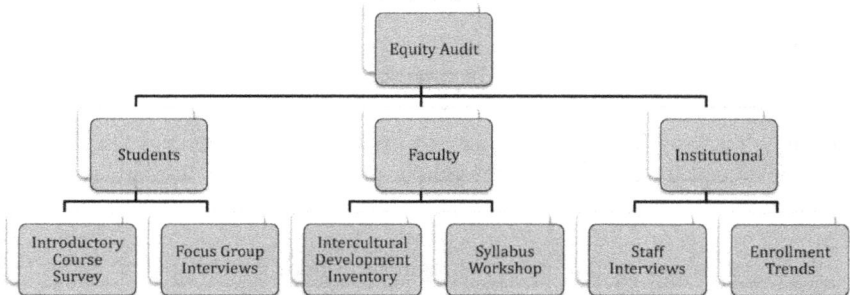

Figure 7.1   Equity Audit Data Sources.

The interviews explored topics such as goals, barriers, strategies, and approaches for supporting U.S. students of color and first-generation college students. We examined enrollment trends over a four-year period, including the number of students with Junior and Senior status in each major who are students of color, male, female, and first generation.

We next briefly discuss how these institutional data (staff interviews and enrollment trends) afforded us a lens through which we were able to understand the first two types of data. For example, we learned that our department's elementary education program has experienced increased numbers of first-generation and male students in the past five years, while the percentage of American students of color enrolled has remained relatively consistent. Through interviews with campus staff who work closely with students in our targeted demographic groups, we learned that U.S. students of color report frequently experiencing acts of microaggression by both faculty and peers across their college experiences. Our campus staff interview subjects all spoke about the importance of connectedness, relationships, and a sense of belonging to student retention. These institutional data provided us with an understanding of the broader context in which our teacher education program exists. Without an appreciation for the realities of the sociocultural factors for our work, we would not have been able to contextualize the data collected from students and faculty in our department. Our analysis of findings from the first two data sets (preservice teacher and faculty experiences and perspectives) will be discussed in detail below.

INTRODUCTORY COURSE SURVEY

Overview and Rationale

To help understand more about the retention of our students in the education program, we developed a survey for all students who completed our required introductory education course. This course is designed to help students learn more about the field of education and often serves to prompt students to decide to pursue an education major or minor. Not all students who take the course are interested in education; some take the course to fulfill other college requirements.

Methodology

Our research team developed a survey that posed Likert questions and open-ended questions about reasons students decided to pursue or not pursue a major or minor in education. Likert items were analyzed utilizing quantitative methods, and open-ended responses were coded utilizing deductive and inductive methods (Corbin and Strauss 2014, 195; Miles, Huberman and Saldana 2013, Ch. 4). We collected data across four consecutive semesters, with 148 students invited to participate in the study by completing the survey, and 126 consented to participate. The surveys were administered during class time. Of the total 126 students who completed the survey, 75 percent were first-year students, with 67 percent identifying as female and 33 percent as male. We were not able to collect data on students' racial and ethnicity due to confidentiality concerns, yet we know that our demographics are similar to those reported in the state of Minnesota and nationally from studying institutional demographic enrollment trends. Participants' responses to the Likert items provided overall thematic patterns, while the open-ended responses offered further detail about these identified themes.

Findings

The findings from our survey data illuminated why students chose to continue or not to continue in the education program. Two-thirds of survey participants indicated their intent to continue in the education program. Participants' responses to open-ended questions indicated that students' choice to continue in the program was impacted by several factors including the desire to work with children, inspiration from former teachers, influence from the education faculty, their work experiences in educational settings, and the ability to positively impact and improve education.

Participants responded to the prompt: "Do the following issues impact your decision to continue to pursue a teaching license?" The responses indicated that sense of belonging (51 percent), relationships with faculty (51 percent), and financial obligations (51 percent) were the most common responses. An analysis of the open-ended responses offered more nuanced explanations of how a sense of belonging impacted decisions to continue in the program. Many students indicated that they felt that they belonged in the program after participation in the introductory course. For example, one respondent stated, "After completing the introductory course, I realized that being around these people and faculty is where I feel most at home. I feel like I belong in this department and with these people. They really helped me to start feeling at home on campus." Another noted, "This (belonging) is a big factor for me. I wanted to feel like I have a place in my major, and the education department really makes a point to do this."

Responses to open-ended items also explained how relationships with faculty impacted their decision to continue in the program. Analysis of these data suggests that relationships with faculty in the education department have been important to respondents and have motivated them to continue in the education program. One respondent stated, "The faculty is encouraging and positive and that makes me want to stay here," while another offered a similar sentiment, "Forming close relationships to professors and using them as role models is a good part of the education program."

Our team hypothesized that certain factors such as the financial outlook of a career in education, or course demands on time for those holding a student job, or access to transportation for PreK-12 school-based field experiences might serve as obstacles or barriers to dissuade students from pursuing an education degree. While open-ended responses mention low salary in education (15 percent), our analysis of survey data suggests that for the majority of survey participants this factor did not deter them from pursuing education. Although survey respondents commented that teaching salaries are considered "low," this did not impact their decision because their desire to teach mattered more. One unique comment about motivation to become a teacher despite financial outlook under-scored the urgency and importance of conducting an equity audit. The respondent stated, "There are not enough males in this field and there are not enough teachers of color. Students need to see teachers that reflect their identities." Many other respondents shared that they have received scholarships and that they view the cost as "worth it" because of the reputation of the program. One respondent noted, "I know that after college, I will have some loans to pay off, but the quality of education I am receiving makes it all worth it."

Despite the cost of higher education and relatively low teacher salary, 83 percent of respondents indicated that work obligations did not impact their decision to continue in education and 79 percent indicated that the need and associated cost of transportation to practicum sites did not impact their decision to continue in the program. In open-ended responses, participants explained that their work is flexible, they can schedule around classes, they work at night, and that classes come before work. Examples of comments included "Work will always come second because I believe my education is the most important focus in my life now," and "I work on campus, so my job is really focused on my school first, then my job."

DISCUSSION

The survey data provides empirical evidence of our need to recruit male students given that the majority of our preservice teachers identified as female. Several strengths of our program were identified through the analysis of survey data, including relationships with faculty and a sense of belonging. These two factors are important for retention. Faculty in our department support our students in the classroom and through one-on-one advising sessions; however, we also recognize that we must continue to develop and refine our implementation of culturally inclusive pedagogies if we can hope to continue to foster a sense of belonging and relational support. While responses indicated a sense of belonging impacting their decisions, comments were mainly geared toward their interactions with faculty. We recognize that other supports may need to be developed to promote a greater sense of belonging, such as peer mentorship. Peer mentorship programs have been found to enhance retention, success, and students' ability to integrate knowledge across academic courses (Chester, Burton, Xenos and Elgar 2013, 35; Collings, Swanson, and Watkins 2014, 937). Most importantly, evidence supports the effectiveness of mentorship in decreasing inequities and supporting underrepresented students (Shotton, Oosahwe, and Cintron 2007, 90).

STUDENT FOCUS GROUPS

Overview and Rationale

To understand the experiences of our students more deeply, we conducted focus groups with students from traditionally underrepresented groups in teacher education. We chose to conduct focus groups because they facilitate engagement through interactive discussions, offer the opportunity to elicit responses to specific questions, and allow for flexibility. For example, focus groups enable researchers to obtain a greater depth of understanding through elaboration and follow-up questions, allow for spontaneity such that participants can bring up topics the researchers had not considered, and the reactions of one participant can stimulate responses from other participants (Lederman 1990, 119–120). In short, focus groups can help faculty and administrators obtain incredible insights into students' experiences (Krueger and Casey 2009, Ch. 1).

Methodology

We conducted three focus groups with participants who self-identified as belonging to groups that are traditionally underrepresented in our education program: first-generation, low-income, students of color, males, and English Learners (ELs). The three groups included (1) underrepresented students who chose to pursue education, (2) underrepresented students who initially chose to pursue education but who later changed majors/minors, and (3) an underrepresented student who completed the introductory education course but chose not to pursue an education major/minor. Although we employed the same focus group protocol for each meeting, one meeting was conducted as an interview with only one participant. The first focus group consisted of nine participants and the second focus group had two participants. These group sizes afforded members an opportunity to share insights and promote a diversity of perspectives but did not put stress on particular individuals (Greenbaum 1998, 3; Krueger and Casey 2009, 67; Vaughn, Schumm, and Sinagub 1996, 48–51).

A trained moderator asked a series of open-ended prompts and allowed participants to verbalize other information they deemed relevant. The prompts invited participants to discuss topics such as factors that led to them pursuing or not pursuing education, barriers and supports to their learning, and their personal experiences as students in education classes. To ensure the effectiveness of the focus groups and interview, we followed the work of prior researchers (Greenbaum 1998, 3, 34, 79–82; Vaughn, Schumm, and Sinagub 1996, 38, 48–51, 76), such that we identified a clear purpose, considered the size compositions of the groups, and selected and trained a moderator utilizing best practices. Each focus group lasted 60–120 minutes.

The sessions were structured to include a description of the purpose of the study, an overview of the major themes and questions to be discussed, and ground rules for participation. The moderator led the discussion utilizing the question prompts, active listening, and facilitation skills. Participants were given the option to complete a demographic information sheet. The sessions were recorded and transcribed, and the transcriptions were de-identified by the moderator to ensure they did not contain identifying information to ensure confidentiality.

We coded data from the focus groups and the interview utilizing deductive and inductive methods (Corbin and Strauss 2014, 195; Miles, Huberman and Saldana 2013, Ch. 4). Two coders independently reviewed the transcripts to identify major themes and subthemes of participants' statements. The two coders then met to compare their themes, and from the comparison determined the themes and subthemes to apply related to participants' statements. The two coders then independently applied the revised themes and subthemes, and then met again to compare their codes. Any discrepancies were resolved by discussion. If a theme did not have high agreement, the coders revisited that theme independently and then compared their codes again.

Findings

The focus groups and interview provided an incredibly rich set of data from our students related to how to support preservice teachers who are traditionally underrepresented in education. The findings pointed to several supports and barriers. First, students described the importance of coordinated fieldwork and partnerships in helping them to feel a sense of belonging to the profession. They described how meaningful our field placements and partnerships are and expressed a desire for even deeper connections with the larger K-12 education community. Second, they described structural barriers related to costs and policies. For example, preservice teachers must complete several expensive licensure exams, must complete certain tasks as dictated by the state, and travel to field placements. Several of these pose challenges for students from underrepresented groups, who may not have access to reliable transportation or the funds to cover such costs. Third, participants described a need to reframe larger societal perceptions of teaching and its status. In the United States today, teachers receive lower wages and less respect than other fields, despite the importance and intensity of the work, and the training required. Fourth, the students described the importance of building an inclusive community for all, both on- and off-campus. This supported the notion that although community building was already an important part of our program, even more focus and intentionality behind fostering such environments would be helpful. Finally, they described how their prior experiences afforded them a deeper knowledge of equity and social justice, and hence it is important to differentiate the teaching of equity literacy based on prior knowledge and experiences.

DISCUSSION

The findings from the focus groups and interview, when triangulated with other data sources included in the equity audit, suggest that a number of barriers exist in recruiting, retaining, and supporting students from underrepresented groups in teacher education. First, financial barriers remain toward becoming a teacher—whether it is through expensive licensure exams, transportation costs, or teacher salaries. While candidates do not report financial barriers as significant while they take the introductory course, these hurdles become apparent later in the program. For students who may be looking to help support their families or assure a stable financial future while repaying student loans, teaching may not be a realistic option. Second, the significant societal perceptions of the teaching profession continue to pose barriers. Although no single teacher education program can break down all barriers, a coordinated effort for advocacy for teachers and teacher educators will be critical. Third, participants described how they sought an enhanced sense of belonging both within the program, and with the field in general. Although this is already a highly emphasized component of our programs and colleges, it still suggests room for growth, and a need to examine cohort-based models and mentorship models for students who are underrepresented—both on-campus and with the field in general. Finally, enhancing differentiation when teaching content related to social justice and equity is particularly meaningful for students from underrepresented groups to provide more scaffolded development of knowledge and experiences. While student perspective was essential for the study, we also recognize that understanding the perceptions of faculty were imperative to this study.

FACULTY IDI

Overview and Rationale

The IDI (Hammer, Bennett, and Wiseman 2003, 421) was chosen as a tool for the equity audit because of its ability to assess individuals and groups in terms of intercultural mindsets and skills. The developmental profiles produced by the IDI provide a lens through which to examine practices and perspectives of faculty in terms of cross-cultural interactions, which can facilitate more inclusive practices throughout the department. The IDI is widely recognized in the field of education as a valid and reliable measure of interculturality and provides accompanying materials for intercultural development (Hammer, Bennett, and Wiseman 2003, 421–422). In order for faculty members to work effectively with diverse preservice teachers and to help all preservice teachers develop skills for inclusive, multicultural education, faculty can benefit from knowing more about their own intercultural assets and blind spots.

Methodology

The IDI is a psychometric assessment that uses responses to fifty prompts to place individuals on a continuum of intercultural development. An invitation to complete the IDI was sent to all education faculty, as well as the two directors of student teaching. These members of the department work directly with preservice teachers through coursework and field experiences. By inviting faculty to complete and debrief the results of the IDI, our research team gathered data on the intercultural competence of faculty and identified strengths and areas for growth. Ten of eighteen eligible department members completed the IDI. A qualified administrator of the IDI (not a department member) administered a group debrief of unidentified results at a department meeting to serve as a training and opportunity for further reflection and development. The IDI debrief and training examined both the current intercultural strengths and blind spots of the department and offered concrete ideas for all individuals to further develop their intercultural skills.

Findings

The IDI provides individual and group profile scores related to Bennett's continuum known as the Developmental Model of Intercultural Sensitivity (Hammer, Bennett, and Wiseman 2003, 439). This continuum identifies individuals' developmental orientation, ranging from monocultural mindsets of *denial* and *polarization* to multicultural or intercultural mindsets of *acceptance* and *adaptation*. In the center of the continuum is *minimization*, an orientation that occupies the most "space," and wherein most adults who complete the IDI find themselves. This orientation at the center of the continuum is where individuals begin to become more culturally aware and skilled (Lou and Bosley 2012, 343). Eighty percent of our faculty who took the IDI were in the *minimization* developmental orientation, and the remaining 20 percent were in the *adaptation* developmental orientation. Hammer describes the *minimization* orientation as "a transitional mindset between the more monocultural orientations of *denial* and *polarization*, and the more intercultural/global worldviews of *acceptance* and *adaptation*. *Minimization* highlights the commonalities in both human *similarity* (basic needs) and *universalism* (universal values and principles) that can mask a deeper understanding of cultural differences" (Hammer 2016, 34). Furthermore, individuals operating in *minimization* may not recognize the institutional privilege they are afforded (Hammer, Bennett, and Wiseman 2003, 425). The *adaptation* orientation "consists of both Cognitive Frame-Shifting (shifting one's cultural perspective) and Behavioral Code-Shifting (changing behavior in authentic and culturally appropriate ways). *Adaptation* enables deep cultural bridging across diverse communities using an increased repertoire of cultural frameworks and practices in navigating cultural commonalities and differences. An *adaptation* mindset sees adaptation in performance (behavior)" (Hammer 2016, 35).

DISCUSSION

Faculty in the department are operating largely in a *minimization* mindset, which means we may not be fully attending to how our own cultural practices and perspectives are perceived by colleagues and candidates from other cultural backgrounds. While the faculty is interested in cultural differences, we are sometimes unsure of how to successfully adapt our mindsets and behaviors to effectively work with others. Furthermore, we may be unsure as to how to be critical of our own and other cultural practices and may be perpetuating institutional privileges we have been afforded. However, some members of the faculty were operating in the developmental orientation of *adaptation*, allowing these individuals to serve as models and mediators for students and colleagues. Faculty members would benefit from a myriad of developmental activities aimed at exploring the beliefs and values behind cultural practices. Specifically, faculty should participate in conversations about how differences and similarities within and between cultures in particular contexts are interpreted, and critically examine accepted practices within the department for ways in which we might exclude members of the community. The equity audit in itself is an example of a critical examination that will benefit the department as a whole. By deeply exploring our cultural practices, knowing we have blind spots in our intercultural understandings, we can better recruit, retain, and support diverse candidates. Reflecting deeply on our IDI results will allow us to move toward *acceptance* and *adaptation* as a department, disrupting institutional privilege in our courses and in our departmental policies. By developing our intercultural mindsets, we will be better positioned to work effectively with candidates from diverse cultural backgrounds, while also honing our development of teachers who will strive for equity and advocacy for their future students.

SYLLABUS WORKSHOP

Overview and Rationale

Through our analysis of departmental data and documents, we identified the syllabus as being a critical document through which faculty and students interact. Further, the policies, content, and other elements of a syllabus may or may not support inclusion and equity for all students. Hence, we researched and drew upon a syllabi review protocol developed by the Rossier School of Education's Center for Urban Education at the University of Southern California (2018, 1–5). According to the Center for Urban Education (2018), syllabus review is an inquiry tool to promote racial/ethnic equity and equity-minded practice (3). Syllabi are important to consider because they perform multiple functions in the academic program. They are contracts, records, learning tools, and communication devices (3). As such, they are a rich source of information about what occurs at the course level. As "artifacts of practice" (4) they can unwittingly reproduce norms that privilege the historically white student populations for which they were originally conceived. With explicit and careful syllabi inquiry, faculty can demystify these norms. They can re-design syllabi in ways that welcome, validate, and more accurately represent the experiences of students who have been traditionally excluded or marginalized in higher education spaces (4). Through critical syllabi inquiry, we began to envision how we could transform our classroom-based practices to better support underrepresented students in our education program. It is important to conduct such syllabi reviews in collegial workshop settings as a way to invite and engage discussion and reflection (Center for Urban Education 2018, 2).

Methodology

Our research team first employed the equity-minded inquiry process outlined by the Center for Urban Education called "the checklist" approach because we were new to equity-minded inquiry and were interested in examining the content, language, and tone of our syllabi (22). Using this, we developed and engaged in departmental and institutional workshops to identify opportunities to transform our syllabi to increase equity and cultural inclusivity. Our workshop approach invited faculty to bring samples of their syllabi and to conduct both a self-reflection and small and large group discussions. Syllabi included those from courses in world language, children's literature, mathematics, and introduction to education. Small groups chose a focal area from the following:

1. Language that conveys the instructor's willingness to help students succeed;
2. Content that fosters diversity, inclusivity, and empowerment;
3. Using a variety of assignments, assessments, and activities that take into account students' diverse backgrounds and promote critical thinking; and
4. Providing opportunities for students to share their cultural knowledge and to engage in discussions of real-world problems from diverse perspectives. (Center for Urban Education 2018, 2).

For each of the four focal areas, we offer a description of the revisions made to the syllabi as a result of the collaborative workshop.

Findings

Focal Area 1: Language that Conveys the Instructor's Willingness to Help Students Succeed

One of the syllabi that was examined and revised during the workshop did not include language explicitly communicating the instructors' willingness to help students succeed. During the departmental syllabus workshop, the statement below was added to the syllabus:

As your professor, I am here to support you in your learning. I will work hard to provide you with:

- *Readings, discussions, activities, and assignments that help you deepen your understanding of the course material;*
- *A positive classroom environment in which everyone feels included, and all voices are heard;*
- *A welcoming attitude to different experiences, ways of thinking, and diverse perspectives on teaching and learning;*
- *Ongoing feedback that is fair and productive, and that helps you improve your learning and experiences;*
- *Supports to help you succeed, and a willingness to connect you with resources;*
- *Reasonable flexibility when things don't go as planned—please don't be afraid to ask for help.*
- *A partnership in which the professor and students work together to promote success in learning for our class, our partner teachers, and the students we work with in the community.*

Focal Area 2: Content that Fosters Diversity, Inclusivity, and Empowerment

Another syllabus examined during the workshop particularly lent itself to the analysis of diverse content because it was a literature course. Required readings included both literary and scholarly texts. We considered whether the focal topics (content) for class sessions and required reading addressed issues of social inequality and promoted social consciousness of equity issues (USC 2018, 2). The existing syllabus included the following statement:

> *We will explore diversity in children's literature, including issues related to the lack of inclusiveness seen in writing and publishing for children in the United States. These issues reflect power inequalities in the publishing industry, in schools, and in the marketplace.*

However, through the process of the syllabus workshop, we identified an area for improvement by increasing the focus on promoting social consciousness of equity issues related to writing and publishing for children. Although the above statement was on the syllabus, the analysis of the course completed at the syllabus workshop identified the fact that this topic warranted more class sessions and required readings than it received at the time. We identified an opportunity to increase the use of class time and required readings on the topic of power inequalities in the children's literature publishing industry. Through the syllabus workshop, this allowed us to increase and deepen students' awareness and exploration of social inequities. While the syllabus itself was not modified, the course practices were transformed from this reflective analysis.

Focal Area 3: Using a Variety of Assignments, Assessments, and Activities that Take into Account Students' Diverse Backgrounds and Promote Critical Thinking

Other syllabi analyzed in the workshop already used a variety of assignments, assessments, and activities taking diverse backgrounds into account and promoting critical thinking, most notably, student choice. For example, one of the syllabi stated:

> *We will average the Gateway, Daily Homework, Videos, and Final Exam scores together according to the following weights. We will decide the final weights in class. The percentages must sum to 100 percent.*
> *Daily Homework (5 percent): 5 percent*
> *Gateways (35–50 percent): Your choice?*
> *Videos (35–50 percent): Your choice?*
> *Final Exam (5–15 percent): Your choice?*

After review and discussion, the instructor created a statement to more explicitly state the rationale connecting the assignment and assessment practices to recognition of students' unique individual needs and backgrounds:

> *In this class, you will help choose how your semester grade will be calculated. This is because I want to acknowledge that different students have different strengths, and I want you to be in the best position to succeed. Thus, this is an opportunity for you to personally weigh the importance of each type of assignment in a way that best reflects your strengths.*

Focal Area 4: Providing Opportunities for Students to Share Their Cultural Knowledge and to Engage in Discussions of Real-World Problems from Diverse Perspectives

In reviewing an additional syllabus during the workshop, the discussion focused on a key assignment that provided students opportunities to share their cultural knowledge. Before engagement in the syllabus workshop, the purpose of this assignment focused on individualism and personal storytelling without attention to positioning the story within larger sociocultural frames or considering it from diverse perspectives. Directions for the assignment stated:

> *Reflective thinking and writing are key components of developing effective teaching practice. In reflective writing, we describe and narrate events in order*

to make sense of our past experiences, the meaning of our current practices, and re-imagine the future as more effective teachers, and more compassionate people.

Drawing on the work of Chávez and Longerbeam (2016, 209–214), this reflective writing assignment was reimagined to reflect the positionality of personal narratives, consideration of real-world issues and diverse perspectives. Directions on the syllabus were changed in the following way:

Throughout this course, you will investigate issues of diversity and equity in educational settings. An important goal is to foster understanding of how social identities (race, ethnicity, gender, (dis)ability, language, class, religion, and sexual orientation) and cultural values and beliefs are constructed and learned. Through this assignment, you will engage in thoughtful self-examination of your beliefs, values, and perspectives about self and others. You will analyze how your social and cultural identities have been constructed through explicit and implicit messages from family stories, communities, schools, and media.

DISCUSSION

The opportunity to engage in this workshop collaboratively, rather than individually, was key to the revisions made. Reflective dialogue with others in a safe space allowed us to envision how we could transform our classroom-based practices to better support underrepresented students in education. While faculty across the institution were invited to attend, participation was optional. The faculty who elected to participate in the syllabus workshop was eager to engage in this work and made substantive, impactful changes to their syllabi. These faculty members expressed overwhelming appreciation for the opportunity to closely examine how their intentions were matching their words in the public contract of the course syllabus. Anecdotally, the changes were well received by students, and future workshops have been requested by faculty across departments.

IMPLICATIONS

The equity audit process provided a rich opportunity for our department to engage in reflective dialogue that led to changes in practice. The equity audit framework allowed us to recognize, respond, and begin to redress some of the biases and inequities in our program (Gorski 2019, 1). We hope to move forward to create and sustain a program that attracts, retains, and graduates more preservice teachers from underrepresented groups. Other departments on campus have requested resources to conduct an equity audit of their own in response to participation in the syllabus review and other presentations on campus. We have had the opportunity to consult with campus leaders about how this framework might be integrated into institutional program reviews, transforming the equity audit process from an optional endeavor to a structural change firmly embedded in the institutional evaluative practices.

Inspired by the findings of our equity audit, we offer the following implications. First, engaging in systematic analysis of data from multiple sources is crucial, as it can provide insight into gaps in knowledge about how programs, faculty, and staff can support student experiences and offer converging evidence. Within this process, it is essential that some of these sources include students' voices and perspectives. However, incorporating student voices and perspectives must occur in a respectful and careful way to ensure students feel safe, unburdened, and not tokenized.

Second, when engaging in analyses of our practice and programs, and considering ways to support professional development, it is essential to structure self-studies and activities in a manner that allows all participants, including staff and faculty, to feel safe and to be vulnerable. This type of work involves critically examining one's own self and practices, in addition to the structures in place within and outside of programs. If participants do not feel safe, it can be an impediment to this work and to the campus community.

Third, when obtaining data from multiple sources, it is important to consider the holistic experiences of our students in the context of the programs, practice, and campus life. We must consider how multiple systems interact to include the experiences of students from underrepresented groups. In addition, building a support system for students should occur in a holistic manner.

Finally, our findings indicate that building community and relationships are vital tasks. We must ensure that a sense of belonging that we build on campuses, and within programs extends to all students. This means that we need to critically examine who we are and recognize privilege within our practices to find ways that we can change to be inclusive to all students. As noted in the introduction to this chapter, equity auditing by itself is not enough to create change. While the audit may reveal practices that foster inequity rather than equity, it remains a preliminary step to transformation. Transformative learning not only challenges assumptions of the world but leads to action (Brown 2006, 706). An example of an action our equity audit yielded was the creation of a mentorship program within our department to support students from underrepresented groups. Teacher education, and higher education in general, cannot continue to solely reflect Euro-American values and ways of knowing, being, and communicating. Both individually and programmatically, we are responsible for transformative change to foster better outcomes for underrepresented students.

Using the equity audit approach our team uncovered individual, departmental, and institutional practices that can be transformed to provide better experiences and outcomes for preservice teachers from underrepresented groups. Such work may help to attract and retain more individuals from underrepresented backgrounds to the field of teacher education and enhance the culturally relevant practices of teachers entering the profession, which could then have a long-term ripple effect on K-12 students and the field of education. More broadly, while the process ought to be modified based on the needs, goals, and expertise of departments or institutions, an equity audit is a powerful tool to identify and reduce inequities commonly experienced by marginalized students. Most importantly, what is learned from the equity audit should be used to inform changes on campus and within programs to enhance equity and support transformative inclusion.

REFERENCES

Brown, Kathleen M. 2006. "Leadership for Social Justice and Equity: Evaluating a Transformative Framework and Andragogy." *Educational Administration Quarterly* 42 (5): 700–45. doi:10.1177/0013161x06290650.

Casey, Leo, Matthew Di Carlo, Burnie Bond, and Esther Quintero. 2015. *"The State of Teacher Diversity in American Education."* Washington, DC: Albert Shanker Institute." http://www.shankerinstitute.org/resource/teacherdiversity.

Castro, Antonio J. 2010. "Themes in the Research on Preservice Teachers' Views of Cultural Diversity: Implications for Researching Millennial Preservice Teachers." *Educational Researcher* 39 (3): 198–210. doi:10.3102/0013189x10363819.

Chávez, Alicia Fedelina, and Susan Diana Longerbeam. 2016. *Teaching Across Cultural Strengths: A Guide to Balancing Integrated and Individuated Cultural Frameworks in College Teaching.* Virginia: Stylus Publishing, LLC.

Chester, Andrea, Lorelle J. Burton, Sophie Xenos, and Karen Elgar. 2013. "Peer Mentoring: Supporting Successful Transition for First Year Undergraduate Psychology Students." *Australian Journal of Psychology* 65 (1): 30–7. doi:10.1111/ajpy.12006.

Collings, Rosalyn, Vivien Swanson, and Ruth Watkins. 2014. "The Impact of Peer Mentoring on Levels of Student Wellbeing, Integration and Retention: A Controlled Comparative Evaluation of Residential Students in UK Higher Education." *Higher Education* 68 (6): 927–42. doi:10.1007/s10734-014-9752-y.

Corbin, Juliet, and Anselm Strauss. 2014. *Basics of Qualitative Research: Techniques and Procedures for Developing Grounded Theory.* Thousand Oaks: SAGE.

Council for the Accreditation of Educator Preparation. 2013. "2013 CAEP Standards." http://caepnet.org/~/media/Files/caep/standards/caep-standards-one-pager-0219.pd f?la=en.

Easton-Brooks, Donald. 2015. "Bridging the Gap and Diversifying Teaching Education." In *The Race Controversy in American Education*, vol. 2, pp. 259–80. Santa Barbara: Praeger.

Greenbaum, Thomas L. 1998. *The Handbook for Focus Group Research*. Thousand Oaks: SAGE.

Gorski, Paul. 2019. "Equity Literacy for Educators: Definitions and Abilities" *Equity Literacy Institute*. Last modified May 22, 2020. https://08a3a74a-dec5-426e-838 5-bdc09490d921.filesusr.com/ugd/38199c_d5fce9c583f345ffad8dc108173fbd1f .pdf.

Gorski, Paul and Katy Swalwell. 2015. "Equity Literacy for All." *Educational Leadership* 72 (6): 34–40.

Groenke, Susan, L. 2010. "Seeing, Inquiring, Witnessing: Using the Equity Audit in Practitioner Inquiry to Rethink Inequity in Public Schools." *English Education* 43 (1): 83–96.

Hammer, Mitchell R. 2016. *The Intercultural Development Inventory (IDI) Resource Guide*. Olney, MD: IDI, LLC.

Hammer, Mitchell R., Milton J. Bennett, and Richard Wiseman. 2003. "Measuring Intercultural Sensitivity: The Intercultural Development Inventory." *International Journal of Intercultural Relations* 27 (4): 421–43. doi:10.1016/ s0147-1767(03)00032-4.

Hussar, William and Tabitha Bailey. 2019. *"Projections of Education Statistics to 2027 (NCES 2019-001)."* U.S. Department of Education, Washington, DC: National Center for Education Statistics.

Krueger, Richard and Mary Anne Casey. 2009. *Focus Groups: A Practical Guide for Applied Research*. Thousand Oaks: SAGE.

Ladson-Billings, Gloria. 2006a. "From the Achievement Gap to the Education Debt: Understanding Achievement in US Schools" *Educational Researcher* 35 (7): 3–12. doi:10.3102/0013189x035007003.

Ladson-Billings, Gloria. 2006b. "Yes, but How Do We Do It?: Practicing Culturally Relevant Pedagogy" In Landsman & Lewis, (eds.), *White Teachers, Diverse Classrooms: A Guide to Building Inclusive Schools, Promoting High Expectations, and Eliminating Racism,* pp. 30–42. Sterling: Stylus.

Lederman, Linda Costigan. 1990. "Assessing Educational Effectiveness: The Focus Group Interview as a Technique for Data Collection." *Communication Education* 39 (2): 117–27. doi:10.1080/03634529009378794.

Lou, Kris Hemming and Gabriel Weber Bosely. 2012. "Facilitating Intercultural Learning Abroad". In *Student Learning Abroad*, pp. 335–60. Sterling: Stylus.

Miles, Matthew B, Michael Huberman, and Johnny Saldana. 2013. *Qualitative Data Analysis: A Methods Sourcebook*. Los Angeles: SAGE.

Milner IV, H. Richard and Tyrone C. Howard. 2013."Counter-narrative as Method: Race, Policy and Research for Teacher Education." *Race Ethnicity and Education* 16 (4): 536–61. doi:10.1080/13613324.2013.817772.

Minnesota Department of Education. 2017. "Report of Teacher Supply and Demand in Minnesota's Public Schools." https://mn.gov/pelsb/assets/2017%20Teacher%20 Supply%20and%20Demand%20Corrected_tcm1113-322217.pdf.

Michell, Lynn. 1999. "Combining Focus Groups and Interviews: Telling How It Is; Telling How It Feels." In *Developing Focus Group Research: Politics, Theory and Practice*, pp. 36–46. Thousand Oaks: SAGE.

Shockman, Elizabeth. 2019. "Bill Aims to Get More Teachers of Color in Minnesota Classrooms." Minnesota Public Radio. https://www.mprnews.org/story/2019/02 /12/bill-aims-to-get-more-teachers-of-color-in-minnesota-classrooms.

Shotton, Heather, E. Star L. Oosahwe and Rosa Cintron. 2007. "Stories of Success: Experiences of American Indian Students in a Peer-mentoring Retention Program." *The Review of Higher Education* 31 (1): 81–107.

Skrla, Linda, James Joseph Scheurich, Juanita Garcia, and Glenn Nolly. 2004. "Equity Audits: A Practical Leadership Tool for Developing Equitable and Excellent Schools." *Educational Administration Quarterly* 40 (1): 133–61. doi:10.1177/0013161x03259148.

Sleeter, Christine E., L. I. Neal, and Kevin K. Kumashiro. 2015. *Diversifying the Teacher Workforce*. New York: Routledge.

Taie, Soheyla, and Rebecca Goldring. 2017. "Characteristics of Public Elementary and Secondary School Teachers in the United States: Results from the 2015–16 National Teacher and Principal Survey First Look (NCES 2017-072)." U.S. Department of Education. Washington, DC: National Center for Education Statistics. Retrieved from https://nces.ed.gov/pubsearch/pubsinfo.asp?pubid=2 017072.

Vaughn, Sharon, Jeanne Shay Schumm and Jane M. Sinagub. 1996. *Focus Group Interviews in Education and Psychology*. Thousand Oaks: SAGE.

Villegas, Ana Maria and Danne E. Davis. 2007. "Approaches to Diversifying the teaching Force: Attending to Issues of Recruitment, Preparation, and Retention." *Teacher Education Quarterly* 34 (4): 137–47.

Villegas, Ana Maria and Jacqueline Jordan Irvine. 2010. "Diversifying the Teaching Force: An Examination of Major Arguments." *The Urban Review* 42 (3): 175–92.

Chapter 8

Lessons and Uses for Studying Inclusivity in Biology

Katherine Furniss, Jacob Jantzer,
Thomas Kirkman, and Kyle McClure

INTRODUCTION

At United States, colleges and universities, introductory biology courses (Biology 101) are among the largest enrolled courses. Existing data and experience indicate that, in the United States, Biology 101 students from systematically disadvantaged groups have poorer outcomes than white students. Furthermore, concern about the differences in the qualitative experience of those students is significant. As a result, Biology 101 represents a high impact inclusion opportunity to improve student experiences by making changes to a single course. We collected data to inform decisions about how to improve the outcomes and experiences of those students. In this chapter, we compile several important lessons for others attempting similar research. First, we learned that coordinating with administrative departments to obtain official data is a difficult process. Recruiting diverse participants was an additional challenge, and researchers had limited time and resources for the research in addition to their typical duties. We also found that while the research reinforced the faculty's anecdotal understanding of student experience, the results did identify areas to target change. Therefore, this evidence-based project focused on the experiences of students from underrepresented minority (URM) groups was particularly valuable for increasing efficiency in curriculum revision. Our research provides a template that can aid in execution of similar projects and smooth the process for institutions or departments engaged in inclusive curriculum revision.

The Becoming Community Initiative on our campuses challenged us to ask ourselves what transformative inclusion means to us. For this group, it means listening to our students, hearing their struggles and accomplishments, taking action to address identified issues, and celebrating successes. We engaged in this work in the context of Biology 101, an introductory biology course. As will be described below, a large fraction of all students pass through this course, so it presents a significant opportunity to address inclusion. Before any transformation can be made, it is necessary to assess the experiences of minoritized groups of students in this foundational course. The information gathered during this preliminary stage will inform the transformative actions to be taken and provide a benchmark to measure changes. In this chapter, we will describe our research process, the theory underlying our approach to transformative inclusion, and the challenges we experienced when carrying out that work.

Institutions that value transformative inclusion must investigate student experiences in courses such as Biology 101, as this is a gateway course for nearly all students interested in Science, Technology, Engineering, and Mathematics (STEM) careers. Students who major in biology, biochemistry, nutrition, and nursing, in addition to most health-related preprofessional programs, are required to take it. Unsurprisingly, this course has high enrollment, especially for first-year students. At the institutions where we carried out our research, combined total undergraduate enrollment is approximately 3,600 students. First-year enrollment is approximately 980 students. Biology 101 typically enrolls approximately 400 students every fall. Therefore, about 40 percent of first-year students take Biology 101 during their first semester. Given the quantity of students enrolled and its timing as a course during the first semester of college, reducing achievement gaps can have a large positive effect.

Our research uncovered significant differences in outcomes for under-represented minority (URM) groups in Biology 101. Achievement gaps are detrimental not only to the individual students but also have broader implications. Attrition of capable students due to achievement gaps contributes to the ongoing shortage of job seekers in STEM fields and to the critical services those careers provide. Additionally, achievement gaps can be barriers for students from URM groups to accessing potentially lucrative and fulfilling careers and reproduce existing inequalities (Hamrick 2019).

Large unanswered questions remain about the experiences of minoritized students in STEM courses, and Biology 101 in particular. These questions are pressing on many levels. First, minimal research has been done on the outcomes and experiences of URM students in small liberal arts colleges.

Therefore, biology faculties have little evidence to reference and incorporate into their work with students.

Second, while biology faculties are invested in student success and inclusion, efforts to deeply analyze disparities have not been undertaken. Lack of time, data, and money had prevented previous close examination of disparities in Biology 101 outcomes and student experience. Additionally, the expertise necessary to design, execute, and analyze this research was not present in the biology department. Solutions to these issues will be discussed later.

Our focus in this chapter is on the process of carrying out the research. Despite institutional support and external funding, we encountered obstacles and complications while completing our work. By sharing our solutions to these difficulties, we hope that other higher-education professionals will be able to avoid or mitigate them. As we will show below, STEM fields must do more to ensure inclusion for all or continue to risk wasting the potential of too many students.

THEORY OF CHANGE

This research begins the process of Planned Approach to Change (Lewin 1947). In this three-step approach, an organization must first *unfreeze* by creating awareness that what is happening does not work for everyone. Our work has a clear role in the process of *unfreezing* by providing information from our students directly to the community members (34–40). For us, this step represents the initial awareness of outcome disparities for students from URM groups compared to nonminority students. While there was little systematic data to rely on, there was some evidence that minority-group students performed less well than nonminority students in Biology 101. The observation of those disparities compelled us to act toward greater inclusion and begin the second step of Lewin's model.

The second step is referred to as *moving* and is broken into four parts: (1) collecting information about the current situation, (2) using the gathered knowledge to identify barriers, (3) creating a plan of action, and (4) taking action. The last step is a *re-freezing* in the current culture and practice (Lewin 1947, 34–40). The results of our research will play a role in the first three parts of the *moving* step. The research will create a local awareness that is more effective than research and data done on a more national scale, or even within other units of the institution. The results will also be used to identify barriers and inform the development of the action plan. Additionally, combining institutional data with student surveys and interviews allows assessment of the action plan.

Table 8.1 **Representation of Race and Ethnicities (expressed in percentage) for U.S Population (U.S. Census Bureau 2019), Science Occupation (National Science Foundation 2017), Fall Enrollment in Postsecondary Institutions (U.S. Dept. of Commerce, Census Bureau, Current Population Survey 2017), and Science Bachelor's Degree (Hamrick, 2019)**

	Population	*Science Occupation*	*Science Bachelor's Degree*	*Fall Enrollment in Postsecondary Institutions*
Black	13.4	6.2	6.6	13.6
Hispanic	18.3	7.0	10.7	18.9
Native American	1.3	0.2	0.4	0.7
More than one race	2.7	1.6	3.4	3.7
White	60.4	62.6	58.5	56.0

Background

In a national context, increased attrition of people from URM groups in STEM fields is common (Chen and Soldier 2013, 18). Little systematic data is available describing rates of enrollment and completion of STEM degree programs for people in these groups. Available information is limited to statistics published in particular research contexts or with little specificity. Table 8.1 compiles data across a variety of sources and illustrates the underrepresentation of black, Hispanic, Native American, and more than one race in science occupations and degrees. Nationally, URM students begin STEM degrees at the same rate as white students; however, they graduate with STEM degrees at a lower rate (Estrada et al. 2016; Beasley and Fischer 2012, 436). Beasley and Fischer found that black and Hispanic students leave STEM majors at higher rates than their gender-matched-white peers (440). Additionally, it is well established on a national level that introductory STEM classes have a high attrition and drop/fail/withdraw rate for all students. This trend was also observed at the institutions where we carried out our research. However, those outcomes are distributed unequally between students from majority groups and students from URM groups (white vs. students of color, first-generation vs. continuing generation, etc.).

   At least some of this attrition can be attributed to the interpersonal cues present in classroom and lab interactions between students from minority groups and their teachers, teaching assistants, and peers (Estrada, Eroy-Revels, and Matsui 2018, 258). For example, smiling is the most common interpersonal cue associated with kindness. Alternatively, avoiding eye contact would have the opposite effect. In our work, we focused on the cues related to the concepts of stereotype threat and kindness cues. Both concepts relate to the sometimes subtle and sometimes overt signals and preconceptions that students and teachers project toward one another.

Stereotype threat, the concern that an individual will confirm a negative stereotype by performing poorly, can affect students' performances. Steele and Aronson initially looked at the effect of stereotype threat on the performance of white and African American students on mathematics tests (1995). They found that black students performed worse on a standardized exam when they were told the results would indicate their intellectual ability. However, when students were told to view the test as a challenge, black students performed similarly to white students (Steele and Aronson 1995, 805). Their work formed the foundation for future attempts to assess the consequences of stereotype threat and develop practices to mitigate its consequences. Particularly, researchers have studied these effects and solutions for women and URMs in the sciences (Steele 2002; Blascovich 2001; Schmader and Johns 2003; Beasley and Fischer 2012).

Their findings demonstrate several key characteristics of learning environments which may exacerbate the effects of stereotype threat. For example, having low numbers of URM students in a classroom can heighten stereotype threat, especially in courses that utilize active learning strategies requiring group work. Also, URM students may experience increased pressure to perform well in a challenging course where students can struggle and may frequently not know or misunderstand concepts (Beasley and Fischer 2012, 436). These examples demonstrate that stereotype threat responses can be triggered by seemingly innocuous teaching techniques. Additionally, it can be extremely difficult to distinguish a student who is "just not putting in the effort" from one who is reacting based on this kind of fear or uncertainty. From behind the teacher's podium, the behaviors and outcomes look the same, even though the causes are quite different.

The inverse of stereotype threat can be thought of as kindness cues (Estrada, Eroy-Revels, Matsui 2018). Kindness cues are essential to developing a sense of social inclusion and belonging. For example, students enter class, especially on the first day, and if they do not know anyone and no one smiles at them, they can feel excluded and it may trigger stereotype threat (Estrada, Eroy-Revels, and Matsui 2018, 263). Feeling included, especially in courses in their major, allows students to develop a social identity that includes their intended discipline (Estrada, Eroy-Revels, Matsui 2018, 266).

The importance of these kindness cues has been echoed on our campus. In a recent panel, students of color were asked what professors do on the first day to let students know that their classroom is a safe space and that they are welcome (Keller et al. 2016). A student quickly answered, "I would look at my professor and see if their eyes rolled straight past me or if they look at me and they smile. Because that's what I'm doing, I am trying to read their face to see whether or not I can feel welcome." A second student chimed in "We can sense it when we feel welcome." Just as with behaviors that can trigger stereotype threat, these kindness cues can be subtle, but their cumulative effect on student comfort and performance is measurable. These small differences are particularly important in the context of STEM-related courses, because those courses are part of a pathway to lucrative career opportunities.

Research demonstrates that incorporating science into one's identity is a strong indicator of persistence in STEM fields, and that persistence opens doors to economic opportunity (Estrada, Eroy-Revels, and Matsui 2018, 266). STEM jobs in the United States are projected to grow by 8.9 percent per year which is 2.5 percent faster than non-STEM occupations. Moreover, those with STEM jobs earn 29 percent more than their peers in non-STEM jobs (U.S. Department of Commerce 2017). However, access to this increasing number of well-paying jobs is not equitable. According to the National Center for Science and Engineering Statistics, racial minority groups (blacks, Hispanics, and Native Americans) are underrepresented in both STEM majors and careers (Hamrick 2019). If students from URM groups are pushed out of STEM-oriented introductory classes, they will likely never gain access to these job opportunities. This is why introductory classes are a critical opportunity for increasing retention of students from URM groups: those early experiences can set the trajectory of a student's education and career.

Many students, particularly those who initially express interest in STEM-related fields, encounter their introductory courses in their first semester. This important period affects a student's future course and career choices. Outcomes in courses in the first semester can influence success in other courses taken in the same semester or later semesters. In fact, success in a course and a sense of belonging can have effects that are seen in higher GPAs and persistence up to two years later (Harackiewicz et al. 2014, 377). Passing Biology 101 is required for many students to move on to the next course in their major. Additionally, the concepts and skills from Biology 101 provide the necessary foundation for these future courses. Therefore, mastery of concepts and skills and the perception of success will affect students as they continue in their STEM degree—or decide to switch majors (Toven-Lindsey et al. 2015, 2).

Currently, demographic changes in the makeup of college student populations further increase the importance of understanding the experiences of underrepresented groups of students. Increasing diversity in a variety of racial/ethnic categories and growth in the proportion of first-generation college students mean that more students will be affected by these early courses. As a result, these established national and local disparities will only be amplified unless educators and institutions take action to mitigate the factors driving differential experiences for majority—and URM students. Achievement gaps, attrition, and the long-term effects all reproduce harm and continue to push interested students out of STEM careers. For students to find success and belonging in STEM careers, it is crucial to understand their Biology 101 experience.

Our research was part of an institution-wide effort to improve inclusivity at a moderately sized liberal arts college in the Midwest. The results of this work will be used to make evidence-based decisions about course design and professional development in all departments, but particularly in STEM disciplines. Once completed, our research will be disseminated to the biology department, and used to modify teaching practices in Biology 101. To provide context for our research, in the next section we will describe the nature of introductory biology at the institution we studied, and the challenges we faced implementing our research strategy.

THE RESEARCH

Biology 101 is the introductory biology course taught at the institution where we did our research. At this institution, underrepresented students enroll in Biology 101 and graduate with science majors in similar percentages to the overall institution's enrollment (table 8.2). It is generally taught in sections of thirty to thirty-five students, with separate lab sections. Each semester there are thirteen to fourteen class sections taught by nine professors and twenty to twenty-one lab sections taught by eleven professors. While some overlap in professors between class and lab exists, most students have a different professor for their class and their lab. This is because staffing and enrollment in courses necessitate the flexibility of separating lab and lecture sections.

Biology 101 classrooms are small lecture format, with a large screen and blackboard at the front, and students seated at tables. While tables could be moved, they typically are left in rows. Chairs in the classroom are on wheels and can allow for small groups to form.

The class and lab experience varies between professors. In addition, there is a wide variety in both general teaching experience and Biology 101 specific

Table 8.2 Demographic Data from 2015 to 2019 for College of Saint Benedict/Saint John's University (CSB/SJU). Values Expressed in Percentages. CSB/SJU Enrollment n = 7575, Sciences n = 2610, Biology 101 n = 2024.

	CSB/SJU enrollment (%)	Sciences (%)	Biology 101 (%)
Black	4.0	4.1	4.6
Hispanic	8.3	9.1	9.6
Native American	0.8	0.9	1.0
More than one race	0.3	0.4	0
White	85.5	84.5	85.5

teaching experience. Most newly hired faculty teach Biology 101. This is often their first semester as a full-time professor, and so they lack prior experience. Some more experienced faculty teach Biology 101 every fall; however, others teach Biology 101 once every three to four years. Therefore, every fall semester Biology 101 instructors are split between about five faculty who teach Biology 101 every year and about four faculty that are either new to the department or teach Biology 101 infrequently.

Not only is teaching experience varied, but pedagogical styles range from mostly active learning to mostly lecture, and some faculty assign regular homework while others do not. While Biology 101 does have shared content and skills goals, the order in which content is delivered and method of teaching and practicing skills is left to the faculty member. Additionally, faculty members may choose a topic area to address those goals. Some choose to address biology by examining biological aspects of race in humans, others aquatic ecology, and so forth. In our data, some students reported that their interests were not aligned with these overarching topics and this detracted from their experience.

Our data shows that students had a wide range of opinion about their Biology 101 professors. Sometimes, different students described the same professors in opposing ways. This is hardly surprising, given existing understandings of student perceptions of professors. It does, however, emphasize the ways in which the same professor and teaching practices can have differing effects from student to student. This demonstrates the importance of professors consciously attending to a diversity of students and student interpretations of their behavior. Particularly for URM students, attending to some of the basic kindness cues could help ensure students feel welcome in the classroom.

Teaching assistants are typically provided in Biology 101 classes, though occasionally a professor may choose not to use one. Teaching assistants are expected to attend every class and facilitate one to two study sessions every week. Teaching assistants are typically students who have earned a B or higher in Biology 101 and range from sophomores through seniors. Teaching assistants receive no uniform training, and while a few professors provide mentoring and training to their teaching assistant, others may not. Our preliminary results indicate that students had widely varying experiences with their teaching assistants. Some were viewed as helpful and open, while others were viewed as incompetent, absent, or unwelcoming. Overall, students did not report the teaching assistants as having a significant impact on their experience in Biology 101.

Biology 101 is generally taken by students in their first semester of college. At the institution we researched, these students typically come directly from high school to college and so are "traditional" college students in age. As in most introductory courses, students exhibit a wide range of prior experience and preparation: some students have taken AP Biology in addition to other science and math classes. However, other students may have taken a biology course as a sophomore in high school and that was their last science course before Biology 101. This varied preparation leads to an array of student experiences in Biology 101. Some find the course to be redundant to their high school courses and express a desire for greater challenge, while others feel the course went too fast and was too hard.

Students in Biology 101 have identified majors in the sciences such as biology, chemistry, and physics, health-related majors like nursing and nutrition science, and preprofessional tracks such as premedicine, preveterinarian, prephysician's assistant as the top three areas for their intended majors. Other majors like those in the humanities, social sciences, and business are selected in much smaller numbers. The top reason students identify for taking Biology 101 is that it is required for their intended major. However, about 40–50 percent of students also say they choose Biology 101 because biology is interesting and useful. Importantly, students have no choice about the courses they are enrolled in for their first semester. So especially for students who may be first-generation college students or from underrepresented groups, there is little opportunity to "stack the deck" of their schedule in the first semester toward courses they believe they will succeed in. Even in this case, several students reported feeling like they knew a lot about biology or were well prepared to succeed but found that Biology 101 was unexpectedly challenging.

Importantly, the challenges presented by staffing, student composition, and variation in instruction are typical of many institutions. Our approach is applicable to any department attempting to increase inclusivity and improve the quality of all students' experience. Common problems face faculty and administrators seeking these improvements: a lack of available data, limited resources, and the need to collaborate across programs to gather a team with the necessary skills to generate solutions.

Research Methods

In this section, we describe the process we used to carry out our research. While many aspects of this process are typical of any social-scientific research, we explain them here in order to shed light on some areas that we believe would be helpful to others carrying out similar projects. At the outset, all the members of the research team shared a commitment to improving inclusivity in general at our institution. That commitment manifested as a shared desire to improve student experience in the classroom, reduce barriers, and understand student perspectives about Biology 101.

As stated before, Biology 101 is a prerequisite for many science and health-related professions. These careers are becoming increasingly important as ways to address the aging human population, human disease, and environmental challenges. Previous research has clearly illustrated the challenges and shortcomings of science classes generally and introductory biology specifically regarding inclusivity. These courses are known to act as gatekeepers to upper division courses and science careers. Reasons for disparity in success often points to stereotype threat, microaggressions, lack of support structures, and a missing sense of belonging (Estrada, Eroy-Revels, and Matsui 2018, 259).

In addition to addressing the general trends described above, the biology department had three primary questions which our research sought to answer. First, did any disparities in Biology 101 outcomes exist that are based on gender, race, or first-generation status? Second, did students from these groups have different experiences from students who were white, continuing generation, and men? Finally, did students from these groups have differing motivations for pursuing STEM and taking Biology 101?

The research team all had some background in pedagogy and teaching best practices. This general knowledge was helpful, but we needed to deepen our understanding of the challenges specific to introductory biology courses. In order to expedite this process, the research team hired a first-year student to assemble an annotated bibliography. This element of the process was successful. The student saved us considerable time and effort gathering resources, particularly as during this early phase of the research we wanted to focus our attention on more time-consuming tasks such as obtaining funding and writing the survey. Our ability to recruit student research assistants was limited because our research involved information about professors and students. However, for the annotated bibliography, the student helped the research team build the background to develop questions that would address previously identified disparities in student experience and outcome, and construct a survey that would be comparable to similar research carried out at other institutions.

The next step in the process was to compile the questions for our survey. Questions regarding demographics required attention to language used to ensure we did not "other" any of our participants. Additionally, length of the survey was an ever-present consideration due to concerns that students would not complete a survey that was too long. As a result, we had to balance the demographic questions we asked against the total length of the survey. We focused on self-identified race, first-generation status, language spoken in the home, gender identity, and identification as LGBTQ+, since these were the categories our experience suggested would have the most impact at our institution.

The questions above, along with questions about student attitudes, motivations, and perceptions as they entered the course, were part of the presurvey. Student participation in the presurvey was voluntary. Students received a series of e-mails requesting their participation in the survey, and professors were asked to provide five to ten minutes in class during the first two weeks of the course and were given standard language to read to the students. Not all professors did this, but students were also able to take the survey on their own time. This differential was probably a significant barrier to gathering a larger sample from the total student population. For other researchers attempting similar projects, getting buy-in from faculty members in the department, or leveraging the authority of department chairs to enforce faculty cooperation might be advisable.

The postsurvey followed the same format of the presurvey (e-mailed link, professors asked to provide time in class during the last two weeks of the course, e-mail reminders). This would allow us to examine any changes in motivations and attitudes about Biology. The postsurvey contained additional questions about the Biology 101 experience. These questions specifically addressed student attitudes and perceptions about their professor, their classmates, as well as pedagogical style and how that affected the student. A subset of these questions can be found at the end of this chapter in Appendix 1: Survey Questions Related to Belonging. Publication of the results of this research along with the complete survey is in progress.

Surveys are an excellent way to collect large amounts of data; however, they may not reveal underlying attitudes due to the prescriptive nature of the questions. Therefore, one-on-one interviews were held in the spring of 2019 for students who took Biology 101 in the Fall of 2018. Students were recruited by posting fliers in several buildings across campus as well as e-mails sent to all Biology 101 students. We made clear that the person doing the interview would be someone outside the department and that no one in the department would be able to identify them based on their demographics or responses.

Interviews were conducted as semistructured retrospective interviews with students recruited directly by the Biology 101 faculty, through a general call for participation, and by existing participants suggesting participation to their peers (snowball sampling). There were thirteen total interviews. Most of the students were nursing majors, and the rest were a mixture of several other majors ranging from English to biology. All the interview participants were women, and three identified as people of color. Several identified as low-income or first-generation, with these identities occasionally overlapping in an individual student. Students discussed their general experience at college as well as their specific experience in Biology 101 in relationship to their identities and personal history.

While the survey and interviews were occurring, we were also examining student records data for Biology 101 students. These data included ACT Math score, letter grade in Biology 101, and grades in other courses during the semester Biology 101 was taken. We looked at these with regards to gender, race, and first-generation status. In addition, we also looked to see if tenured versus nontenured professor made a difference overall or regarding the previous categories.

In order to do these analyses, we had to obtain student information from the Registrar as well as receive Institutional Review Board (IRB) approval for the surveys and interviews. We had a positive experience with our school's IRB. The IRB committee members were helpful with their feedback explaining the sort of justifications required and the required limits on our use of personal identifiable student data. We had a less favorable outcome in attempting to gain access to student records and in the end, we were not able to gain access to all the data we sought. Administrative concerns were expressed in terms of the Family Educational Rights and Privacy Act (FERPA) and sometimes in terms of overworked and understaffed administrators. The privacy concerns precluded sharing the data directly, but the administrative staff were too overworked with their primary tasks to run the analysis for us and provide us with the results. For other researchers, assessing the resources available and administrative infrastructure at an institution may help in avoiding or mitigating similar problems and obstacles. Additionally, institutional prioritization of this work could emphasize the importance of this research and therefore increase the likelihood of administrators making this information available.

Challenges Encountered and Possible Solutions

As mentioned earlier, the biology department had a lack of information or evidence about inclusivity, outcomes, and student perceptions. In order for individual faculty to prioritize research on these topics, it is important that the time and effort put forth by faculty is recognized and valued by departments and the institution. For example, research in this area should count toward tenure and promotion. For those in non-tenure-track positions, it should be explicitly valued during yearly review and continuation of contract decisions.

Additionally, funding to support this work is essential. The infusion of grant funding from an external source allowed our research team to form from disparate academic homes and conduct an in-depth, multimethod examination of inclusion in Biology 101. Assistance identifying and applying for grants related to inclusivity should be supported by institutional offices, and internal funding should be available whenever possible.

The institution can also prioritize inclusivity work by facilitating formation of interdisciplinary teams. The formation of this group was in some ways a random process. Required expertise outside of a typical biologist's training was necessary for our research. The biologist had previously interacted casually with another group member on the topic. The remaining two group members were found by sending many e-mails out and being pointed in the direction that eventually led to the final two group members. Having the larger institution facilitate individuals finding interested group members with expertise in needed areas would remove a barrier to initiating research.

Our research team is a collection of faculty with differing backgrounds. One social scientist (a sociologist), two lab scientists (a biologist and physicist), and one from the humanities (English). On paper, the collection of various skills was a boon for the group—and in many ways this was a reality. However, it also caused some bottlenecks and difficulties as the project progressed.

One source of delay in the project was the amount of work required of the social scientist. In order to maintain confidentiality, student interviews were only accessed by the English and sociology faculty, who carried out the transcription and qualitative analysis. During the research, the English faculty member left the research team when they got another job at a distant location. The new job prevented them from continuing any participation in our project. This meant that the sociologist was now responsible for all interview-related duties. As a result, the project necessarily faced delays. None of the other team members had a background in qualitative research, and while the biologist or physicist might have been able to help with transcription, they were prevented from doing so by confidentiality concerns.

Similarly, quantitative analysis duties were unshared among our team members. The physicist oversaw data analysis and concerns about confidentiality (particularly with student records from the Registrar's Office) made sharing analysis duties difficult. While this was an anticipated part of the structure for our research group, it meant that the physicist was less able to contribute to other elements of the team.

The departure of the humanist from the team also illustrates one of the other significant barriers to completing the research successfully—the adjunct status of the faculty members. Only one member of the team (the physicist) was tenure-track. As adjuncts, none of the other three members of the research team were carrying out this work as a part of their contract. Additionally, they were in a position of weakness in terms of job security. Particularly for the biologist, being the bearer of criticism had shades of risk.

The instability of the team which results from team members being non-tenure-track greatly increases the risk the project will be delayed or derailed. Unfortunately, a reality of the current job market in academia is that adjunct or term faculty members are incentivized to do service and research that extends well beyond the scope of their contracts in order to remain desirable candidates for continued work at their current jobs or to prospective new employers. Coupled with the real desire these faculty members have to be useful and contribute to their institutions, it is unlikely they will solely teach, even at liberal arts colleges and universities where teaching is the main emphasis. Term faculty can make valuable contributions—this project demonstrates that. However, caution should be taken when teams are largely made up of term faculty, and one or more team members are likely to leave the institution over the course of a multiyear project.

Survey design was an important focus as it was a major form of data collection. With few examples of surveys that readily applied to our area of interest, we designed our own, and this has attendant problems. As is common in survey research, our results indicated that students may not have been interpreting some questions in the way intended. While we were able to pilot our survey with a group of students from the previous year, the subsequent revisions may have introduced new communication problems. More thorough testing, including having a group of students test take the survey and then meet with a faculty member to provide feedback on the wording, would have been helpful.

As mentioned, an undergraduate student was utilized during the early stage of literature review and we would highly recommend utilizing students in this role of literature search. Our student produced a high quality and useful annotated bibliography. Additionally, we would recommend identifying political science or education majors to help conduct interviews and complete transcription and coding. These areas were a bottleneck in this project and the inclusion of students could benefit the faculty while providing valuable experience to the students.

The research team decided to use an internal survey tool (Forms Manager). While several of the faculty had used the tool before, none had extensive familiarity with all of the features. Therefore, the first round of surveys in fall 2018 had been set up in a way where the pre- and post-survey responses couldn't be connected. Therefore, we could not match pre- and posttest surveys together. This kind of technology problem is partially not only due to the inexperience of the team members in creating pre- and posttest designs in the Forms Manager tool but also due to the need to coordinate with the Registrar's Office. Originally, we intended for the Registrar's Office to send out the invitation to participate, and then they would be able to link the students' academic records with their survey responses. Moreover, misunderstanding about how that was to happen led to the research team inadvertently setting up the survey in such a way that it was not possible to connect pre- and posttest participants' data to other student records. Since much institutional research requires interfacing with many units of the institution, attention should be paid to ensuring that each party knows which duties it has claimed.

Another survey issue, as with most surveys, was the response rate. Of the 389 students enrolled in Biology 101 in fall 2018, 78 percent took the presurvey and 53 percent took the postsurvey. Of the 396 students enrolled in

Biology 101 in fall 2019, 45 percent took the presurvey and 47 percent took the postsurvey. This is an acceptable but not ideal response rate, despite our efforts to utilize best practices for this sort of research (Dillman, Smyth, and Melani Christian 2009, 233). It would be worthwhile to determine ways to better advertise and promote the survey with students as well as determine what incentives work best for students. One explanation for the decreased rates in fall 2019 was fewer professors providing time in class for students to complete the survey. Each department should determine the best way to provide this time.

Much like survey completion, there were issues with interviewee recruitment. Most of the interviewees were similar in their demographics (white women, continuing generation students, majoring in nursing). Interviews were done during a semester when many other minigrants studying campus inclusivity were also being executed. It is possible that students of color, first-generation, and so forth felt fatigued by all the requests for their time and input. Institutions should be mindful about coordinating and staggering research projects that require student input. Additionally, fliers and e-mails can be lost in the barrage of fliers and e-mails students are exposed to. Perhaps individual fliers handed out in class by Biology 101 professors would make a more direct impact on recruitment of interviewees. Lastly, it is possible that students feared retaliation. While it was clearly stated that a faculty member not involved or connected to the biology department would be completing the interviews and identifying information would be removed, students may not have internalized this or feared it would not be followed. This concern is another reason why having students in education or political science majors be the interviewees and transcribers could be beneficial.

Was It Worthwhile?

The clear answer to this is yes! Reading about what has been experienced and done in other departments is helpful, but nothing is more motivating that hearing from your own students. The timing of the research project and results was also beneficial. The biology department underwent program review during the research project and received the results during the process of developing an action plan. The coinciding of the two meant action plan items specific for Biology 101 could be guided by the results. The research results allowed for a narrowing down of relevant actions to take and ensured the department responded to their students' needs.

In addition to providing recommendations for changes, we were also able to celebrate successes with biology faculty. We do not observe a difference in grades between women and men in Biology 101. One explanation for the parity of performance between men and women in Biology 101 at this institution is that the women hear many empowering messages across multiple mediums. A second possibility is that Biology 101 is predominantly taught by women faculty. In fall 2019, of the thirteen sections, ten were taught by women. The three sections with male professors had female teaching assistants. Additionally, women are in the obvious majority (67 percent) in the Biology 101 classroom. Finally, some research has identified race as the primary identity related to feelings of stereotype threat, while gender had a minimal role (Beasley and Fischer 2012, 437).

Our results indicate that a greater understanding of our students' experiences and perspectives as well as a consideration of inclusivity in this high enrollment, required course is important. Biology 101 grades, survey responses, and interview data suggest that there are disparities in outcomes and experiences for URM students at this institution. For example, interview responses reveal that students' experiences were often not directly discriminatory, but a confluence of identities/factors often made the courses especially difficult for URM students. While these students generally didn't feel they were particularly excluded or treated differently in the class, they did experience being a social outsider and this may indirectly impede their success. In turn, they will be less likely to continue into careers in STEM and medicine, with all the detrimental effects noted before.

CONCLUSION

These results point to the value of this type of inclusivity research. Restrictions on time and resources require that inclusivity work be targeted at the areas of greatest need. In our case, while we saw that current efforts to include women have largely been successful, additional work is necessary to achieve similar benefits for URM students. Knowing this information improves the chances of success in inclusivity initiatives in the future and helps to point to further research necessary to better understand the specific needs of URM students. None of this would be possible without our work, and therein lies the value of inclusivity research for all institutions seeking greater equality for students.

Overall, this project is only a small part of the important work of building inclusive campus environments. We were successful in carrying out our project, but we encountered challenges that we hope others can learn from. Particularly, budgeting adequate time for projects, expecting difficulty accessing student records, getting buy-in from faculty members, and ensuring the integrity of the data collection process are all pitfalls we hope others can avoid. In the end, our research has pointed to several possible areas the Biology 101 faculty can engage in which should help to reduce students' experiences of stereotype threat and improve outcomes.

APPENDIX 1: SURVEY QUESTIONS
RELATED TO BELONGING

1. I was well prepared for Biology 101.
2. My Biology 101 professor cares about me as a person.
3. I am comfortable asking questions in Biology 101.
4. The professor takes my questions and concerns seriously.
5. I feel uncomfortable seeking help from my professor outside of class.
6. I feel my grade reflects my knowledge.
7. Sometimes I feel I don't belong in the class.
8. I often feel excluded from peer or group interactions.
9. I have a community of classmates and we help each other learn.
10. My race affects the way my classmates think about me.
11. My race affects the way my professor thinks about me.
12. My gender affects the way my classmates think about me.
13. My gender affects the way my professor thinks about me.
14. My confidence in my academic abilities grew as a result of the course.
15. Interactions with my classmates contributes to my academic confidence.
16. My learning style was not reflected in class activities and assignments.
17. Understanding Biology 101 content is fundamental for my career goals.
18. Academically, it is important to me to do well in Biology 101.
19. Personally, I want to do well in Biology 101.
20. I am in fact doing well in Biology 101.
21. I had a bad experience in Biology 101, so I changed my academic plans.

REFERENCES

Beasley, Maya A., and Fischer, Mary J. 2012. "Why They Leave: The Impact of Stereotype Threat on the Attrition of Women and Minorities from Science, Math and Engineering Majors." *Social Psychology of Education: An International Journal* 15 (4): 427–48. doi:10.1007/s11218-012-9185-3.

Blascovich, J., Spencer, S. J., Quinn, D. M., and Steele, C. M. 2001. "African Americans and High Blood Pressure: The Role of Stereotype Threat." *Psychological Science* 12 (3): 225–29. doi:10.1111/1467-9280.00340.

Chen, X., and Soldier, M. 2013. "*STEM Attrition: College Students' Paths into and out of STEM: Fields Statistical Analysis Report (2013).*" Washington, DC: National Center for Education Statistics. www.nces.ed.gov/pubs2014/ 2014001.rev.pdf.

College of Saint Benedict and Saint John's University Digital Commons. 2016. "What CSBSJU Students of Color Want Their Faculty to Know." YouTube video, April 4, 2016. https://www.youtube.com/watch?v=M773AoyOIZA.

Dillman, D. A., Smyth, J. D., and Christian, L. Melani. 2009. *Internet, Mail, and Mixed-Mode Surveys: The Tailored Design Method.* Hoboken, NJ: John Wiley & Sons, Inc.

Estrada, M., Burnett, M., Campbell, A. G., Campbell, P. B., Denetclaw, W. F., Gutiérrez, C. G., Hurtado, S., John, G. H., Matsui, J., McGee, R., Okpodu, C. M., Robinson, T. J., Summers, M. F., Werner-Washburne, M., and Zavala, M. 2016. "Improving Underrepresented Minority Student Persistence in STEM." *CBE Life Sciences Education* 15 (3): es5. doi:10.1187/cbe.16-01-0038.

Estrada, M., Eroy-Reveles, A., and Matsui, J. 2018. "The Influence of Affirming Kindness and Community on Broadening Participation in STEM Career Pathways." *Social Issues and Policy Review* 12 (1): 258–97. doi:10.1111/sipr.12046.

Hamrick, Karen. National Science Foundation, National Center for Science and Engineering Statistics. 2019. *Women, Minorities, and Persons with Disabilities in Science and Engineering: 2019*. Special Report NSF 19-304. Alexandria, VA. https://ncses.nsf.gov/pubs/nsf19304/digest/field-of-degree-minorities.

Harackiewicz, J. M., Canning, E. A., Tibbetts, Y., Giffen, C. J., Blair, S. S., Rouse, D. I., & Hyde, J. S. 2014. "Closing the Social Class Achievement Gap for First-Generation Students in Undergraduate Biology." *Journal of Educational Psychology* 106 (2): 375–89. doi:10.1037/a0034679.

Lewin, Kurt. 1947. "Frontiers in Group Dynamics: Concept, Method and Reality in Social Science; Social Equilibria and Social." *Human Relations* 1 (1): 5–41. doi:10.1177/001872674700100103.

National Science Foundation, National Center for Science and Engineering Statistics, National Survey of College Graduates. 2017. See table 9-7. https://ncses.nsf.gov/pubs/nsf19304/assets/data/tables/wmpd19-sr-tab09-007.xlsx.

Schmader, T., and Johns, M. 2003. "Converging Evidence that Stereotype Threat Reduces Working Memory Capacity." *Journal of Personality and Social Psychology* 85 (3): 440–52. doi:10.1037/0022-3514.85.3.440.

Steele, C. M., and Aronson, J. 1995. "Stereotype Threat and the Intellectual Test Performance of African Americans." *Journal of Personality and Social Psychology* 69 (5): 797–811. doi:10.1037/0022-3514.69.5.797.

Steele, C. M., Spencer, S. J., and Aronson, J. 2002b. "Contending with Group Image: The Psychology of Stereotype and Social Identity Threat." In *Advances in Experimental Social Psychology*, edited by Mark Zanna and James Olson, vol. 34, pp. 379–440. San Diego, CA, USA: Academic Press.

Toven-Lindsey, B., Levis-Fitzgerald, M., Barber, P. H., and Hasson, T. 2015. "Increasing Persistence in Undergraduate Science Majors: A Model for Institutional Support of Underrepresented Students." *CBE Life Sciences Education* 14 (2): ar12. doi:10.1187/cbe.14-05-0082.

US Census Bureau Quick Facts. Available at https://www.census.gov/quickfacts/fact/table/US/PST045219.

U.S. Department of Commerce. 2017. *STEM Jobs: 2017 Update*. https://www.commerce.gov/news/reports/2017/03/stem-jobs-2017-update.

U.S. Department of Commerce, Census Bureau, Current Population Survey (CPS), October Supplement, 2000, 2010, and 2017. See Digest of Education Statistics 2018, table 306.30 https://nces.ed.gov/programs/digest/d18/tables/dt18_306.30.asp?referrer=report.

Chapter 9

Building Inclusivity in the Spanish Classroom

Bridging the Gaps between Latinx and Heritage Speakers and Second-Language Learners

Emily Kuffner, Tania Gómez, and Sarah Schaaf

According to the US Census Bureau, Hispanics constituted 18.3 percent of the nation's total population in 2019 making this group the nation's largest ethnic or racial minority. One outcome of this rapid demographic growth is that Latinx[1] students have been pursuing college education in increasing numbers. In the higher education blog Cuellar (2018) reported that in 2015, 67 percent of Latinx students enrolled in college immediately after high school as compared to 49 percent in 2000. Therefore, understanding the diversity among this population can help colleges and universities more intentionally serve and support their success. Likewise, the Latinx population has recently grown in areas that traditionally have had less Latinx representation due to increased internal migration from states in the Southwest, South, and Northeast United States to cities in the Midwest, North Carolina, and Washington (Cuellar 2018). This geographic shift creates new challenges for institutions of higher education as they serve an increasingly diverse population and offer support to underrepresented communities. Since the Latinx population constitutes such a large segment of the population, institutional efforts to promote diversity and increase inclusivity must include significant attention to the needs of Latinx students. Moreover, demographic shifts also demand attention to language instruction, since some estimates indicate that the United States will contain 128 million Spanish speakers by 2060 (Milla 2019, 1) and bilingualism is projected to continue to rise.[2]

Like many other institutions across the United States, ours have seen a significant rise in Latinx population. According to admissions data, the rise went from 2.5 percent in 2010 to around 8 percent of the student body in 2019–2020 (272 out of a total student body of 3,463 in fall 2019). Concurrently, our campuses have been affected by racial and ethnic tensions that can divide the student body. The most notable example occurred during the 2016 election when a group of seemingly intoxicated young men were filmed loudly chanting "Build that Wall" on the bus that connects our campuses. The incident was filmed and posted on social media, provoking community outcry and protests by students who demanded that the administration act to promote inclusion and address perceived anti-Latinx bias. In this chapter, the authors who are all teachers of Spanish, examine the academic and administrative challenges of teaching language courses in two small, majority white, rural, joint liberal arts colleges where there is minimal exposure to Spanish-speaking populations outside of the classroom. We argue that the language classroom is an ideal space to build cultural bridges toward transformative inclusivity that we hope can reduce ethnically charged incidents such as the aforementioned. We also reiterate, as many other authors have suggested (see Milla 2019; Carreira and Kagan 2011; Bowles, Toth, and Adams 2014; Potowski 2002, among others), that the needs of Latinx students are distinct from other "students of color" and that the category "students of color" used by our own institutions and many others, while part of a well-intentioned desire to promote diversity and inclusion, can obscure significant differences in the pedagogical needs of distinct minority groups, especially those who decide to attend language courses or courses in which Spanish is the main means of communication.

In order to discuss the challenges and opportunities for inclusion and language learning posed by changing demographics, we first briefly summarize linguistic research that indicates that heritage speakers of Spanish and learners of Spanish as a second language should be in separate classrooms. We then turn to the challenges posed by such findings for smaller institutions, whose less populous student body often does not allow for the implementation of such a model. Then, we consider how to use mixed classrooms of both heritage learners and second-language learners as a space to build cultural bridges that allow us to simultaneously reach two very distinct student populations and increase cross-cultural and language competency. Our approach incorporates direct observations of students in mixed classrooms, observation of a pilot course, and research data from anonymous student surveys that indicate the nuanced nature of the challenges to building a truly inclusive classroom environment. Lastly, we present strategies we have begun to implement in order to reenvision the language classroom as a critical site for building inclusivity in an era of declining support for the humanities. We suggest that language departments should become focal points to create dynamic outreach networks to and for Latinx students. This meaningful connection can provide a point of departure that could assist institutional efforts to promote diversity and inclusion.

CHALLENGES OF INTEGRATING HERITAGE SPEAKERS IN THE CLASSROOM

Studies have demonstrated that Latinx students are a remarkably diverse group in terms of racial identity, language skills, cultural and socioeconomic background, and other factors that create a diverse spectrum of needs (see Beaudrie 2012; Carreira 2007; Potowski 2002, among others.). Admissions data from our institution substantiates this finding and indicates the diversity of students who identify as heritage speakers. Some may have Spanish-language skills, while others will have had no exposure to Spanish. According to Torres, Cabo and Beusterien, even among recent immigrants, "due to becoming acculturated to mainstream US culture, they [heritage speakers] are oftentimes left with meager knowledge of their family history and ancestry" (2017, 271). With regard to language skills, upon entering the American education system, students whose first language is not English quickly develop linguistic competency in English. Use of the Spanish language, therefore, serves a social and familial role so that although a heritage speaker may not be fluent in Spanish, the language may be an important element of cultural identity.

Although Latinxs may have significant exposure to Spanish, this is usually provided in nonacademic contexts so that their linguistic competency cannot be compared to the "traditional" second-language students, who have learned Spanish in a purely academic setting. Bowles, Toth, and Adams (2014, 499) indicate that

> [Latinxs] often possess a more restricted lexicon and range of registers than monolingual speakers. . . . They also have shown difficulties in [. . . grammatical constructs such as . . .] gender agreement (Montrul, Foote, and Perpiñan 2008; Polinsky 2006), tense, aspect, mood distinctions (Lynch 1999; Montrul 2002; Polinsky 2006; Silva-Corvalán 1994), and differential object marking (Montrul and Bowles 2008), among other [. . .] [linguistic differences].

Given the distinct linguistic characteristics of Latinxs exposed to Spanish, researchers in language learning and teaching normally refer to them as heritage speakers. A heritage speaker is defined as an "individual who was raised in a home where [. . .] [Spanish] is spoken, who speaks or only understands the heritage language and who is to some degree bilingual in English and the heritage language" (Valdés 2001, 1). These students may struggle to find an entry point into an academic system and language classrooms that are set up to meet the needs of monolingual students.

Studies of second-language acquisition indicate that heritage speakers who decide to enroll in language courses have significantly different pedagogical needs than "traditional" second-language learners.[3] While second-language learners often feel stronger in writing than speaking skills, the reverse is generally true for heritage speakers. At our institutions, students must obtain proficiency in a second language by either being exempted if they are already proficient in English and at least one other language or by completing the third semester of language instruction. Written intake questionnaires administered by our office of Academic Advising to incoming freshmen who stated that they were already proficient in a language other than English ask students to describe their listening and speaking skills in that language. One student, who we will call "Jaime,"[4] states: "I grew up speaking Spanish. At one point, it was my first language. Once I started attending pre-school, I grew accustomed to English." Other students identify their level of fluency as low, such as "Leslie" who in the same questionnaire states "I think that I'm good at understanding the language but have trouble speaking" it. The majority of heritage speakers self-assessed stronger speaking than writing or reading skills. Many students explained that, while they speak Spanish in the home, they read and write primarily or only in English, such as "Robin," "at home I only speak and listen to Spanish, I would like to perfect my reading and writing." Since heritage learners often have much more advanced oral abilities than reading or writing skills, they can give the impression of greater fluency than they possess (Boon and Polinsky 2015, 7).

As a result of the continuing increase in the number of heritage students entering higher education, including for our context, many language departments and instructors have worked on designing or adapting language placement exams that work for this particular group of students (see Fairclough, Belpoliti, and Bermejo 2010; Fairclough 2006, among others). While some rely on standardized tests such as the Avant Spanish Heritage Language (SHL)—a test that measures grammar, verb use, spelling, and vocabulary unique to heritage learners—other institutions prefer creating their own tests of students' language competency in which they include a language background questionnaire (Fairclough 2006, 595; Potowski 2002, 41). The standardized tests are designed with the second-language learner student in mind, and even those specifically designed for heritage students contain grammar-based questions that assume familiarity with metalinguistic terms, which can lead to students being misplaced in a class that is too advanced for their linguistic competence (Boon and Polinsky 2015, 10). Misplacement creates challenges for the heritage learner who does not possess the same background in the formal study of grammar as their second-language learner peers at an equivalent level of oral fluency. Our institution piloted the placement by using the Avant SHL test, but nonetheless encountered misplacements of heritage speakers within our language curriculum. For this reason, we have reverted to a time-consuming process of individualized interviews with heritage learners. This has created institutional challenges since these interviews can only be conducted by trained faculty, of which we have a select few, and students and their advisors may be unaware that overriding test placement is an option for them.

Although heritage speaker programs foster increased cultural awareness and strengthen affiliation to Hispanic communities, they also present pedagogical issues for teachers. Heritage speakers often feel that they are "not good at" the heritage language or that their form of the language is "incorrect" since they frequently experience criticism from native speakers for grammatical or lexical errors in the heritage language. In addition, they may face discrimination or marginalization for speaking a non-English language. As such, building positive affective experiences and confidence are often important elements of language learning for heritage speakers. Alongside these heritage language programs, many researchers, policymakers, administrators, and practitioners have worked on easing the experiences of heritage speakers in academic settings. Examples include the National Heritage Language Resource Center (at the University of California, Los Angeles), which is devoted to heritage language education and research; the Heritage Language Journal; the Alliance for the Advancement of Heritage Languages at the Center for Applied Linguistics; conferences and workshops devoted to heritage language issues; and many journal articles, books, and dissertations.

Of colleges and universities with a significant Latinx population (>5 percent), approximately 40 percent implement heritage learner courses, and this number is increasing (Carreira 2012b, 227). Although programs such as these are more likely to be offered at larger institutions (Beaudrie 2012, 204), our smaller student body makes maintaining separate classrooms very difficult. Likewise, the Midwest is behind the national trend, and there are fewer classes specifically designed for heritage learners despite growing Latinx populations (Beaudrie 2012, 204). Therefore, as is the case at our institution, instruction of heritage speakers and second-language learners usually still takes place in "mixed" classrooms. This presents several drawbacks for each group of learners. Second-language learners can be challenged to move toward greater cross-cultural competency, and many may see Latinx culture as "other" or "foreign," creating a cultural divide within the mixed classroom. In terms of affective needs, second-language learners can feel inferior to and intimidated by heritage language learners' greater oral fluency. Conversely, heritage speakers may be intimidated by second-language learners' greater exposure to explicit grammar instruction. Challenges for heritage language learners can come from the instructors themselves, who often privilege one variant of Spanish as "'correct'" and label students' heritage dialect and tendency to speak in a more informal register as incorrect.[5] Furthermore, heritage learners perceive the mixed classroom as a challenge since they tend to underestimate their own Spanish fluency, pronunciation, and comprehension, while the teacher tends to overestimate their ability based on oral fluency (Beaudrie 2012). Beaudrie concludes that "traditional foreign language classes are unsatisfactory for SHL [Spanish Heritage Language] students and . . . separate language courses for heritage language learners are necessary to meet their specific needs" (Beaudrie 2012, 213). Improving outreach to Latinx students and building a strong heritage speaker program that meets the needs of heritage speakers could increase institutional affiliation in these underserved groups. While the literature documents that offering separate heritage language classes has pedagogical benefits for both heritage learners and second-language learners, praxis often lags behind research. For example, our department attempted to create a heritage speaker class to allow heritage speakers to increase their lexicon, learn some of the grammar rules governing Spanish, and prepare them for academic work in Spanish. However, low enrollment prevented us from being able to continue offering such a course. This is often an administrative impediment, since heritage speaker courses are likely to be under-enrolled at least initially.

Additionally, the declining support for humanities in higher education presents administrative challenges in getting smaller sections approved. Statistically, languages are often the first programs or departments to be cut in moments of budget crisis and non-English language classes were more affected by the 2008 recession, with 12 percent of language programs cut compared to 6 percent of humanities programs in general (Johnson 2019). The *Chronicle of Higher Education* reports that 651 non-English language programs were cut from colleges and universities across the country in the last three years (Johnson 2019). Although we believe that implementing heritage language courses at our institutions could give us a competitive edge in providing exemplary academic services to an increasing Latinx population, we have come to see the creation of a separate heritage speaker track as a long-term ideal, while the immediate reality requires that we find best practices to teach mixed classes. Thus, we seek to utilize our classroom as a space to build cultural bridges that allow us to simultaneously reach two very distinct student populations and increase cross-cultural competency while building language skills. Since mixed classrooms often focus primarily on the needs of second-language learners, creating language-learning practices that address heritage speakers' needs is an issue of inclusivity. We will return to this argument subsequently to describe some initiatives and activities we have implemented or will be implementing soon to optimize the use of mixed classroom spaces.

MIXED CLASSROOMS AS A CULTURAL BRIDGE: OUR RESEARCH AND FINDINGS

To address the distinct pedagogical challenges, language programs specifically designed for heritage speakers have emerged around the country (see Beaudrie 2012; Boon and Polinsky 2015). These programs' goals are to increase the opportunities to use and to be exposed to the heritage language, to challenge dominant social hierarchies, to model and construct positive linguistic and cultural identities, and to serve as a site for the development of literacy skills in the heritage language. The heritage language classroom can be empowering for students whose culture has been marginalized and effaced within mainstream US culture.

While our department was implementing a pilot course for heritage speakers that was ultimately cut due to low enrollment, our institutions sought to improve the overall campus climate with regard to inclusivity. With funding from the Andrew W. Mellon Foundation, our institutions surveyed student opinions regarding perceived inclusivity and found that students of color often felt they were subtly marginalized through racialized microaggressions and other forms of exclusionary behavior in and out of the classroom.[6] Our team of researchers sought further funding to survey the perceptions of our Latinx population, since we hypothesized that their perspectives may have been subsumed within a broad category of "people of color" that some Latinx people may not identify with and that obscures ethnic identity within racialized identity categories.

We initially surveyed all students in language classes or attending language events; however, we found that out of the seventy-six surveys we collected, only six were from heritage speakers. Therefore, we conducted a second survey targeting heritage speakers using admissions data, keeping the results anonymous, that resulted in a further sixty-three surveys from Latinx students who self-identified as heritage speakers. The survey consisted of six multiple choice questions asking students to identify their gender (male/female/ other), academic year, whether they identified as Hispanic/Latino (yes /partly (some)/ no), whether Spanish was spoken in the home or community they grew up in, ranking whether they personally felt included in the campus community on a scale of one to five, and whether the institutions are perceived as a welcoming environment for Latinx/Hispanic students (yes/ somewhat /no). The second half of the survey presented seven more open-ended questions asking students to identify services they are aware of on campus for Latinx/

Hispanic students, clubs and organizations for Latinx/Hispanic students they were aware of, asking if they had participated in these clubs and organizations and if so how this affected sense of community at our organization, and for additional comments and suggestions "to better integrate the Latinx or Hispanic community" within the broader institutional community. This research bore out our initial hypothesis that Latinx identities were not fully encompassed by the category of "students of color" since several students asserted that institutional events focused on minority issues and efforts to improve the campus climate for "students of color" are implicitly aimed at black students and that Latinxs are marginalized and their identity obscured even within a well-intentioned effort to improve inclusivity.

Research data from the aforementioned heritage speaker survey indicates the nuanced nature of the challenges to building a truly inclusive classroom environment. For example, while many students felt that the student-run Latin American cultural club was an integral part of their feelings of belonging on campus, such as "Mariel" who states that the club "is the reason I feel like I have a place and a voice on campus. Its where I feel at home and my authentic self. It makes me proud of where I came from and my culture," minority groups within the Latinx community such as Afro-Latinos sometimes feel unwelcome at the same club, with several students commenting that the club is, in "Miguel's" words "mostly Mexican . . . and I feel like they don't include that [Afro-Latinx identity]," is "focused on the Mexican-American culture, and not the rest of the Hispanic countries and cultures," or that, as "Nina" asserted, if you "don't look Latinx" you don't fit in. "Ana" commented that "I have been told by other Hispanic/Latinx students that . . . I'm not really a Mexican especially since I don't look like it . . . I know my appearance is the first to be judged on and I frequently feel out of place so I don't attend events I would like to attend." As these anecdotes attest, students who belong to the dominant minority group—those who identified as Mexican-American—within the diversity of Latinx identities had a distinct experience from those who hold a more marginalized Latinx identity, including those who "look White," and those who are Afro-Latinx, as well as students whose heritage is non-Mexican. Thus, even with efforts to promote inclusivity and greater representation, students with marginalized identities can experience micro or even macroaggressions and patterns of exclusion.[7]

Heritage speakers' experience at a primarily white institution has allowed them to suggest a number of pathways to greater inclusivity. For example, students in the above-mentioned heritage speaker survey would like to see our campuses become sanctuary schools to build affirming relationships and create a familial-like environment among students, faculty, and staff members.[8] Heritage speakers also call for psychological and physical safe school spaces as well as a variety of events that could help them affirm their racial/

ethnic pride. Our survey data demonstrates that Latinx students would like to see more recognition of their heritage celebrations, stating "I want Hispanic Heritage to be taken as seriously as MLK day." Building caring relationships between students, faculty, and staff members has been a challenge for our institutions—as well as many others—due to factors such as our rural location and the lack of diversity among faculty in comparison to the student body.[9] It is not surprising to see that Departments of Spanish or Hispanic Studies, in our institution and nationally, are often the only department in which Latinx professors are well represented. A rural location also creates a challenge to attract a diverse faculty body. An area with little ethnic and racial diversity may not be an attractive place to live for members of underrepresented groups.

In response, our administration joined the Consortium for Faculty Diversity in 2017 which seeks to increase the racial diversity of faculty members. With an ever-increasing population of Latinx students, we should actively be seeking to hire more Latinx faculty, staff, and administrators who can serve as mentors and role models to our students. Faculty mentorship is a key means to retain students and for Latinx students to see their culture reflected in the curriculum. However, this work should be rewarded through service credit or other forms of institutional recognition so that underrepresented faculty are not simply given more workload and responsibility.

In creating a familial-like school environment, we argue—as confirmed by our survey data—for the need to create dynamic outreach networks to Hispanic and Latinx students to build institutional affiliation among this growing demographic. For example, our campuses, which adhere to a Catholic religious affiliation, have a campus ministry that puts on bilingual cultural event celebrations such as Our Lady of Guadalupe mass or *Las posadas* celebrations (a Christmas tradition). Such events can be key moments to create community among Latinx students and can also benefit second-language learners who are able to come into contact with Spanish outside the classroom. Several other events to create a familial-like environment have been proposed in the institutional plan *Actions Toward a More Inclusive CSB/SJU 2017-2019* (Actions 2017) that describes institutional strategies to promote inclusivity and diversity. Some of these events include a mass in Spanish once a month on campus, participation Latinx cultural celebrations such as *la Quinceañera Mass* and *Día de los Muertos*, and the presence of Latinx speakers on our campuses.

The last pathway to inclusiveness reported by Latinx students—and directly connected with creating a familial-like school environment—was their desire to see more on-campus events available that allow them to express racial and ethnic pride and see current events addressed. Thus, students asked that the current immigration debates be addressed directly in the classroom, seeing this as a way to support students who felt that their heritage was under attack. One student, "Tony," stated that "both my parents being non-citizens are the possibility of being deported [*sic*], my brothers taking to foster care, and I have to leave school for work and regain my brothers—it is a constant thought behind my back how I could lose everything" and "Tony" wanted others to understand "our current situation and how much we [immigrants] have done for the United States." Other events could include lectures delivered by Latinx speakers, films in which immigration topics are raised, and student cosponsored events such as cooking classes and Latin dance nights.

USING MIXED CLASSROOMS TO
FOSTER CAMPUS-WIDE CHANGE

Latinx students polled during our research also felt that the majority white population of our colleges did not understand or respect their cultures. Without detracting from the importance of the aforementioned campus-wide solutions, we propose to consider how to use mixed heritage and second-language learner classrooms as a space to build cultural bridges that allow us to simultaneously reach two very distinct student populations and increase cross-cultural competency while building language skills. We assert that promoting a cultural environment that draws on the strengths of heritage learners to add cultural focus in mixed classes can allow us to address issues of identity, biculturalism, and bilingualism that can foster second-language learners' understanding of the politics of language and identity. On the other hand, this must be done while avoiding tokenizing heritage speaker students by putting them in a position of representing all members of their culture(s). Similarly, heritage speakers cannot be expected to use their greater oral fluency to act as unpaid tutors who assist second-language learners during class.

The language classroom can provide an ideal space to examine the structural practices of racism in other cultures that can nuance student views of the nature of race and racism. By studying Latinx identities, students confront race as a constructed category by grappling with different definitions of race that trouble US-centric categories such as "person of color" or categories such as "white" that do not exist in the same way in other countries. Consequently, we believe it is essential to build transnational content into entry-level courses such as First-Year Experience and similar courses and to continue to build transnational analysis throughout all students' college careers. By building cross-cultural understandings of identity categories, students are forced to confront their own socially constructed racial categories.

On the other hand, any account of culture in the language classroom must keep in the forefront that students need to make connections with their own culture and be aware of the diversity of the Spanish-speaking world, including within the United States. Intercultural knowledge about other Latinx groups in the United States could have an impact on the heritage speakers' community of practice and perspectives (Burgo 2017, 8). One way this can be done is to effectively and mindfully pair or group learners to draw on the strengths of each type of learner: mixed groups of heritage speakers and second-language learners should perform tasks that are challenging to both types of learners, and should divide work so that each works in an area that is of greater challenge to them. This can allow heritage learners to assist second-language learners to maintain a fluent conversation through their greater oral ability and larger command of vocabulary, while second-language learners can support heritage speakers in writing tasks using their usually higher grammatical and orthographic competence. Having a mixed-level language class also necessitates the inclusion of differentiated tasks that learners can complete at their own rate since second-language learners will often complete writing tasks more quickly, while heritage speakers may complete oral tasks more rapidly. However, "it is important to strive to equalize the amount of work and the interest level of the activities . . . such that all students feel that they are being treated fairly" (Carreira 2012, 17). The mixed classroom approach also allows heritage speakers to reinforce their identities, reconnect with their heritage culture, and expand their cultural competence by becoming aware of other Latino groups in the United States or other Spanish-speaking countries cultures.

THE LANGUAGE CLASSROOM AS
CULTURAL AMBASSADOR

The language classroom can be a powerful site to build inclusivity and awareness of Latinx culture that can impact and change the broader campus culture, and we have implemented a number of strategies and programs based on our research that we believe could be replicated or adapted to other institutions and by other departments. First, we believe that the language classroom can be a powerful space to build cultural awareness of the United States as a Spanish-speaking country. The United States has the second-largest number of Spanish speakers of any nation after Mexico, and the number is increasing daily (Burgen 2015). However, if Spanish as a heritage language is not culturally valued, we risk losing the rich resource of bilingual language skills since subsequent generations become more dominant in English, gradually losing the heritage language over several generations. By making the language classroom a space that recognizes the value of heritage language and culture within our largely immigrant nation, we can provide students with a powerful sense of pride in their culture that may inspire them to keep language skills vibrant.

Spanish is not a foreign language in the United States, yet language textbooks rarely present the United States as a site of Spanish-speaking culture. Our cultural offerings must include a profound recognition of the United States as a Spanish-speaking country. For example, instructional material might include visual analysis of Latinx murals in cities such as Minneapolis or San Francisco, readings taken from Spanish-language authors who write in the United States, or from the growing number of works written in Spanglish or other bilingual forms. By seeking out a local Hispanic cultural context, we can also support our second-language learners—who on our campuses may have come from an area where they have never had contact with Spanish as a native language—to appreciate the rich Hispanic heritage of the United States and see the applicability of classroom language learning to their post-college experience. This content will also benefit heritage speakers who wish to see more respect and visibility given to Hispanic cultures.

Another opportunity to build community between second-language learners and heritage speakers may lie in linguistic contact zones. By utilizing materials written in stigmatized variants that bridge the boundaries of language through 'Spanglish' and related mixed language variants, we can provide fertile territory to address the living and evolving nature of language in a way that could raise confidence in both linguistic groups. Second-language learners may find these texts more accessible than texts written entirely in Spanish, while heritage learners are provided with an example of multiidentity cultural expression; these materials may also raise the linguistic confidence and improve attitudes of heritage speakers who speak a stigmatized variants analyzed in class.

Due to the rural location of our institution and the demographics of Latinxs in our area, we seek connections with the local community to increase visibility of local Latinx cultures in order to encourage student engagement. Such efforts include local excursions to Latinx supermarkets and restaurants and other Latinx-owned businesses. We strive to invite local speakers from surrounding communities who are Latinx business owners or who serve Latinx communities such as interpreters, health-care providers, and others. While there is no perceptible Latinx presence in the town closest to our campuses, there is a significant Latinx population in other towns as close as a few miles away, a fact of which students not from the local community may not be aware. We also seek out local volunteer opportunities to provide that allow students to engage with the Spanish language in an authentic context. For example, our students volunteer as interpreters for a food bank in a neighboring town that contains a significant Latinx population, mostly recent immigrants who work in the local meat-packing plant. Other informal interpreting opportunities include the yearly Christmas toy drive. This opportunity exposes students to Spanish as a spoken language within the United States and does not require a high level of linguistic ability. Similarly, we build connections with local institutions that serve a Spanish-speaking population such as the Catholic Church in the aforementioned town that holds Spanish-language masses weekly. Students from our campuses frequently visit the congregation to volunteer in various capacities, such as giving flu shots.

We believe that it is also important to offer events that are not academically but culturally motivated. For example, musical events provide another opportunity to create cultural affiliation. On several occasions, we have invited a local Salsa band to perform on our campuses. By exposing heritage speakers and second-language learners to Spanish through lyrics and through dance instruction in Spanish (offered by one of the members of the aforementioned Salsa band) students are able to participate without being restricted by their background knowledge or language skills. Such activities lower affective filters, thereby increasing motivation to participate in future events. Likewise, this event highlights Hispanic cultural heritage in our area and racial diversity and cultural history through brief explanations of musical origins given by the lead singer, and through the diverse racial composition of the band itself which contains several Afro-Cuban members. Having local and national community members present on our campuses has assisted in creating institutional affiliation in the Latinx and heritage speaker populations on current topics such as immigration, economy, social movements in Latin America, and so forth. These events have been very well attended, attracting up to two hundred students and are offered free of charge to all members of the community. We believe that holding free events is especially important to create an inclusive environment since even a low entry cost can be a barrier for students who may be struggling to meet basic needs (see Heying and Nash's chapter on food insecurity in this volume). We also seek to raise the visibility of Spanish and English/Spanish contact languages on campus by using Spanish-language content in posters and other promotional materials around campus to provide an authentic example of Spanish as a US language. Long-term, we also hope to develop a podcast with student-created content that would highlight Latinx culture on-campus and in the surrounding community and that would contain content in both English and Spanish.

Creating a truly inclusive community requires that we foreground marginalized categories within Latinx identities. Student comments regarding the way that a student club devoted to promoting Latinx heritages excludes certain groups like Afro-Latinxs even within an effort to combat stigma highlights the need to pay attention to patterns of exclusion within subordinated identities. In response to this problem, we have begun a targeted response to bring greater visibility to ethnic and racial variety within the Latinx population in and outside the United States. In building strategies to address racial and ethnic diversity within the Latinx population, we have invited an expert to address the differing needs of heritage speakers in the language classroom in order to increase awareness of the significant presence and distinct pedagogical needs of these students. In this event, the members of our language departments, most of whom did not receive formal training during their graduate work in teaching heritage students, were given strategies to better meet the needs of these students. The event was open to the community in general and was attended by a number of students including heritage speakers, members of other departments, and even teachers from local secondary schools. The speaker also offered a lunch workshop that targeted heritage speakers and was specifically designed for students who were considering careers in education and those majoring in Hispanic Studies.

A book discussion group open to students, faculty, and staff might also provide an opportunity to address racial and linguistic diversity. Such groups could include readings and discussions about the stigmatized variants of Spanish, the journeys of immigrants in the United States, and the experiences of Latinx in higher education. Also, it would be significant to include Latinx writers who have published with the heartfelt intention of sharing their own experiences as immigrants in this country. For example, Junot Díaz's *The Brief Wondrous Life of Oscar Wao*, or Esmerelda Santiago's *When I was Puerto Rican,* or T.C. Boyle's *The Tortilla Curtain.* Similarly, we seek to incorporate works from well-known authors including Erika Sánchez (novelist, poet, and essayist), Luis Trelles (journalist) and Sandra Cisneros (poet and novelist). It is also suggested that faculty from Hispanic Studies or Spanish departments create book or reading suggestion lists that could be incorporated into our common curriculum courses. Increasing faculty familiarity with US Latinx writing and critical theory may encourage the analysis of Latinx heritage across departments.

CONCLUSION

In summary and as discussed throughout this chapter, despite the growth of the Latinx population across the country and efforts made by some colleges and language departments, the trend is to continue to have mixed classrooms in which heritage speakers and second-language learners are grouped together. Since this academic model fails to take full advantage of the rich bilingual resource presented by heritage language speakers, we have suggested several pathways to transform the language classroom into a critical site to build inclusivity, strengthen diversity and promote cultural competency while at the same time enriching heritage speakers and second-language learners' linguistic experience by utilizing the strengths of each to complement learning and support the others' weaknesses.

Instead of waiting until incidents of cultural misunderstanding, exclusionary behavior and/or institutional discrimination occur, we need to prepare students, staff, and faculty to engage in productive classroom and institutional discussions through collaborative work. Offering academic and nonacademic opportunities and events on campus and in nearby communities fosters inclusivity for our Latinx student population and as a result, we can contribute to a vibrant and evolving meaning of "heritage" that is beneficial to both Spanish-language instruction and heritage studies. Therefore, the activities and events outlined above are not just ancillary curricular appendages but rather indispensable additions to Spanish programs. It is important to note that the activities proposed here are limited by the geographical scope and the financial restrictions of our institution. We will continue to study the impact of such activities on our own campus and encourage other institutions to collect similar data on student perceptions of campus climate and institutional affiliation among marginalized groups, including Latinx and heritage speaker students. Although Heritage languages are in danger of dying out over the course of only a few generations if the language is not fostered, valued, and encouraged, the multicultural and multilingual nature of our student body should present an opportunity for the humanities as students come into our classrooms with rich cultural and linguistic resources that will allow them to proceed quickly to advanced level classes. We hope that our research will assist our department in designing future curricula and will inform our community and faculty at large in curricular and pedagogical decisions as Latinx populations continue to grow.

While our work with heritage students focuses on language teaching, our approach could be adapted to a number of disciplines within the humanities by addressing the need to include more interdisciplinary and translinguistic content across the curriculum. We urge other institutions to pay greater attention to Latinx identities and cultures and to intersectional forces of race, gender, and class within Latinx identities as an integral part of efforts to promote inclusion on campus, both in the language classroom and across the curriculum. As the number of heritage speakers increases across the United States, campuses will need to consciously take their needs into account in order to create pathways to success for all students.

NOTES

1. Because of their diversity, there are various terms to describe this minoritized group. The first term, "Hispanic," may encompass individuals who identify

as Afro-Hispanic, white, indigenous, or as a mixture of these racialized categories. "Hispanic" includes individuals with heritages from Spanish-speaking countries. Another term, "Latinos/Latinas," refers to individuals with ancestry in Latin America. In recent years, the term "Latinx" has also emerged—a term adopted for gender inclusivity that captures multiple intersectional identities—to refer to US born people who have a diversity of experiences with the Spanish language and its culture. The preference of identification varies by region and by institution. In this chapter, we use the term "Latinxs" when referring to the group in general terms, but heritage speakers when discussing Latinxs with reference to their participation in courses where Spanish is the main means of communication or learning.

2. According to Francois Grosjean (2018), there was a steady increase of the percentage of bilinguals between 1980 and 2016. In 1980, the percentage of bilinguals was 10.68 percent whereas in 2016, it was 20.14 percent, practically a doubling of the number. Adding a few percentage points to take into account those not included in the survey, the proportion of bilinguals today is probably around 22 percent of the total population.

3. According to Bowles, Toth, and Adams 2014, there are several linguistic reasons that explain why heritage speakers enroll in college Spanish classes including maintaining their speaking and listening skills, developing literacy skills, and broadening their knowledge of formal and professional registers. In addition, affective reasons include the desire to connect socially and individually with their ethnic background and form cultural connections with Spanish-speaking communities.

4. All names used are pseudonyms.

5. As Boon and Polinsky assert, this bias can be conscious or unconscious (2014, 10). Valdés et Al. demonstrate that educator bias favored certain varieties of academic Spanish over others (Valdés et al. 2008).

6. Recent scholarship has developed the term racial microaggressions to explain the "racial stereotypes, insults, and alienation . . . students [of color] . . . experience from peers, staff, and faculty at the university" (Morales, 2014: 49).

7. Macroaggressions occur at a structural level encompassing actions that are intended to exclude, either by action or by omission (Osanloo, Boske, and Newcomb, 2016: 6).

8. Delgado (2019: 253) defines sanctuary schools as institutions that "at minimum have openly expressed an unwillingness to cooperate with Immigration and Customs Enforcement (ICE) when there is an effort to arrest someone who is undocumented" or refuse to allow ICE on campus without a warrant.

9. Despite efforts designed to diversify the academy across colleges and universities in the United States, persons of color continue to be underrepresented in faculty positions in higher education (see Rucks-Ahidiana, 2019; Smith, Yosso, and Solorzano, 2006; Trower and Chait 2002). According to the National Center for Education Statistics, in fall of 2013 among all postsecondary institutions in the United States, faculty of color included Black/African Americans (6 percent), Latina/os (5 percent), Asian/Pacific Islanders (10 percent), and American Indian/Alaska Natives. By 2017, among all full-time professors nationally, the numbers indicate a worrisome decline in Black/African American and Latinx professors: 81 percent were white, 11

percent were Asian/Pacific Islander and Black/African Americans and Hispanics each accounted for 2 percent (NCES 2017). The disparities are more extreme when relative seniority and prestige of academic positions is factored in; Latinx professors make up about 7 percent of lecturer and 8 percent of instructor positions, but only 3 percent of full professors (NCES 2017).

REFERENCES

"Actions toward a more inclusive CSB/SJU 2017-2019." 2017. Report. College of Saint Benedict and Saint John's University.

Beaudrie, Sara M. 2012. "Research on University-Based Spanish Heritage Language Programs in the United States: The Current State of Affairs." In *Spanish as a Heritage Language in the United States: The State of the Field*, edited by Sara M. Beaudrie and Marta Fairclough, pp. 203–222. Georgetown: Georgetown University Press.

Boon, Erin, and Maria Polinsky. 2015. "From Silence to Voice: Empowering Heritage Language Speakers in the 21 Century." *Informes del Observatorio del Instituto Cervantes* 1–27. doi:10.15427/OR007-01/2015EN.

Bowles, Melissa, Paul Toth, and Rebecca Adams. 2014. "A Comparison of L2-L2 and L2 Heritage Learner Interactions in Spanish Language." *The Modern Language Journal* 98 (2): 497–517. doi:10.1111/modl.12086.

Bowles, Melissa, and Silvina Montrul. 2014. "Heritage Spanish Speakers in University Language courses: A Decade of Difference." *ADFL Bulletin* 43 (1): 112–122. doi:10.1632/adfl.43.1.112.

Burgen, Stephen, 2015. "US Now Has More Spanish Speakers than Spain- Only Mexico Has More." *The Guardian.* June 29. https://www.theguardian.com/us-news/2015/jun/29/us-second-biggest-spanish-speaking-country.

Burgo, Clara. 2017. "Culture and Instruction in the Spanish Heritage Language Classroom." *Philologica Canariensia* 23: 7–17.

Carreira, María. 2007. "Spanish-for-Native-Speaker matters: Narrowing the Latino Achievement Gap Through Spanish Language Instruction." *Heritage Language Journal* 5 (1): 147–171.

———. 2012a. "Basic Principles for Teaching Mixed Classes." *National Heritage Language Resource Center.* http://nhlrc.ucla.edu/.

———. 2012b. "Meeting the Needs of Heritage Language Learners: Approaches, Strategies and Research." In *Spanish as a Heritage Language in the United States: The State of the Field*, edited by Sara M. Beaudrie and Marta Fairclough, pp. 223–240. Georgetown: Georgetown University Press.

Carreira, María, and Olga Kagan. 2011. "The Results of the National Heritage Language Survey: Implications for Teaching, Curriculum Design and Professional Development." *Foreign Language Annals* 44 (1): 40–64. doi:10.1111/j.1944-9720.2010.01118.x.

Cuellar, Marcela. 2018. "Understanding Latinx College Student Diversity and Why It Matters." *Higher Education Today.* A blog by American Council on Education.

https://www.higheredtoday.org/2018/01/29/understanding-latinx-college-student
-diversity-matters/https://www.higheredtoday.org/2018/01/29/understanding-lati
nx-college-student-diversity-matters/.

Delgado, Olga. 2019. "Sanctuary Cities, Communities, and Organizations: A Nation
at a Crossroads." *Social Work with Groups Journal* 42 (3): 253–255. doi:10.1080
/01609513.2018.1560120.

Fairclough, Marta. 2006. "Language Placement Exams for Heritage Speakers of
Spanish: Learning from Students' Mistakes." *Foreign Language Annals* 39 (4):
595–604. doi:10.1111/j.1944-9720.2006.tb02278.x.

Fairclough, Marta, Flavia Belpoliti and Encarna Bermejo. 2010. "Developing an
Electronic Placement Examination for Heritage Learners of Spanish: Challenges
and Payoffs." *Hispania* 93 (2): 270–289.

Grosjean, Francois. 2018. "The Amazing Rise of Bilingualism in the United States."
Psychology Today. https://www.psychologytoday.com/us/blog/life-bilingual/
201809/the-amazing-rise-bilingualism-in-the-united-states.

Johnson, Steven. 2019. "Colleges Lose a 'Stunning' 651 Foreign Language Programs
in Three Years." *Chronicle of Higher Education,* January 22. https://www.chronicl
e.com/article/Colleges-Lose-a-Stunning-/245526.

Lynch, Andrew. 1999. "The Subjunctive in Miami Cuban Spanish: Bilingualism,
Contact, and Language Variability." Doctoral dissertation. University of Minnesota,
Minneapolis, MN.

Milla, Fabiola. 2019. *Designing a Curriculum to Engage Heritage Speakers in a
Spanish Classroom.* Master Theses Projects, Otterbein University.

Morales, Erica. 2014. "Intersectional Impact: Black Students and Race, Gender and
Class Microaggressions in Higher Education." *Race, Gender and Class* 21 (3/4):
48–66.

Montrul, Silvina. 2002. *Incomplete Acquisition in Bilingualism: Re-examining the
Age Factor.* Philadelphia: John Benjamins.

Montrul, Silvina and Melissa Bowles. 2008. "Negative Evidence in Instructed
Heritage Language Acquisition: A preliminary Study of Differential Object
Marking." In *Selected Proceedings of the 2007 Second Language Research Forum,*
edited by Melissa Bowles, Rebecca, Foote, Silvia, Perpiñán, & Rakesh Bhatt, pp.
252–262. Somerville, MA: Cascadilla Proceedings Project.

Montrul, Silvina, Rebecca Foote and Silvia Perpiñán. 2008. "Gender Agreement in
Adult Second Language Learners and Spanish Heritage Speakers: The Effects
of Age and Context of Acquisition." *Language Learning* 58 (3): 503–553.
doi:10.1111/j.1467-9922.2008.00449.x.

National Center for Education Statistics. 2017. "*The Condition of Education 2017
(NCES 2017 144).*" Washington, DC: U.S. Department of Education. https://nces
.ed.gov/fastfacts/display.asp?id=61.

Osanloo, Azadeh, Christa Boske and Whitney Newcomb. 2016. "Deconstructing
Macroaggressions, Microaggressions, and Structural Racism in Education:
Developing a Conceptual Model for the Intersection of Social Justice Practice
and Intercultural Education." *International Journal of Organizational Theory and
Development* 4 (1): 1–18.

Polinsky, Maria. 2006. "American Russian: Incomplete Acquisition." *Journal of Slavic Linguistics* 14 (3): 191–262.

Potowski, Kim. 2002. "Experiences of Spanish Heritage Speakers in University Foreign Language Courses and Implications for Teacher Training." *ADFL Bulletin* 33 (3): 35–42. doi:10.1632/adfl.33.3.35.

Rucks-Ahidiana, Zadawi. 2019. "The Inequities of the Tenure-Track System." Inside Higher Ed. https://www.insidehighered.com/advice/2019/06/07/nonwhite-faculty -face-significant-disadvantages-tenure-track-opinion.

Silva-Corvalán, Carmen. 1994. *Language Contact and Change: Spanish in Los Angeles*. Oxford: Oxford University.

Smith, William, Tara Yosso and Daniel Solorzano. 2006. "Challenging Racial Battle Fatigue on Historically White Campuses: A Critical Race Examination of Race Related Stress." In *Faculty of Color Teaching in Predominantly White Colleges and Universities*, edited by Christine Stanley, pp. 299–327. Bolton, MA: Anker Publishing.

Torres, Julio, Diego Cabo and John Beusterien. 2017. "What's Next? Heritage Language Learners Shape New Paths in Spanish Teaching." *Hispania* 100 (5): 217–276. doi:10.1353/hpn.2018.0066.

Tromer, Cathy and Richard Chait. 2002. "Faculty Diversity: Too Little for Too Long." *Harvard Magazine* 104 (4): 33–38.

Valdés, Guadalupe. 2001. "Heritage Language Students: Profiles and Possibilities." In *Heritage Languages in America: Preserving a National Resource*, edited by J. Peyton, J. Ranard, and S. McGinnis, pp. 37–80. McHenry, IL: Center for Applied Linguistics and Delta Systems.

———. 2006. "Making Connections: Second Language Acquisition Research and Heritage Language Teaching."In *The Art of Teaching Spanish: Second Language Acquisition from Research to Praxis,* edited by Rafael Salaberry and Barbara A. Lafford, pp. 193–212. Georgetown: Georgetown University Press.

Valdés, Guadalupe, Sonia V. González, Dania López García, and Patricio Márquez. 2008. "Heritage Languages and Ideologies of Language: Unexamined Challenges." In *Heritage Language Education: A New Field Emerging,* edited by Donna Brinton, Olga Kagan, Susan Bauckus, pp. 107–130. New York: Routledge.

Webb, John B. and Barbara L. Miller. 2000. *Teaching Heritage Language Learners: Voices from the Classroom.* New York: American Council on the Teaching of Foreign Languages.

Chapter 10

Creating an Inclusive Learning Environment in Exercise Science Education

Mary Stenson, Donald V. Fischer,
Janelle Hinchley, and Janna LaFountaine

INTRODUCTION

Exercise Science is the study of biological, sociocultural, and behavioral aspects of human movement with primary application to human health and exercise/sport performance. There are numerous subdisciplines within exercise science such as exercise physiology, kinesiology, sport psychology, sport nutrition, and physical activity epidemiology (Dunn 2009, 270). While other terms are used to describe the field such as kinesiology or sport studies, we will use the term "exercise science" to describe programs of study that include both natural and social science aspects of the discipline (Dunn 2009, 270). We chose this terminology because it most closely resembles our own department, ESSS, at a small, private, liberal arts college in the Midwest United States. We offer a minor course of study with three full-time faculty. A new major in Exercise and Health Science will begin in fall 2020. Exercise science programs typically serve students interested in cardiac rehabilitation, coaching, personal fitness training, corporate wellness, strength and conditioning, global and public health, and physiology or biomechanics research. Additionally, students can pursue graduate studies in exercise science, medicine, physical therapy, nursing, occupational therapy, sports medicine, and teaching. Increasingly, exercise science programs are important for serving students interested in rapidly growing allied health fields the most common of which are physical therapy, occupational therapy, cardiac rehabilitation, and athletic training (Barfield et al. 2012, 164).

Exercise science and related allied health fields have limited representation of minoritized individuals (Brooks et al. 2013, 147; Barfield et al. 2012, 165). Exercise science undergraduate programs and the larger allied health workforce served by those programs have not kept pace with shifting population demographics in the United States (Hodge and Wiggins 2010, 36; Brooks et al. 2013, 147). For example, in 2015, only 7.7 percent of occupational therapists identified as racial or ethnic minorities ("Salary & Workforce Survey" n.d.). Additionally, in 2016–2017 the American Physical Therapy Association indicated that merely 18.3 percent of physical therapists identified as racial or ethnic minorities ("Physical Therapy Workforce Data" n.d.).

Exercise Science is a unique discipline because its subdisciplines encompass natural and social sciences. For example, most undergraduate programs include areas of study in the natural sciences such as exercise physiology and biomechanics, as well as social science courses such as sport and exercise psychology and sport sociology (Brooks et al. 2013, 153). Humanities and social sciences seem to lend themselves to discussions of diversity and inclusion in ways that are less tangible for the natural sciences. Students often disassociate natural science courses with nonscience courses where discussions of sociocultural issues commonly take place (Favero and Van Hoomissen 2019, 561). In 2013, Brooks and colleagues listed leading journals which published works on diversity and inclusion in kinesiology and exercise science; however, the journals and topics listed were in social science subdisciplines (Brooks et al. 2013, 149). While other STEM fields have made progress toward discussions about increasing diversity, there is little discussion of diversity in natural science-based subdisciplines of exercise science (Bergstrom 2018, 1; Johnson 2019, 365; Killpack and Melón 2016, 1; Dunn 2009, 271).

Much like other STEM fields, exercise science and its subdisciplines are built on a small subset of privileged voices that often fail to recognize the diversity that exists among humans (Ram, Starek, and Johnson 2004, 251). To best support inclusion in the field of exercise science, faculty and administrators need to be prepared to welcome and support an increasingly diverse student body (Brooks et al. 2013, 147; Hodge and Wiggins 2010, 36), call attention to gaps and blind spots in exercise science research on and by minoritized groups (Favero and Van Hoomissen 2019, 562; Lujan and DiCarlo 2018, 414; Ram, Starek, and Johnson 2004, 251), and create space for discussions about diversity and inclusion in health and human performance. These changes are especially necessary at primarily white and undergraduate institutions where the pipelines into exercise science and allied health careers begin (Hodge and Corbett 2013, 163; Hodge and Wiggins 2010, 45).

Bowen and Bok (1998) note that diversity in higher education "helps institutions achieve three objectives central to their mission—identifying individuals with high potential, permitting students to benefit educationally from diversity on campus, and addressing long-term societal needs" (Bowen and Bok 1998, 278). In addition to striving for greater representation of minoritized individuals in exercise science, we must also create space in our programs for open dialogue about diversity that allows all students to benefit. Discussions of diversity in exercise science are important because we will increasingly see diverse students in our classrooms, laboratories, clinics, athletic teams, and fitness facilities (Brooks et al. 2013, 145; Finch and Blankenship 2011, 32). Students will ultimately work with people in clinical or public settings which necessitate an awareness of diversity and inclusion (Hulme 2010, 272). This awareness will help students be better healthcare professionals. Additionally, awareness of the influence of power structures (e.g., race, gender, and class) and how they affect health and human performance are essential to developing client-centered exercise science professionals with the agency to create change. The American Medical Association, for example, has emphasized the importance of integrating cultural knowledge into premedicine coursework ("The Core Competencies for Entering Medical Students" n.d.). Moreover, there is inherent value in recruiting and retaining diverse students and faculty such that we all benefit from diverse perspectives (Brooks et al. 2013, 147). Broader and more diverse perspectives allow for varied approaches to problem-solving, increased awareness of the perspectives of others, and decreased use of stereotypes (Brooks et al. 2013, 147).

As educators, we need to be able to support our diverse students and create environments in and out of the classroom in which people feel supported to learn in community with others. We also want to develop faculty who feel comfortable addressing bias in research and practice that marginalizes diverse persons (e.g., most physiology is based on the male model or we make incorrect assumptions about race without proper evidence which then affect health care). Throughout this chapter, we will refer to the model described by Lowrie and Robinson (2013), wherein exercise science departments can build effective, inclusive learning communities by understanding and engaging the self, others, and the systems in which we learn, work, and live (Lowrie and Robinson 2013, 174). Understanding and engaging must be followed by assessment, adjustments, and closing the feedback loops such that changes are continuously assessed for effectiveness (Banta and Blaich 2011, 26).

Brooks and colleagues (2013) call on the exercise science community to "continue to conduct research on curriculum impact, students' attitudes and behaviors, learning outcomes, and student retention, and supporting the educational value and benefits of diversity" (Brooks et al. 2013, 147). In answering Brooks's call, we were drawn to Lowrie and Robinson's (2013) emphasis on the importance of "departments to self-reflect and ask if they are addressing the needs regarding the recruitment and retention of students and faculty of color" (Lowrie and Robinson 2013, 171). When we began the process of self-reflection as a department, we fully recognized that we have low representation of minoritized students, which is consistent with our institutions as a whole; however, we genuinely want to build an inclusive community where students and faculty of color feel they are welcome. The inclusive climate we strive for "requires inclusive leadership; respect for multiple identities of the full community; an understanding of the value of the collective demographics; and a willingness and commitment to engaging in the educational process of learning about self, other, and the system in which the community exists" (Lowrie and Robinson 2013, 172).

Through self-reflection, we realized that we were not taking an active approach toward transformative inclusion and our course content surrounding diversity and inclusion was limited to social science courses (e.g., Culture and Sport, Gender and Sport). We recognized we were not helping our students understand the "intersectionality of science and sociocultural issues" (Favero and Van Hoomissen 2019, 561). A result of our self-reflection was to identify ways to highlight diversity and inclusion efforts in exercise science that are useful inside and outside the classroom as well as across the various natural and social science subdisciplines of exercise science. We strive to engage all faculty and students in discussions of privilege, discrimination, and inclusion and not simply rely on our social science and humanities faculty or minoritized faculty to take on the work of inclusion in our department. As white faculty, we can recognize our own privilege and be advocates and allies for change and effective mentors for all of our students and colleagues (Lowrie and Robinson 2013, 174).

The goal of this chapter is to empower other exercise science professionals to examine their own diversity and inclusion practices and to provide concrete examples of actionable change. In the spring of 2018, we embarked on a process of self-reflection and information gathering by prioritizing increasing awareness of the needs of our minoritized students. We sought to determine if our current practices were effective at creating an inclusive program both inside and outside the classroom. From the information we gained from our students, conversations with campus partners and inclusion leaders, and investigations of how other programs create inclusive learning communities, we developed and began implementing a number of actionable steps toward improving access and inclusion in our own exercise science program that may serve as a model for others.

OUR PROCESS

Our primary goal was to examine the effectiveness of our small ESSS department in creating an accessible and inclusive community for students. We wanted to reflect on and gather student perceptions of the departmental climate for students from minoritized groups including factors that influence the students' perceptions of the climate, the perceived strengths and weaknesses of the department in providing an inclusive learning environment, and suggestions for change. We also wanted to gauge the accessibility and equity of the curriculum and cocurricular opportunities. Finally, we wanted to determine if the department provided a sufficient number of opportunities within and outside courses for students to engage in discussions of diversity and inclusion. Our goal in exploring these issues was to learn how we might create a more inclusive learning community.

We used a mixed-methods design to answer our questions. Quantitative data was obtained from various institutional offices and through a survey sent to students enrolled in ESSS courses (16.6 percent response rate; $N = 90$). Qualitative data was obtained from open-ended survey questions and focus groups of students enrolled in ESSS classes in the previous two years. Because of the small numbers of minoritized students at our institutions and within our department, we chose not to statistically compare responses of minoritized to nonminoritized students.

The student survey consisted of demographic questions, forced-choice questions, and open-ended questions about how students perceive the culture of the department and courses in areas of diversity, inclusivity, and accessibility. ESSS faculty developed the survey questions from a foundation of questions from the institutions' student senior survey and in consultation with campus partners and inclusion leaders. At the end of the survey and through an e-mail announcement, students were recruited to participate in small focus groups. The focus groups were conducted in a semistructured manner by a facilitator not associated with the department. Preplanned questions were developed in response to student survey data to help us better understand student responses. In addition to the preplanned questions, the facilitator asked follow-up questions to obtain more detailed responses when necessary.

Additional demographic data about students enrolled in ESSS courses were obtained from the Registrar, the institutional Office for Planning and Strategy, and Student Accessibility Services. Each office provided different information about our students in aggregate data only. None of the researchers had access to individual student data obtained from these offices. The Registrar provided course enrollment data and general demographic data including race/ethnicity, gender, and first-generation college status. The Office for Planning and Strategy provided aggregated data on family income, SAT/

ACT scores, and selected data from student entrance and exit surveys for our minoritized and nonminoritized students. Student Accessibility Services provided the number of ESSS students eligible for learning accommodations.

The demographic data and forced-choice survey responses provided detailed information about who our students were, and their general perspectives on our departmental practices in areas of course content, pedagogies, and student-faculty relationships both inside and outside the classroom. Overall, we found that although there are very few minoritized students in our department, the department student population is similar to the institutional profile. The focus group and open-ended responses helped us give context to the survey and demographic data to further understand the perspectives of our students. In analyzing the qualitative data, we identified three main conclusions: content promotes awareness, effective inclusive pedagogies, and strong relationships.

First, we identified that our students, especially our minoritized students, perceive we are doing an adequate job of promoting inclusive and accessible environments within and outside of our courses. For example, some students shared the following feedback:

- "A lot of students have the mindset that because it's a science class, it is not the place to bring it up, but most of the professors are great and open to discussion." (minoritized student)
- "I personally appreciate if it [diversity] is acknowledged even once, and I feel that the ESSS professors don't mind putting aside class material to discuss these issues." (minoritized student)
- "They are always professional and fair. Example: men v. women pay in the workplace. My professor said that women deserve equal pay for equal work." (minoritized student)
- "It [discussions of race and ethnicity] is satisfactory but could be bolstered by the social aspect." (minoritized student)
- "Health and Fitness touches on socioeconomic status and gender, as well as location and access to service, but we don't talk a lot about other social identities." (non-minoritized student)

In reviewing student responses, we took pride in many of our students' comments about our willingness to be open, approachable, welcoming, and inclusive. Overall, our students felt we discussed content in a way that increased awareness of social issues and connected those issues to class content at an introductory level.

Second, ESSS students noted that department faculty effectively used inclusive and accessible pedagogies. Students felt faculty would be comfortable and willing to have conversations about controversial topics, faculty valued all students' opinions, and made sure everyone in the class was heard. For instance, our minoritized students shared the following comments:

- "If I asked to talk about [controversial topics], I think that they would be more than willing."
- "While stuff in the news may not be directly addressed, professors are aware and understanding of students' want to participate."
- "They make it clear that you cannot hide in the back, you must be involved in dialogue."
- "The professors value everyone's opinion and don't put anyone down. They express this through their tone of voice, what they say after you speak, and expanding on students' points."

We also found that our use of small group work in many classes was viewed favorably, especially because small groups help students find ways to engage with each other such that they can learn from each person's unique experiences and perspectives (Finch and Blankenship 2011, n.p.). Students also commented that they find our courses to be academically challenging and that our faculty make sure students know they are a resource and are available to help.

Third, most students commented on the strength of their relationships with faculty. They indicated that we were approachable, welcoming, accessible, and that they perceived us to be comfortable talking about difficult concepts. For example, our minoritized students shared the following:

- "All of the professors make you have name cards, so they learn your name. To me, this shows that they want to know you and your opinion. There is a wide range of acceptable answers, but professors can challenge your thinking. They want to make sure you can make informed arguments."
- "Our professors are very good on inclusivity—they just see us as students who want to learn and help you anyway they can. My professor is willing to meet with me inside and outside classroom."

Students indicated that their level of comfort and strength of relationships with ESSS faculty were our strongest characteristics. This is notable because strong mentoring relationships are listed as one of the most important contributors for future success of minoritized students and faculty (Hodge 1997, 181; Hodge, Brooks, and Harrison 2013, 205; Johnson 2019, 370; Hodge and Corbett 2013, 163).

From our examination of focus group and open-ended survey responses, we were able to identify areas of needed change in our departmental practices in three areas: (1) content promoting awareness of diversity, (2) inclusive pedagogies, and (3) building strong relationships. In the area of course content, we recognize that there are important and relevant topics we can cover in more depth. Students were especially interested in more thoughtful discussions about gender and sexuality issues in sport, especially the experiences of women and LGBTQ+ athletes. Within the theme of inclusive pedagogy, we can better prepare our faculty for leading discussions about controversial social topics and explicitly integrating current social issues into the course content in an intentional way. Many minoritized and non-minoritized students commented that they did not see connections between courses addressing natural science content and discussions about diversity, equity, justice, and inclusion. In the theme of strong relationships, we can continue to build strong mentoring relationships with our students by making ourselves accessible for conversations outside of the classroom, encouraging constructive dialogue on social issues, and helping students become agents of change.

Finally, we developed two main outcomes or goals to work toward in addressing student suggestions in our course content, pedagogies, and student relationships. The first is that we will strive to intentionally integrate topics of diversity, equity, justice, and inclusion in our courses. While there is evidence of this practice currently, we feel that making explicit connections between these topics and class content will help students more clearly see how content, even in our natural science-based courses, can be influenced by issues of diversity, equity, justice, and inclusion. Connecting course content to these topics will inform students about how evidence-based decision-making is influenced by disciplinary ethnocentrism. The second goal is to model and intentionally encourage students to be agents of social change by explicitly encouraging their participation in campus events and helping students develop the skills they will need to influence change on campus and in the broader community. Our hope is that by working through Lowrie and Robinson's (2013) model of examining self, others, and systems we can create an inclusive learning community for all of our students and faculty (Lowrie and Robinson 2013, 174).

The following section is a description of our plan for integrating what we learned into our curriculum, our pedagogies, and our interactions with students. While we are making efforts toward many of the ideas and action items we discuss here, we still have work to do. We truly consider this a cyclical model of change in which we will continuously assess, adjust, and close the feedback loop with our students.

ACTIONABLE STEPS

What follows is a description of the actionable items generated as a result of our research. These action items involve maintaining or enhancing positive elements of the program, as well as implementing new mechanisms to promote the diversity of our faculty and students, and to ensure access, equity, justice, and inclusion for the department. Please note that this is not an exhaustive list of the actions we could or should take, rather, a description of one exercise science department's journey toward being an inclusive, student-centered learning community. We are sharing our plan so others can learn from our experience working toward transformative inclusion.

It is important to note the ESSS department had a unique opportunity to envision and promote diversity and a more inclusive climate within the department. For many years, the department offered a minor curriculum; however, a major curriculum in Exercise and Health Science will begin in fall 2020. The implementation of the new major provided an opportunity to reexamine structures and processes used to recruit and retain faculty and students from diverse backgrounds, and to help position them for success. Through revision of the curriculum, establishment of new learning outcomes, development of a new assessment plan, and revision of content within existing courses, the department could make large structural changes to create a more inclusive learning environment.

Clear Mission and Values

We began our work toward creating a more inclusive environment with a clear mission, philosophy, and set of core values (Lowrie and Robinson 2013, 172). The ESSS department created a handbook to describe these elements to students, faculty, administration, and outside individuals. The language of the handbook describes departmental expectations, provides examples of what inclusion looks like, and identifies structures and processes that will promote a climate of inclusion. For example, the Mission Statement includes the following:

> *The department fosters inclusive and integrated learning, critical thinking, strong communication skills, and exploration of culture and gender related issues, as well as provides leadership and service opportunities for students.*

Additionally, the Philosophy Statement outlines our commitment to an inclusive learning environment. In addition to other commitments, we state:

> *Within an inclusive and socially just learning environment that fosters a climate of respect and excellence, students and faculty members work as a team to*

examine and understand the human experience of sport, exercise, and physical activity.

Within our Core Values, we include Respect and Empathy which are described as:

We value people and the dignity inherent to the human experience. We value one another as human beings by taking seriously and appreciating what the other person or persons bring to the encounter, being open and receptive to experiences or perspectives that are different from our own.

Assessment Practices

Included in the department handbook is a well-designed assessment plan that is consistent with many of the best practices in academic assessment (Maki 2010). While students were not directly involved in the development of the curricular learning objectives and assessment rubrics, both the learning objectives and rubrics will be vetted by ESSS students, including students from minoritized groups, and modified as necessary to help ensure departmental assessment is inclusive (Montenegro and Jankowski 2017, 8).

The academic assessment plan emphasizes direct measures of student learning in multiple courses within the curriculum, with summative assessment in the capstone courses. The capstone experience is fulfilled by either an independent undergraduate research project or an internship experience, both of which allow students to design their own learning experience in partnership with a faculty moderator. The use of student-designed artifacts promotes an inclusive method of assessment, providing opportunity to demonstrate learning in a way that is authentic to each student (Montenegro and Jankowski 2017, 8). By embedding direct measures of student learning in multiple courses throughout the curriculum, the department will be able to monitor student progress over time (Astin 1993).

In addition to student and alumni(ae) surveys that will provide indirect evidence of the student learning environment inside and outside the department, the assessment plan also includes measures of access, equity, and inclusion provided by institutional reports. These data will include student enrollment, retention, graduation rates, and participation rates in high-impact practices. The department is also examining ways to solicit feedback from students who started but chose not to complete the major or minor. We believe these voices may provide unique perspectives in helping the department to understand the barriers to access and inclusion within the department. We are also investigating valid and reliable ways to formatively assess equity, justice, and inclusion within the classroom to facilitate faculty mentoring.

The use of data to inform departmental decisions, rather than subjective perceptions or intuition of faculty, is important in maintaining or enhancing an inclusive climate (Hodge, Brooks, and Harrison 2013, 205; Banaji, Bazerman, and Chugh 2003, 61). The ESSS department will analyze assessment data in multiple ways in order to identify themes and inequities between student groups (Montenegro and Jankowski 2017, 13). Engaging all faculty members in interpreting assessment data will promote a shared understanding and ownership of the assessment process (Banta and Blaich 2011, 23). The department uses assessment results to inform decisions related to pedagogy, the curriculum, cocurricular experiences, faculty development, and resource allocation in order to both enhance student learning and promote an inclusive learning environment. The department will also share the assessment results, and decisions informed by the results, with students and the academic administration (Banta and Blaich 2011, 26; Montenegro and Jankowski 2017, 8; Astin 1993).

The department handbook also describes a cyclical process within the assessment plan. That is, if departmental or curricular structures or processes are modified to enhance student learning, the quality of the students' educational experience, or the learning environment, the data stream will be resampled after an appropriate length of time to determine whether the modification resulted in the desired change. Continuous improvement ensures the department provides the highest quality educational experience for all students (Banta and Blaich 2011, 26; Astin 1993).

Similar to departmental assessment, evaluation of student progress toward learning objectives in individual courses is an opportunity for faculty to model equity, justice, and inclusion to students. This begins with each faculty member acknowledging they have implicit biases that could affect their ability to create an inclusive learning environment. By acknowledging the potential for implicit biases, the faculty member can intentionally examine aspects of the assessment process where blind spots may exist, gather more information as needed, and make decisions that promote equity, justice, and inclusion (Banaji, Bazerman, and Chugh 2003, 61).

As an example, ESSS faculty are expected to engage students in transparent and open discussions about the course content and learning outcomes in ways that help students appreciate the relevance to the students' academic or career goals (Simon and Taylor 2009, 57). In creating assessments of student learning, faculty should ensure the knowledge and skills assessed are connected to course goals and expected outcomes. Faculty should allow students multiple opportunities to engage in formative assessment using multiple methods of assessment, allowing students to express their knowledge in ways that are authentic to the manner in which they constructed their understanding of the course material (Chandler, Zaloudek, and Carlson 2017, 159–162). Additionally, assignments should be accompanied by well-constructed, valid, and reliable rubrics to minimize the influence of implicit biases on the evaluation of student work (Malouff 2008, 192; Chowdhury 2018, 66). Faculty should provide feedback on where students met and fell short of expectations, and assist student development of metacognition skills by helping them examine why they met or failed to meet expectations and what can be done to promote future success (Hattie and Timperley 2007, 86–96). When possible, ESSS faculty also minimize implicit biases by using personal identification numbers in place of names on assignments (Malouff 2008, 192). Clear communication with students regarding learning objectives and the process of evaluation of student work within each course and across the curriculum improves transparency and contributes to a truly collaborative and inclusive learning environment.

Faculty Hiring

The department handbook also serves an important function in the faculty search and hiring process by articulating the qualities of inclusivity expected of all faculty who teach in the department (Hodge, Brooks, and Harrison 2013, 205; Lowrie and Robinson 2013, 170; Culp 2016, 280; Laursen 2019). The handbook reaffirms the department's commitment to recruit, hire, and support a vibrant and diverse faculty. In the handbook, we pledge to utilize an institutionally appointed Search Advocate who will help us identify and mitigate potential cognitive and structural biases in our hiring practices (OSU Search Advocate Program Oregon State University 2017).

The department handbook directs all faculty members to intentionally deepen and broaden their understanding of inclusive teaching, mentoring, and advising through professional development opportunities which should be shared among departmental colleagues (Keith and Russell 2013, 191; Johnson 2019, 370). By encouraging faculty colleagues to willingly and authentically mentor each other, we enable dynamic and synergistic partnerships and model the department philosophy and core values for our students.

The department also has a responsibility to promote vibrant and multi-faceted diversity within the classroom. To promote diversity of the students within the classroom, the department will continue to work collaboratively with the Admissions Department to identify and recruit students from diverse backgrounds to campus (Hodge, Brooks, and Harrison 2013, 208; Lowrie and Robinson 2013, 170; Keith and Russell 2013, 194). We will enhance outreach programs in high schools and community colleges in order to create pipelines for minoritized students. We will also partner with institutional programs, such as Upward Bound and Intercultural Leadership Education and Development, to actively recruit and retain first-generation college students from minoritized groups. The brochures and advertisements for the Exercise and Health Science major explicitly describe the department's commitment to providing students an inclusive and socially just learning environment, as well as methods used to promote diversity, equity, justice, and inclusion within the department. Our communications with prospective students explain the short-term and long-term benefits of learning in an inclusive department climate.

The department also has a responsibility to create and maintain an overall learning environment that will help position every student for success inside and outside the classroom (DiGiacinto 2014, 182). The ESSS department partners with existing programs on campus whose aims foster a more diverse campus community. As an example, ESSS faculty work with the Writing Center to tailor writing assistance to the disciplinary needs of our students. We also partner with the Office of Experience and Professional Development (OEPD) to ensure ample opportunities for professional networking and career exploration though events such as panel discussions and immersion experiences, professional development opportunities to enhance resume and interview skills, and career fair opportunities. Finally, we plan to partner with the Emerging Scholars Program, developed by an ESSS faculty member. The program provides first-year students who are traditionally underrepresented in their fields an opportunity to participate in undergraduate research as first-year students. The ESSS department also commits to hiring minoritized students into laboratory and research assistant positions where students receive meaningful mentorship in the research process (Johnson 2019, 370). Because of the lack of diversity in exercise science and allied health fields, we strive to create a community in our department in which minoritized students feel they can make important contributions in these fields.

In addition to building meaningful mentoring relationships with our minoritized students, we commit to educating all of our students about the privileges they have to influence social change. We will continue to promote a climate of equity, justice, and inclusion by initiating and maintaining conversations about topics related to diversity and inclusion (Hodge, Brooks, and Harrison 2013, 206). As an example, the department hosted a dialogue session on the topic of white privilege that resulted in a robust discussion of inclusivity, and the lack there of, in sport and society. We will continue to use this dialogue session model to engage students in a discussion related to challenges to sport and exercise participation faced by women and LGBTQ+ athletes, a topic our students expressed an interest in discussing more fully. We also hope to move the discussions beyond awareness of diversity toward explicit discussion of social change, which is in direct response to the results of our self-reflection and student feedback.

Curriculum

The Exercise and Health Science major curriculum was intentionally constructed to equip our graduates with the knowledge and skills to function effectively as ethical, client-centered health and exercise professionals and encourage their willingness to be agents of change in promoting equity, justice, and inclusion. A hallmark of the curriculum is the Introduction to Exercise and Health Science course completed during the student's first year of college. The course will help students build community, transition to college, explore potential careers in exercise and health fields, and develop academic skills critical to success within the major. Students who find social support and connect with departmental and institutional resources are more likely to have a sense of direction and persist in the face of obstacles (Karp, Hughes, and O'Gara 2010, 80). In addition to the several high-impact practices embedded in the course, each student will collaborate with the OEPD to embark on a process of self-discovery, career exploration, goal setting, and academic and experiential planning. The collaboration is intended to encourage every student to take ownership of their education and build a personalized experiential plan for success.

A second hallmark of the major is the emphasis on ethical, evidence-based, and client-centered decision-making. Evidence-based decision-making will be introduced in the Introductory course and reinforced with the study of culture, social diversity, and ethics in advanced courses. In the major curriculum, more emphasis is placed on culture and social diversity by moving from half semester courses addressing culture and gender in sport to required full semester courses. The move provides students more time to process what they learn in a more meaningful way. In practicing evidence-based decision-making skills, students will have natural opportunities to explore and discuss issues related to race, ethnicity, gender, social class, ability level, religion, and sexual orientation (Hulme 2010, 275). Specific issues encountered by health and exercise professionals may include nutritional and performance implications associated with fasting during Ramadan, thermoregulation issues experienced by Muslim women due to full body covering, and issues using normative comparisons to evaluate the fitness of transgendered individuals. Service-learning projects embedded in advanced courses will also provide opportunities for each student to enhance their understanding of cultural diversity, act on our core values, and promote inclusivity in tangible ways (Culp 2016, 272; Lowrie and Robinson 2013, 174). The curriculum is not only designed to increase awareness of diversity, but it is also intended to help students become agents of change beyond the classroom.

Individual Courses and Faculty Members

We strive to cocreate with students a learning environment where every student can access and interpret information, and express what they have learned, in ways that honor their experiences, culture, gender, and cognitive and physical abilities. To create this environment, ESSS faculty are committed to bringing the department philosophy and core values into each classroom and student experience. What follows are examples of actionable steps faculty are asked to take into their classes to create an inclusive learning environment.

Individual faculty members should convey course expectations to students through a thoughtful and well-constructed syllabus, by engaging students in multiple conversations about course expectations, and by modeling expected behaviors and values for students (Daly and Vangelisti 2003, 895). Syllabi should be constructed to clearly and explicitly explain that equity, justice, and inclusion are important aspects of the course, a message that should be reiterated and modeled by the faculty member throughout the course (Tanner 2013, 328). Equity, justice, and inclusion should be described as both a lens through which information is examined and a process through which an inclusive learning community is created. By taking the time to explain and engage students in discussions about the importance and relevance of course expectations, the faculty member empowers every student to be successful in the course.

The faculty member's modeling of equity, justice, and inclusion also helps set the foundation for authentic and respectful relationships with students enrolled in the course, which promotes student learning (Daly and Vangelisti 2003, 892; Tanner 2013, 328). For example, faculty should use respectful and inclusive language, seek student input and feedback regarding the course, learn about each student, and appropriately disclose aspects of their own life (Daly and Vangelisti 2003, 892–897; Chandler, Zaloudek, and Carlson 2017, 162–165). Affinity for learning can also be enhanced by an optimistic attitude, bringing energy to the classroom through vocal expressiveness and body language, and promoting self-confidence through mastery-oriented feedback and affirmations (Daly and Vangelisti 2003, 892–895; Chandler, Zaloudek, and Carlson 2017, 162–165).

A climate of equity, justice, and inclusion is also promoted by openly acknowledging and valuing the uniqueness of each person enrolled in the course. This may take place before the class meets for the first time by soliciting information from students about their preferred name, preferred pronouns, and potential challenges or barriers to success in the course (Killpack and Melón 2016, np; Tanner 2013, 327). With the information, the faculty member is better informed to make equitable decisions about relevant aspects of the course, such as when assignments are due, how groups are created, when coursework is to be completed outside of class, and attendance of evening or weekend events. Additionally, we often connect students to resources that can assist with food insecurity, mental health, and tuition-related issues. Learning about students enables faculty to show respect for every student enrolled in the class by recognizing the beliefs, values, and experiences they bring with them to the course (Johnson 2019, 370).

Faculty can model respect for diversity by making all students aware of the diversity that surrounds them every day. From our findings, our students were appreciative when faculty recognized current events and used them to engage students in conversations about equity, justice, and inclusion. Additionally, students appreciated when faculty began class with an acknowledgment of religious holy days and/or historical events associated with the date, particularly events related to social justice. Finally, faculty can support students by attending on campus events associated with diversity, equity, justice, and inclusion, including cultural festivals, student forums, and invited speakers. As one student in our focus group stated, "Students know which faculty members show up to those types of events."

Faculty can intentionally select course content and materials which promote diversity and inclusion, and an affinity for learning. Faculty should adopt textbooks and course readings that include images and sidebars that highlight human diversity in all its forms (Frank 2018, 162; Favero and Van Hoomissen 2019, 562) or that are written by scientists from minoritized groups (Killpack and Melón 2016, np). As an example, an exercise physiology textbook may highlight ethnic diversity in the images of athletes, while a biomechanics textbook may highlight the diversity of human movement abilities by applying concepts to various forms of ambulation. Ideally, human diversity should be overtly addressed within the text and course readings. Additionally, faculty should recognize the contributions of scientists from diverse backgrounds by informing students of the rationale for selecting the readings and explaining why it is important to recognize scientists from minoritized groups (Killpack and Melón 2016, np).

Because every student has a unique set of experiences, gifts, and abilities that influence how they learn, ESSS faculty strive to use student-centered pedagogies and principles of universal design for learning (UDL) (Rose et al. 2006, 2–5; Chandler, Zaloudek, and Carlson 2017, 153). Utilizing UDL principles, we intentionally provide course content in multiple forms, such as text, graphics, audio, and video so students can select the method of learning that best matches their profile of perceptual and cognitive strengths (Rose et al. 2006, 1–7; Chandler, Zaloudek, and Carlson 2017, 154). UDL also includes the faculty member's responsibility to prepare course materials to be accessible to students with sensory, physical, and learning disabilities (Rose et al. 2006, 1–7; Burgstahler 2003, 183) and, when possible, select course materials that are available to students at low cost or no cost (Buczynski 2007, 169). Additionally, the use of technology, such as adaptive keyboards and talk-to-text software, may enhance some student's ability to express what they know (Rose et al. 2006, 1–7; Chandler, Zaloudek, and Carlson 2017, 159–162).

In our work, we found that a course-based undergraduate research experience (CURE) is an effective and influential learning experience for students, especially students from minoritized backgrounds (Laursen 2019, 18–22). Embedded CUREs help students develop greater self-efficacy, self-determination, and problem-solving strategies compared to students who complete the same course without an embedded CURE (Olimpo et al. 2016, np). Academic skill development, such as analytical thinking and data interpretation, is also enhanced by CUREs (Brownell et al. 2015, 3). Unfortunately, students from minoritized backgrounds do not often seek opportunities to engage in undergraduate research (Bangera and Brownell 2014, 602). By embedding CUREs, students are introduced to research and potentially are inspired to seek further research opportunities and consider a graduate education in exercise science (Bangera and Brownell 2014, 604–605).

CONCLUSION

The goal of this project was to assess our department's effectiveness in creating an inclusive learning community inside and outside the classroom such that all students have access and support to be successful. We view the goal of an inclusive community not as an endpoint, but rather a dynamic and ongoing journey which we must continue to evaluate and adjust to in order to meet the changing needs of our students. We plan to continue to answer the call by Brooks and colleagues to "continue to conduct research on curriculum impact, students' attitudes and behaviors, learning outcomes, and student retention, and supporting the educational value and benefits of diversity" (Brooks et al. 2013, 147). Based on what we learned through this process, we recommend other exercise science undergraduate programs begin with assessment of student demographics, student perceptions of the effectiveness and inclusivity of the learning community, and self-reflection of the community cultivated by the department or program using a model similar to that provided by Lowrie and Robinson (2013, 174). Programs should evaluate ways to continue improving strengths and amending weaknesses which should be integrated into an action plan with short- and long-term actionable measures. Action plans should identify ways to enhance diversity, equity, justice, and inclusion at the department, curriculum, and individual course or faculty member levels. Connecting with campus partners and campus leadership for support in carrying out the action plan should be a top priority. As implementation of the action plan continues, departments should reassess student perceptions and adjust as necessary. Finally, departments should be transparent with students about their process, findings, and action plan progress to demonstrate the department or program's commitment to diversity and inclusion. Overall, this process has taught us a great deal about who our students are, what we do well, and what we can do to build on an already strong foundation of inclusion in our department.

REFERENCES

American Physical Therapy Association. "Physical Therapy Workforce Data." n.d. Accessed June 18, 2020. https://www.apta.org/your-career/careers-in-physical-therapy/workforce-data.

American Occupational Therapy Association. "Salary & Workforce Survey." n.d. Accessed June 18, 2020. https://www.aota.org/Education-Careers/Advance-Career/Salary-Workforce-Survey.aspx.

Association of American Medical Colleges. "The Core Competencies for Entering Medical Students." n.d. Accessed June 14, 2020. https://students-residents.aamc.org/applying-medical-school/article/core-competencies/.

Astin, Alexander W. 1993. "Principles of Good Practice for Assessing Student Learning." *Leadership Abstracts* 6 (4): 1–3.

Banaji, Mahzarin R., M. H. Bazerman, and D. Chugh. 2003. "How (Un) Ethical Are You?" *Harvard Business Review* 81 (12): 56–64, 125.

Bangera, G., and Brownell, S. E. 2014. "Course-Based Undergraduate Research Experiences Can Make Scientific Research More Inclusive." *CBE Life Sciences Education* 13 (4): 602–6. doi:10.1187/cbe.14-06-0099.

Banta, Trudy W., and Charles Blaich. 2011. "Closing the Assessment Loop." *Change: The Magazine of Higher Learning* 43 (1): 22–27.

Barfield, J. P., D. C. Cobler, Eddie T. C. Lam, James Zhang, and George Chitiyo. 2012. "Differences between African-American and Caucasian Students on Enrollment Influences and Barriers in Kinesiology-Based Allied Health Education Programs." *Advances in Physiology Education* 36 (2): 164–9. doi:10.1152/advan.00129.2011.

Bergstrom, Rachel A. 2018. "Motion Sickness as Metaphor: Engaging with Diversity in STEM." *Advances in Physiology Education* 43 (1): 1–6. doi:10.1152/advan.00185.2018.

Bowen, William G., and Derek Bok. 1998. *The Shape of the River: Long-Term Consequences of Considering Race in College and University Admissions.* Anniversary edition. Princeton, NJ: Princeton University Press.

Brooks, Dana D., Louis Harrison, Michael Norris, and Dawn Norwood. 2013. "Why We Should Care About Diversity in Kinesiology." *Kinesiology Review* 2 (3): 145–55. doi:10.1123/krj.2.3.145.

Brownell, S. E., Hekmat-Scafe, D. S., Singla, V., Chandler Seawell, P., Conklin Imam, J. F., Eddy, S. L., Stearns, T., and Cyert, M. S. 2015. "A High-Enrollment Course-Based Undergraduate Research Experience Improves Student Conceptions of Scientific Thinking and Ability to Interpret Data." *CBE Life Sciences Education* 14 (2): 14:ar21. doi:10.1187/cbe.14-05-0092.

Buczynski, James A. 2007. "Faculty Begin to Replace Textbooks with 'Freely' Accessible Online Resources." *Internet Reference Services Quarterly* 11 (4): 169–79. doi:10.1300/J136v11n04_11.

Burgstahler, Sheryl. 2003. "Accommodating Students with Disabilities: Professional Development Needs of Faculty." *To Improve the Academy* 21 (1): 179–95. doi:10.1002/j.2334-4822.2003.tb00387.x.

Chandler, Renee, Julie A. Zaloudek, and Kitrina Carlson. 2017. "How Do You Intentionally Design to Maximize Success in the Academically Diverse Classroom?" *New Directions for Teaching and Learning* 2017 (151): 151–69. doi:10.1002/tl.20254.

Chowdhury, Faieza. 2018. "Application of Rubrics in the Classroom: A Vital Tool for Improvement in Assessment, Feedback and Learning." *International Education Studies* 12 (1): 61. doi:10.5539/ies.v12n1p61.

Culp, Brian. 2016. "Social Justice and the Future of Higher Education Kinesiology." *Quest* 68 (3): 271–83. doi:10.1080/00336297.2016.1180308.

Daly, John A., and Anita L. Vangelisti. 2003. "Skillfully Instructing Learners: How Communicators Effectively Convey Messages." In *Handbook of Communication and Social Interaction Skills*, pp. 871–908. Mahwah, NJ: Lawrence Erlbaum Associates Publishers.

DiGiacinto, Kacey. 2014. "Diversifying Kinesiology: Untapped Potential of Historically Black Colleges and Universities." *Quest* 66 (2): 181–90. doi:10.1080/00336297.2014.895951.

Dunn, John M. 2009. "The Times Are a Changing: Implications for Kinesiology." *Quest* 61 (3): 268–77. doi:10.1080/00336297.2009.10483615.

Favero, Terence G., and Jacqueline D. Van Hoomissen. 2019. "Leveraging Undergraduate Research to Identify Culturally Relevant Examples in the Anatomy and Physiology Curriculum." *Advances in Physiology Education* 43 (4): 561–66. doi:10.1152/advan.00023.2019.

Finch, Laura M., and Bonnie Blankenship. 2011. "Dealing with Differences Across the Profession: Introduction." *Journal of Physical Education, Recreation and Dance; Reston* 82 (8): 31–32.

Frank, Anna Marie. 2018. "The Times, They Need A Changing: Infusing Social Justice Into Kinesiology Requires Collaboration." *Quest* 70 (2): 155–65. doi:10.1080/00336297.2018.1438298.

Hattie, John, and Helen Timperley. 2007. "The Power of Feedback." *Review of Educational Research* 77 (1): 81–112. doi:10.3102/003465430298487.

Hodge, Samuel R. 1997. "Mentoring: Perspectives of Physical Education Graduate Students from Diverse Cultural Backgrounds." *Physical Educator* 54 (4): 181.

Hodge, Samuel R., Dana D. Brooks, and Louis Harrison. 2013. "Summary and Conclusions: How Can We Help Enhance Diversity in Kinesiology?" *Kinesiology Review* 2 (3): 203–15. doi:10.1123/krj.2.3.203.

Hodge, Samuel R., and Doris R. Corbett. 2013. "Diversity in Kinesiology: Theoretical and Contemporary Considerations." *Kinesiology Review* 2 (3): 156–69. doi:10.1123/krj.2.3.156.

Hodge, Samuel R., and David K. Wiggins. 2010. "The African American Experience in Physical Education and Kinesiology: Plight, Pitfalls, and Possibilities." *Quest* 62 (1): 35–60. doi:10.1080/00336297.2010.10483631.

Hulme, Polly A. 2010. "Cultural Considerations in Evidence-Based Practice." *Journal of Transcultural Nursing: Official Journal of the Transcultural Nursing Society* 21 (3): 271–80. doi:10.1177/1043659609358782.

Johnson, Kathryn. 2019. "Implementing Inclusive Practices in an Active Learning STEM Classroom." *Advances in Physiology Education* 43 (2): 207–10. doi:10.1152/advan.00045.2019.

Karp, Melinda Mechur, Katherine L. Hughes, and Lauren O'Gara. 2010. "An Exploration of Tinto's Integration Framework for Community College Students." *Journal of College Student Retention: Research, Theory and Practice* 12 (1): 69–86. doi:10.2190/CS.12.1.e.

Keith, NiCole R., and Jared A. Russell. 2013. "Creating a Climate of Organizational Diversity: Models of Best Practice." *Kinesiology Review* 2 (3): 190–202. doi:10.1123/krj.2.3.190.

Killpack, Tess L., and Laverne C. Melón. 2016. "Toward Inclusive STEM Classrooms: What Personal Role Do Faculty Play?" *CBE—Life Sciences Education* 15 (3): es3. doi:10.1187/cbe.16-01-0020.

Laursen, Sandra. 2019. *Levers for Change : An Assessment of Progress on Changing STEM Instruction*. Washington, D.C.: American Association for the Advancement of Science.

Lowrie, Patricia M., and Leah E. Robinson. 2013. "Creating an Inclusive Culture and Climate That Supports Excellence in Kinesiology." *Kinesiology Review* 2 (3): 170–80. doi:10.1123/krj.2.3.170.

Lujan, Heidi L., and Stephen E. DiCarlo. 2018. "The 'African Gene' Theory: It Is Time to Stop Teaching and Promoting the Slavery Hypertension Hypothesis." *Advances in Physiology Education* 42 (3): 412–6. doi:10.1152/advan.00070.2018.

Maki, Peggy. 2010. *Assessing for Learning : Building a Sustainable Commitment across the Institution*, 2nd edition. Sterling, Va: Stylus Pub.

Malouff, John. 2008. "Bias in Grading" *College Teaching* 56 (3): 191–2.

Montenegro, E., and N. A. Jankowski. 2017. *Equity and Assessment: Moving towards Culturally Responsive Assessment*. Urbana, IL: National Institute for Learning Outcomes Assessment.

Olimpo, Jeffrey T., Ginger R. Fisher, Sue Ellen DeChenne-Peters, and Graham F. Hatfull. 2016. "Development and Evaluation of the Tigriopus Course-Based Undergraduate Research Experience: Impacts on Students' Content Knowledge, Attitudes, and Motivation in a Majors Introductory Biology Course." *CBE—Life Sciences Education* 15 (4): ar72. doi:10.1187/cbe.15-11-0228.

Oregon State University. 2017. "OSU Search Advocate Program." OSU Search Advocate Program. January 13, 2017. https://searchadvocate.oregonstate.edu/about.

Ram, Nilam, Joanna Starek, and Jay Johnson. 2004. "Race, Ethnicity, and Sexual Orientation: Still a Void in Sport and Exercise Psychology?" *Journal of Sport and Exercise Psychology* 26 (2): 250–68. doi:10.1123/jsep.26.2.250.

Rose, David H., Wendy S. Harbour, Catherine Sam Johnston, Samantha G. Daley, and Linda Abarbanell. 2006. "Universal Design for Learning in Postsecondary Education: Reflections on Principles and Their Application." *Journal of Postsecondary Education and Disability* 19 (2): 135–51.

Simon, Beth, and Jared Taylor. 2009. "What Is the Value of Course-Specific Learning Goals?" *Journal of College Science Teaching* 39 (2): 52–7.

Tanner, Kimberly D. 2013. "Structure Matters: Twenty-One Teaching Strategies to Promote Student Engagement and Cultivate Classroom Equity." *CBE—Life Sciences Education* 12 (3): 322–31.

Conclusion

Amanda Macht Jantzer and Kyhl Lyndgaard

We finished editing this volume during the incredible summer of 2020. Still reeling from the COVID-19 pandemic, we collectively confronted anew the crisis of systemic racism and police brutality. Beginning in our home state of Minnesota, we witnessed the power of collective action as activism spread from the streets of Minneapolis across the country and across the globe. Justice cannot, and should not, wait. In this context, the inclusion work chronicled here takes on a new urgency. As professionals in higher education, we must acknowledge and uncover the ways our institutions exist in, and contribute to, unjust systems of power and oppression. Moreover, awareness is not enough; we face a mandate for change.

Situated within this context, what changes are needed to create more truly inclusive, diverse, equitable, and just institutions of higher education in the United States? Throughout this volume, faculty, staff, and students provide a range of answers to this pressing question. Some focus on a particular course. Some focus on changing a single department. Some focus on a unique student population. Some focus on issues that cut across a single institution. On their own, these singular efforts have value for illustrating the process of change and reform. These models can and should be extended and replicated in other classes, in other departments, with other student populations, and across other institutions nationwide. However, we argue that the true value of this work is the collective force of these individual change efforts. Altogether, these inclusion initiatives illustrate how a broad coalition of change-makers can use the tools of science and inquiry to center the voices of the marginalized and translate these insights into persistent action that changes systems. The Inclusion Research Initiative illustrates how leaders in higher education can leverage institutional resources to prioritize inclusion and justice work on college campuses, creating a climate that enables students, faculty, staff, and administrators to engage in this work and become emergent leaders in turn. This is how transformative change can happen.

The main theme that cuts across these efforts is that each team embraced inquiry as a point of entry into pursuing this inclusion work. These faculty, staff, and students began by asking important questions about the barriers to inclusion, diversity, equity, and justice in our campus community. How many students experience food insecurity on campus and what factors increase this risk (Heying and Nash)? What institutional practices and polices discriminate against marginalized students (Bacon, Jantzer, and Kramer)? How can colleges and universities "redress a legacy of injustice" (Gordon, Winters, and Benway)? What is the lived experience and perception of the campus climate of students from underrepresented religious communities on campus (Sheehan, Conway, Schrupp, Scott, and Lewi)? How do faculty build inclusivity in Spanish classrooms for heritage speakers as well as second-language learners (Kuffner, Gómez, and Schaaf)? These pressing questions, and more, drove this inclusion work on our campuses. They represent a diversity of considerations from multiple points of influence in a campus community. Informed by ecological leadership theory (Jantzer, Wielkiewicz, and Stelzner), this diversity of input and perspective is a key component of effective organizational change toward multiculturalism and social justice on campus. By tapping into a broad base of emergent leaders, existing networks were strengthened and extended across departments and programs to examine long-standing issues in the community. A critical mass was achieved which allowed each team to see that their work was not happening in isolation, and that this sometimes painful work was driven by solid methodologies of inquiry in a larger ecosystem which supported their work.

Importantly, these efforts overwhelmingly center the need to elicit the lived experiences, perspectives, and voices of marginalized students. These perspectives were gathered using quantitative and qualitative methodologies as students gave their time and energy to voice their truth. However, these efforts do not merely elicit student participation. Many teams also included student collaboration in the underlying process of research and change. Frequently drawing upon standpoint theory, faculty and staff emphasized the importance of collaborating with students, particularly students from marginalized groups, in articulating research questions that would truly resonate with student peers, gathering data through peer-to-peer interviews, and following the lead of students in creating change initiatives. Given that the faculty and staff at our institutions predominantly identify as white, along with other privileged identity statuses, this emphasis on elevating student voices is particularly important for creating the sorts of changes that are truly needed and will be embraced.

From these initial questions and voices, leaders emerged from across the institutions. As the administrators of the Inclusion Research Initiative, we quickly realized that this effort was much more than simply providing a bit of research funding. At the outset, we were overwhelmed—and gratified—by the response to our call for proposals. Faculty and staff reported that they had been waiting for just this opportunity. Many said that they had engaged in deep learning, self-examination, and awareness raising as part of prior inclusion initiatives on campus. Now, they were ready for action. They wanted to learn more about the anecdotal problems they had observed on campus. They wanted to follow-up on the stories they had begun to hear. They wanted to use the tools of science and scholarship to gather data. They wanted to better understand and communicate the scope of problems. And importantly, they wanted to do something about it. And they did.

We quickly began to observe the sort of emergent leadership articulated in Jantzer, Wielkiewicz, and Stelzner's ecological model. Teams of faculty, staff, and students mobilized to communicate the results of their research across the campus community and beyond. They pulled together working groups with stakeholders and leaders across the campuses to examine options and institute lasting changes, like changing the university food plan to reduce the risk of hunger for first-year students. They uncovered details about our institutional history of injustice related to Native boarding schools and engaged institutional and tribal leaders in difficult but meaningful dialogues to build new partnerships, share information, and begin the process of truth which must occur before reconciliation. They helped marginalized students find community and feel less alone. These efforts led to new trainings, a new workshop series, a new conference, new efforts to create a resource center, new collaborations with local and state officials, new pilot programs, informed new program review requirements, and more. Given a climate of support, leaders emerged from this process and inspired additional leaders. In this way, the Inclusion Research Initiative took on a life of its own with a still-expanding sphere of influence across the complex institutional ecosystem. It became something truly transformational. And this gives us guidance for the future, in which even more will be needed.

As Hinton and Enke articulated in their call for action in the forward to this volume, these efforts provide some models for beginning the work of transformative inclusion. This research and theory can inform the creation of more inclusive classrooms, departments, and institutions. We have learned from these efforts and will continue to apply these lessons to pursue change on our own campuses. We hope that others in institutions of higher education will as well. But this is not enough. In the context of the twin crises of COVID-19 and racism in the United States, we are all called to do more. We must center anti-racism work. We must go beyond awareness to engaged action. We must dismantle oppressive structures in our colleges and universities and broader communities. These are the changes we need.

Index

Page references for figures are italicized.

About the Contributors

Pamela L. Bacon, PhD, is dean of the faculty and a professor of psychology at the College of Saint Benedict and Saint John's University. She is a social psychologist whose primary areas of research include the relational self-construal and stereotyping, prejudice, and discrimination.

Belen Benway is a junior, communication major at the College of Saint Benedict. She is from Red Wing, Minnesota and is Mdewakanton Sioux from the Prairie Island Indian Community. She has been working as an undergraduate research assistant.

Catherine M. Bohn-Gettler, PhD, is a professor in the Education Department at the College of Saint Benedict and Saint John's University. She is an educational psychologist whose scholarship focuses on the interrelations between how emotions and cognition influence learning and comprehension. She utilizes this frame to study issues of equity, education, and development.

Emily J. Booth is an undergraduate student at the College of Saint Benedict pursuing a psychology major and music minor. She has worked as a psychology department as an office assistant, behavioral statistics teaching assistant, and through her work on an empirical research project across campus focused on the relationship between transportation and student's sense of belongingness. She was a recipient of the competitive 2020 Jackson Fellowship and worked to complete an internship in social justice with NCCJ-STL.

Chris Conway, PhD, is an assistant professor in the Department of Theology at the College of Saint Benedict and Saint John's University. He received his

PhD in Comparative Theology from Boston College. His research is primarily on Christian and Hindu spiritual practices and devotional traditions.

Kathryn A. E. Enke, PhD, is chief of staff and lead Title IX Coordinator at the College of Saint Benedict. She is a past chair of the board of directors for the National Association of Presidential Assistants in Higher Education. She regularly teaches a course on personal leadership and the private college to doctoral students at the University of Minnesota. Her research focuses broadly on the ways that individuals' identities mediate their experiences in higher education.

Diana Fenton, EdD, is an assistant professor in the Education Department at the College of Saint Benedict and Saint John's University. Dr. Fenton's research and teaching focus is in the area of science and technology in education.

Donald V. Fischer, MSPT, is a professor in the Exercise Science and Sport Studies Department at the College of Saint Benedict and Saint John's University. He is a physical therapist, athletic trainer, and strength and conditioning coach. His primary scholarly interests are in the areas of dynamic postural stability and injuries due to sport participation.

Katherine Furniss, PhD, is currently a teaching assistant professor at the University of Minnesota—Twin Cities and a former visiting assistant professor at the College of Saint Benedict and Saint John's University. She is developing and delivering courses for biomanufacturing professionals to develop a partnership between industry and academia. She has taught a variety of biology courses as well as first-year seminar. Areas of interest include genetic diversity, biology education, and andragogy research.

Tania Gómez, PhD, is an associate professor in the Department of Hispanic Studies at the College of Saint Benedict and Saint John's University. Her main areas of interest include language teaching and testing, sociolinguistics, and pragmatics. Her latest publication describes the strategies used for apologizing in Spanish.

Theodor P. Gordon, PhD, is a visiting assistant professor at the College of Saint Benedict and Saint John's University. He is the author of *Cahuilla Nation Activism and the Tribal Casino Movement*, published by the University of Nevada Press. He earned his PhD in sociocultural anthropology from the University of California, Riverside.

Emily K. Heying, PhD, is an associate professor of nutrition at the College of Saint Benedict and Saint John's University. She teaches nutritional biochemistry, global malnutrition, and undergraduate research seminars. She is interested in how best to alleviate food insecurity among students at liberal arts institutions.

Janelle Hinchley, MSW and LICSW, is a visiting assistant professor at the College of Saint Benedict and Saint John's University. She currently teaches in the gender studies program and her scholarly interests include inclusive pedagogy, multicultural intelligence, and issues related to gender equity.

Mary Dana Hinton, PhD, is president emerita of the College of Saint Benedict and is currently the president of Hollins University. She is a member of the board of directors for the American Association of Colleges and Universities (AAC&U), the Council of Independent Colleges (CIC), Interfaith Youth Core (IFYC), and the University Leadership Council. She founded the Liberal Arts Illuminated Conference and teaches in the University of Pennsylvania Graduate School of Education doctoral program in higher education management, the Institute for Administrators in Catholic Higher Education (IACHE) and the CIC President's Institute New President Program. She was the principal investigator for the *Faculty Formation to Support Liberal Learning for All* grant and the *Becoming Community* initiative, funded by the Andrew W. Mellon Foundation.

Madeleine H. Israelson, PhD, is an assistant professor of literacy education at the College of Saint Benedict and Saint John's University. Her research interests include equity/social justice pedagogy, early literacy instruction, and technology integration.

Amanda Macht Jantzer, PhD, is an assistant professor of psychology at the College of Saint Benedict and Saint John's University (CSB/SJU). She is a counseling psychologist and her primary scholarly interests are in the areas of multicultural and social justice psychology, inclusion in higher education, vocational psychology, and interpersonal violence. She is the co-administrator of the *Becoming Community* grant and of the Mellon Inclusion Research Initiative at CSB/SJU, both funded by the Andrew W. Mellon Foundation.

Jacob Jantzer, PhD, is a visiting assistant professor at the College of Saint Benedict and Saint John's University where he teaches gender studies, sociology, and first-year seminar. A sociologist by training, his areas of interests include gender identity, criminology, and human sexuality.

Robert A. Kachelski, PhD, is an associate professor of psychology at the College of Saint Benedict and Saint John's University with interests in the areas of attention, perception, memory, and language.

Thomas Kirkman, PhD, is an associate professor at the College of Saint Benedict and Saint John's University where he teaches physics courses. Areas of interest include mathematical physics, observational astronomy, and statistical analysis of STEM students.

Jennifer S. Kramer, PhD, is an associate professor in the Communication Department at the College of Saint Benedict and Saint John's University. Her primary area of research is patient/medical provider communication from the perspective of those who are marginalized.

Emily Kuffner, PhD, is an assistant professor in the Department of Modern Languages and Literatures at California State University, Fullerton. Her research is on Golden Age (sixteenth-and seventeenth-century) Spanish Literature and Gender Studies, and her book examines prostitution in this era. Her teaching interests include inclusive pedagogy in language, culture, and Spanish literature.

Janna LaFountaine, MS, is a professor in the Exercise Science and Sport Studies Department at the College of Saint Benedict and Saint John's University. Her teaching responsibilities include courses related to gender, culture and sport ethics. Janna has led a variety of study abroad programs, is the coaching education coordinator, sport management department contact, and in her thirtieth year teaching in higher educa-tion. She has published and presented on the topics of female coaches who work with boys' teams, social support, and international volleyball players, stress and female athletes, and most recently female high school coaches' perspectives.

Rediet Negede Lewi graduated from the College of Saint Benedict in 2019 with a BA in Psychology and a minor in Theology. During her time there, she served as a student interfaith leader at the Jay Phillips Center for Interfaith Learning. She is currently pursuing her MA in medical anthropology at the School of Oriental and African Studies, University of London.

Kyhl Lyndgaard, PhD, is a visiting assistant professor of environmental studies and director of the Writing Center at the College of Saint Benedict and Saint John's University (CSB/SJU). His research interests focus on environmental justice, and he is the author of *Captivity Literature and the Environment: Nineteenth-Century American Cross-Cultural Collaborations* (Routledge, 2016) and coeditor of *Currents of the Universal Being: Explorations in the Literature of Energy* (Texas Tech University Press, 2015). He was the administrator of the *Faculty Development to Engage Increasingly Diverse Students* grant and co-administrator of the Mellon Inclusion Research Initiative at CSB/SJU, both funded by the Andrew W. Mellon Foundation.

Kyle McClure, MA, is a success coach for Summit Scholars in the TRIO Student Support Services at the University of Minnesota-Morris. He taught first-year seminar at the College of Saint Benedict and Saint John's University for three years. His areas of interest include first-year writing and first-year experience.

Jonathan Nash, PhD, is an associate professor of history at the College of Saint Benedict and Saint John's University. Academic interests include early America, early U.S. Republic, American Revolution, Atlantic World, history of childhood, and crime and punishment in the antebellum United States.

Terri L. Rodriguez, PhD, is a professor in the Education Department at the College of Saint Benedict and Saint John's University. Her research focuses on teacher preparation for diversity, equity, and social justice. She is coauthor of *Supporting Muslim Students: A Guide to Understanding the Diverse Issues of Today's Classrooms* (2017) published by Rowman & Littlefield.

Sarah Schaaf, MA, is an instructor in the Department of Hispanic Studies at the College of Saint Benedict and Saint John's University. She is the language coordinator for the department and her primary scholarly interests include sociolinguistics, heritage learners, and inclusion in language pedagogy.

Maria Schrupp graduated from the College of Saint Benedict in 2020 with a BA in sociology with a concentration in anthropology and a minor in Hispanic Studies. During her time there, she served as a student inter-faith leader at the Jay Phillips Center for Interfaith Learning. She has conducted undergraduate research centered around the themes of migration and environmental anthropology. She intends to pursue graduate studies in anthropology.

D'Havian Scott is a senior at the College of Saint Benedict pursuing a BA in sociology with a concentration in anthropology and a minor in psychology. D'Havian is an international student from The Bahamas. In her time at CSB/SJU, she has been involved with the Jackson and Fleishhacker Center for Ethical Leadership in Action Fellowships and has taken part in student development as a Residential and Community Advisor.

Megan Sheehan, PhD, is an assistant professor in the Sociology Department at the College of Saint Benedict and Saint John's University. She received her PhD in anthropology from the University of Arizona. Her research primarily explores Latin American labor migration to Chile, where she has conducted ethnographic fieldwork on transnational migration, racialization, and the cultural production of urban space.

Allison Spenader, PhD, is an associate professor specializing in World Languages and ESL pedagogy in the Education Department at the College of Saint Benedict and Saint John's University. Her research focuses on content-based instruction in language teaching, and intercultural development and language acquisition in study abroad contexts.

Stephen P. Stelzner, PhD, is a professor of psychology at the College of Saint Benedict and Saint John's University. His areas of research include organizational behavior, leadership, community intervention/change, work stress, sport stress/anxiety, youth sports, and cooperative learning in the classroom.

Mary Stenson, PhD, is an associate professor in the Exercise Science and Sport Studies Department at the College of Saint Benedict and Saint John's University. She is an exercise physiologist and mentors several undergraduate researchers each year. Her primary scholarly interests are in the areas of human performance and recovery from exercise, sedentary behaviors, and health and wellness of college students.

Richard M. Wielkiewicz, PhD, is a professor of psychology at the College of Saint Benedict and Saint John's University. His main scholarly interests are in the areas of leadership theory, tests and measures, and evolutionary psychology.

Claire Winters is a senior environmental studies and sociology double major at the College of Saint Benedict. She is from Minneapolis, Minnesota, and has been working as an undergraduate research assistant.

Brandyn Woodard, MA, has been working in international and multicultural education since 1999. He has a bachelor's degree in Spanish and a master's degree in human resources development. He currently serves as the director of Intercultural and International Student Services and co-administrator of the Becoming Community grant, funded by the Mellon Foundation, at the College of Saint Benedict and Saint John's University.

www.ingramcontent.com/pod-product-compliance
Lightning Source LLC
Chambersburg PA
CBHW022309280326
41932CB00010B/1036